LEARNING
TO SAIL

The *Peedie*. Twenty-one feet over all, gaff-rigged, shoal draft, with outside ballast and ample sail. Smart, able, and close-winded; an ideal boat for the beginner.

LEARNING
TO SAIL

H. A. Calahan

DOVER PUBLICATIONS, INC.
Mineola, New York

Bibliographical Note

This Dover edition, first published in 1999, is an unabridged republication of the new edition of the work (with Supplementary Chapter), originally published in 1933 by The Macmillan Company, New York.

Library of Congress Cataloging-in-Publication Data

Calahan, H. A. (Harold Augustin), b. 1889.
    Learning to sail / H.A. Calahan.
        p. cm.
    Reprint. Originally published: New York : Macmillan, 1932. With
supplementary ch.
    ISBN 0-486-40728-4 (pbk.)
    1. Sailing

GV811 .C3 1999
797.1'24—dc21

99-050132

Manufactured in the United States of America
Dover Publications, Inc., 31 East 2nd Street, Mineola, N.Y. 11501

TO

"Mrs. Peedie"

Who is "a cook and a captain bold,
And the mate of the *Nancy* brig,
And a bo'sun tight, and a midshipmite,
And the crew of the captain's gig."

FOREWORD

THIS book is written for the landlubber. It begins at the beginning, and gives just enough information to enable anyone to take out a small boat and bring her back in safety. I feel there is need for such a book. Nearly everything that has been written on the subject of sailing assumes a knowledge on the part of the reader that frequently does not exist, and nearly every author is so wrapped up in his subject that he is writing above the head of the tyro.

The recent discoveries in the science of aerodynamics have brought forth excellent books for the advanced student, but boats have been sailed successfully for countless centuries by sailors who had no appreciation whatever of the theory of what makes a boat go to windward. So this book is written from the practical rather than the theoretical point of view and endeavors to teach sailing as an old sailor rather than a modern scientist would teach it. After the reader has become proficient and can handle his boat in all weathers and all waters—that is the time for him to study the more advanced works on the subject.

The book touches only incidentally the allied arts of racing and cruising. There are several good books on these subjects; but they presuppose that the reader has mastered the art of plain sailing. It has been necessary to draw the line somewhere, so it has been drawn pretty sharply at the point where other books begin.

The material for this book has been gathered in thirty-three years of hard sailing, of getting into trouble and out of it. And although it is written for the beginner, there is much that will be of inestimable value to the old timer. The more we know about boats the more we realize how much remains to be learned.

The book is written for American sailors who are learning to sail small, open or half-decked American boats in the inland waters of the Atlantic Coast of North America. Sailors on the Great Lakes, the Pacific, and elsewhere will, of course, have to apply their own corrections for local conditions of weather, wind, and tide, but in general, anyone learning to sail any boat anywhere will find the book helpful.

The author has borne in mind that the reader may be sailing deep water or shoal; handling a centerboard or a keel boat; rigged with gaff-headed sail or Marconi; and necessarily, a certain redundancy results.

If, at times, the book adopts a preaching tone, it must be borne in mind that preaching (or profanity) is of the essence of all teaching of seamanship. There is little difference between the printed word and the raucous shout of the old salt: "Hey! young feller—better slack off that outhaul if yer don't want ter stretch yer mains'l all outer shape!"

The printed preaching at least has the merit of privacy.

CONTENTS

CONTENTS

ILLUSTRATIONS

CHAPTER I

WHAT IT'S ALL ABOUT

HERE, on shore, life is a hurly-burly.

Out there on the water is escape.

Here, "the world is too much with us." Out there we are alone. A mile from shore, and we are in a world of our own. And what a world! A world of water and wind and sky. A world of ever-changing, inexhaustible beauty. A world, moody and capricious, perhaps; but always fair and square. Sometimes soothing and benign, sometimes boisterous and gay, sometimes lowering, threatening, mad, and dangerous; but always giving fair warning, always playing the game with all the cards on the table if we but know them when we see them.

You cannot find that world of waters in a motor boat. The motor boat carries part of the shore with it; and at the approach of the shore, the gods of the deep go into hiding. The motor boat stinks of the highway and the factory. It roars with the noise of the city. It vibrates to the tempo of a mechanical age.

And, worst of all, you lose the thrill of the gambling when you play with loaded dice.

No, you cannot find the world of waters in a motor boat. You cannot help but find it in a sailboat, for that world of water and sky, wind and tide, is not

1

only about you but part of you. If it fights you, it drives you as well. It is your motor as well as your resistance—your safeguard as well as your enemy.

Of all man-made things there is nothing so lovely as a sailboat. It is a living thing with a soul and feelings—responsive as a saddle horse, loyal as a dog, and thoroughly downright decent. Every sailboat has a character all its own. No builder has ever succeeded in turning out two boats exactly alike. Their measurements may be identical, but the difference is in their character.

Sailing boats are wise. They display a sound shrewdness born of the wind and the wave. And they will impart that wisdom to a sympathetic and attentive helmsman.

Yes, they are wise. If you are mean or niggardly, cowardly or slovenly, selfish, overbearing or cruel, rest assured your boat will find you out.

Yet in stress of storm or adversity, no boat has ever failed to give her best when called on by her master. It may be a poor best. She may be old and rotten and leaking like a basket. The odds against her may be overwhelming. But she will always, always go gallantly into battle, win through if possible, and, if not, die fighting.

To sail this glorious creature, to be her master and her friend, to enter with her into the challenging, whimsical realm of the sea—that is the noblest and the best-compensated of all the arts.

For it gives so much that can never be bought by money. Humility—and self-confidence; courage—and kindness; strength—and gentleness; these are the gifts to the sailor.

And there are other gifts too numerous to mention: long, lazy, sunny hours ghosting through a silent calm; crashing, smashing drives to windward with the lee rail buried, the stinging spray tossed high, the wide wake smoking behind you; tense, sharp battles with eager, ingenious squalls when you must fence with sheet and tiller to parry every thrust and lunge of your gusty opponent. And triumph! That rocky point you weather after a long battle with the tide. It is yours —you have earned it. The landfall you make in a fog, sailing out of the nowhere right up to your mooring— that is better than the solution to the finest mystery story. The gun that announces your victory when you romp first across the finish line in a hard-fought race —that is music divine. The snug warmth of your cabin with a mile of cold gray sea outside is the coziest of homes. Out there, when you are on your own, alone with your ship and the stars, the petty annoyances of life ashore are swiftly dwarfed to their real proportions.

And the sport of the sailor never ends. It is enjoyed by age as well as youth. It is with you in winter as well as in summer, for ice and snow are no barriers to dreaming and planning. A larger boat, a change in rig, a new bottom paint, an alteration here or there, new cruises planned—this is your winter yachting.

You can never learn it all. If you live to be a thousand, you can never learn it all. The art of sailing is as old as mankind and as new as the cat's-paw you see scurrying down from windward. This book is just the barest beginning.

CHAPTER II

THE SELECTION OF A BOAT

A CHARMING young couple of my acquaintance determined to learn to sail. Therefore they set out to buy the sort of boat that would be "just right for a beginner." Their purchase was a dory, about nine feet over all, with a very short rig. It was represented to them as the right boat for a beginner for the following reasons:

First, it was small.

Second, there was not enough sail to get them into trouble.

They spent the summer in Mamaroneck Harbor where there is more than a seven-foot rise and fall of tide and where the current is just what might be expected with a tide of that character. Furthermore, the harbor is very well sheltered, so that in ordinary weather the breeze is extremely light. They spent the summer trying to get a hundred feet from their mooring and finally gave up in disgust. I sailed their boat one day in an endeavor to encourage them, and learned in five minutes why they were giving up the idea of sailing and were taking to gardening instead. The boat was too small.

It had a sail that was useful only in a gale of wind, and a gale is no time for a beginner. When it was blowing hard, they dared not sail; when it was not blowing

4

hard, they *could* not sail. My first advice in the selection of a boat is to get one that is neither too large nor too small, and it is better to get a boat that is too large than a boat that is too small. My second advice is to get a boat that is properly rigged. And it is better to get a boat that is over-rigged than to get a boat that is under-rigged.

Most beginners seek a safe boat. They would do better to get a dangerous boat. To my mind, the safest boat for a beginner is about twenty-one or twenty-two feet over all, and preferably a boat that has been built in a one-design racing class. The majority of one-design boats are generally pretty safe. A racing boat in an open class—that is to say, a boat that is built to certain restrictions of size and sail area—is generally cut down in the factor of safety to make for the factor of speed. But when a number of boats are built from the same designs and specifications, the class usually tries to turn out a safe, able, workable boat, and the speed factor is left to take care of itself. The winner in a one-design racing class usually wins because of the care and the proper tuning up of his boat and his judgment and helmsmanship in the course of the race.

In general, a boat should not be less than twenty-one feet over all because it is impossible to build a boat much smaller that will behave like a real boat and will have the stability and dependable qualities particularly necessary to a beginner. A boat should not be much larger than twenty-one feet over all, because of the difficulty presented in the physical handling of a large sail area.

Most small boats on the Atlantic seaboard are either cat-rigged or sloop-rigged. The true catboat is recognized by her excessive beam or width. She has a single large mast located in the very bows of the boat. On that mast she carries a single large sail. In the development of the catboat for racing purposes, there have been many deviations from the original catboat hull. The boats have been built longer and narrower. They have developed long overhangs forward and aft, and the mast has crept aft to a point sometimes five feet from the bow. They are still catboats in that they carry a single large sail and in that the mast is directly over the forward end of the water line. If you must have a catboat, try to select the old type with the straight stem and the broad beam.

In my opinion, however, the catboat is not the boat for a beginner for the following reasons:

1. The single large sail is very hard to handle in that it is all in one piece.

2. A catboat running before the wind in anything like a sea has a bad habit of rolling. Inasmuch as the sail is almost at right angles to the boat on this point of sailing, the end of the boom is quite likely to get into the water, with dire consequences.

3. A catboat is more likely to jibe accidentally, for it has no jib or small forward sail to give warning of this danger.

4. The catboat is very likely to broach to in altering her course from a run before the wind to any course to windward. Unless the sheet is skillfully trimmed at this time, capsizing is likely to result.

5. The catboat is a poor teacher. Generally they carry very heavy weather helms, so that it is as difficult to acquire good helmsmanship with a catboat as it is to develop the "good hands" of horsemanship with a hard-mouthed horse.

So my vote would be against the catboat.

Photo M. Rosenfeld
FIG. 1   FIG. 2

FIG. 1. A boat with a Marconi, or jib-headed, mainsail
FIG. 2. A boat with a gaff-headed mainsail

My preference for the beginner is a small sloop. Most sloops, which can be readily found, are of the knockabout type. That is to say, they have a jib (a small triangular sail in front of the mast) and a mainsail. They have no bowsprit, but their jib stay (the wire rope on which the jib is hoisted) runs from the head of the mast to the very bow of the boat. The mainsail may be of the Marconi type (see Figure 1) or of the gaff-rig type (see Figure 2).

The word Marconi is a misnomer. A triangular or jib-headed sail is by no means new. It was formerly called the leg-of-mutton rig, but some years ago when the present vogue for the Marconi sail was started, the masts were made very tall and were all curved. It was so difficult to keep a tall, curved mast in the boat that a very elaborate system of wire stays was necessary. These wire stays made the mast look more like a radio tower than anything else, and the nickname "Marconi" mast was applied, and for some reason has stuck ever since.

For the beginner, I strongly urge the selection of a gaff-headed sail. The gaff rig is not so fast on the wind as the Marconi rig, but the mast is shorter and therefore handier. Many maintain that the weight of the gaff (the spar at the top or head of the sail) more than overcomes the leverage of the mast. In my own sailing, I have not been able to detect any material difference. But the gaff rig has certain definite advantages so far as the beginner is concerned.

In the first place, the beginner can probably make his sail set much better with the aid of a gaff, and the ability to hoist a sail properly is no small part of one's success in learning to sail. In the second place, the mainsail can be shortened very quickly on all points of sailing except to windward by simply lowering the peak—or the end of the gaff farthest away from the mast. In the third place, a gaff-headed sail is secured to the mast by hoops, while a Marconi sail, because of the necessity for elaborate stays, is fastened with slides that work along a track on the after side of the mast. These slides not infrequently catch in the track, and when that happens it is very difficult to get the sail either up or down. This is often embarrassing even to an old salt and may cause no end of difficulty to the beginner.

Let us, then, start looking for a boat about twenty-one or twenty-two feet over all, sloop rigged, with a gaff-headed mainsail. Let us look for a good average boat, not one that is too fast, and certainly not one that is too safe. To a certain extent, speed and safety go together. A boat that is under-rigged or over-ballasted or otherwise slow and logy is the sort of boat in which a beginner gets into trouble.

It is essential that the boat selected shall be suitable for the waters to be sailed. It is impossible to sail a deep-draft boat in shallow waters. If you are sailing on Great South Bay, Barnegat Bay, shoal waters in certain parts of the Chesapeake, it is most necessary that the boat shall draw very little water and shall provide lateral resistance to the water by means of a centerboard. The centerboard is the sliding keel which works up and down in a narrow box known as the centerboard trunk.

If, on the other hand, you are sailing such waters as Long Island Sound, Buzzards Bay, Peconic Bay, or any of the deeper waters of the New England coast, the boat with the deep keel is more suitable. It is possible, of course, to sail a shoal-draft boat in deep water, whereas the reverse is not possible. If you are limited by the depth of water to a shoal-draft boat, by all means choose a gaff rig. With very few exceptions,

the Marconi rig has proved unsatisfactory in centerboard boats.

In general, the boat should be designed and built by
men who have intimate knowledge of local conditions,
and the best type of boat for any particular locality
is the boat most nearly resembling the majority of
other boats in that locality.

CHAPTER III

THE MOORING

MORE damage is usually done to a boat in the first few days in the hands of a beginner than in several years of its normal life. So right at this point let us consider that you have bought your boat and must take care of her even before you have learned to sail. She should be delivered to you by the vendor, or you should have her sailed to your anchorage by someone who knows how. Do not attempt to sail a boat until you are thoroughly familiar with everything about her.

The first consideration, then, is the anchorage. Your anchorage should be in a spot as well protected as possible from the heaviest storms which you are likely to get. On the Atlantic seaboard of the North American continent, most of the bad storms come from the east or northeast or southeast. If possible, therefore, select an anchorage that is protected from this wind. Do not lie too near to other boats, and before you select your anchorage watch the way the other boats swing when the wind changes.

A large boat anchored to a long line will describe the extremity of a very large circle. If you anchor your small boat on a shorter line within the radius of that circle, you may swing perfectly clear on most winds; but there may be one quarter from which the wind will blow in which you will be uncomfortably close to the other boat. Your position should be such that the other boat will swing clear of your boat and of your mooring line, regardless of the direction the wind may blow. Furthermore, you must remember that in heavy storms boats frequently drag their moorings. If a boat that is to windward of you drags and you do not, there is apt to be a serious collision. So look carefully at your neighbors and at the way they swing

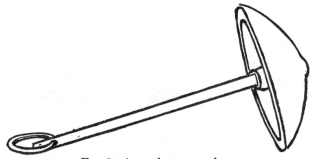

Fig. 3. A mushroom anchor

Allow them plenty of room with a little to spare in case of dragging. If your prevailing storms are to the east, get out your mooring so that it is not directly to the west of any boat.

I have never known of a mooring to be too large or too heavy. I have known many to be too small and too light. The size of a mooring depends a great deal on the depth of the water and the exposure of your position. The type of mooring must be selected with regard to the holding characteristics of the bottom. An anchor that will hold beautifully in sand will pull

right through a mud bottom. An anchor that will sink
deeply into mud, will slide across the top of sand. Local
fishermen and yachtsmen who have anchored in a
locality for many years can best give advice on the
nature of the mooring to be used. In general, a heavy
mushroom anchor (see Figure 3), is a dependable type
or mooring. For a boat twenty-two feet over all, I
would recommend a mushroom anchor weighing not
less than a hundred and fifty pounds.

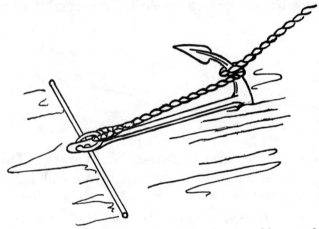

FIG. 4. A double fluke anchor fouled by its cable turned
around the upper fluke

Whatever your choice of mooring, bear in mind that
it should have one important characteristic: it must
be free from any possibility of fouling. The ordinary
double-fluke anchor, even though it may be very large
and heavy, is not suitable as a mooring anchor because
in light airs your boat is apt to be tide-borne in such
a way that your chain will wrap itself around the
fluke and the pull on the anchor will come in exactly

the wrong direction. An anchor thus fouled (see Figure 4), is easily pulled out of the bottom, and the boat marches on to the shore and destruction.

Your mooring should be shackled to chain. The shackle pin (see Figure 5), may screw into the shackle or may pass through the shackle and be secured by a cotter pin on the other side. Use an iron shackle, an iron pin, and an iron cotter pin. Do not permit brass or bronze to be in any part of your mooring line. Brass or bronze sets up an electrolytic condition when

FIG. 5. Shackles

FIG. 6. A thimble

in proximity to iron immersed in sea water. This is likely to eat out the pin so that you will have no security whatever. Your mooring chain should be long and heavy. Chain is sold by the pound, but the heavier the chain, the less the cost per pound.

A heavy chain to my mind is a good investment because it outlasts the light chain by so many years and because even when badly rusted it still has a large factor of safety. Furthermore, a heavy chain makes a perfectly good anchor all by itself. If your chain is heavy enough, there will be no strain whatever on the anchor except in the strongest blows. Moreover, the pull of your boat upon the chain must lift that chain off the bottom before any direct pull can come on the anchor, and this in itself eases the strain.

Another consideration to bear in mind is the fact that in common with everyone else in the world, you will probably want to buy a larger boat after a few years of the small one, and a heavy mooring will hold a large boat as well as a small one; whereas a small chain that will be sufficient for a small boat will be too light for a large one. I recommend that your chain be not less than $\frac{3}{8}''$ section, and a half-inch or $\frac{5}{8}''$ might prove a good investment. Chain must be used instead of rope because it lies along the bottom and rope will rot out in a short time.

The length of the chain should be determined by two considerations:

1. The amount of room in your anchorage.
2. The depth of the water.

Most authorities maintain that the chain should be seven times the depth of the water at high tide. But it must be borne in mind the depth of the water at high tide means depth of the water at the highest tide that will come in the heaviest storms. At the western end of Long Island Sound, the tides reach immense heights in east wind storms because the storms blow all of the Sound down into the western end. If normally you have a seven foot rise of tide but have a twenty foot rise of tide in a heavy storm, you should plan your mooring for the twenty-foot tide rather than for the seven-foot tide. It is a good plan to secure a heavy weight like the fly wheel of an old automobile motor about fifteen feet from your mooring anchor.

This adds to the weight of the chain and makes a spring before any direct pull can come on the anchor itself.

Many authorities maintain that there should be a swivel between the chain and the buoy. In many years of mooring boats to chains, however, I have had my chain kink up only once. On that occasion, my boat was off on a cruise and the chain was fouled by the propellor of a motor boat. It is extremely doubtful if any swivel would have prevented kinking in such a case. Therefore my own experience teaches that a swivel is unnecessary. It is likely soon to fail to operate because of rust. And, worst of all, a swivel introduces a weak member into the mooring line. Therefore swivels are not recommended.

There are many ways of terminating the anchor to a buoy. The two favorite methods seem to be the following:

First the chain is made fast to the bottom of a large can buoy, a globular iron affair with a strong wrought iron rod running through it. To the upper end of the rod is a line ten or fifteen feet feet long which runs to the boat. The boat end of the line may be floated by a few corks so that it may be picked up readily from your boat.

The second method in general use is to shackle your heavy mooring line directly to the chain. The other end of the line is made fast to a light line leading to a small cork buoy which is readily picked up. When you come up to such a buoy, you pick up the buoy and pull in the light line until you come to the heavy mooring line. The mooring line for a twenty-two foot boat need not be particularly heavy—¾" diameter should be sufficient—but it should be new. A new line should be used at the start of each season, and this line should be discarded and renewed the first or second week in August. If the boat stays in the water until November, it is well to renew the line a third time early in October.

Both ends of a mooring line should have a loop spliced into it, and at this stage of your sailing career it would be well to get a local fisherman to do the splicing for you. Wherever iron touches rope, that is, where the rope is shackled onto the chain, the loop splice should be protected by a galvanized iron thimble. (See Figure 6). Where the mooring rope passes over the bow of your boat, it must be protected by wrapping in canvas. Another satisfactory method is to cut a length of rubber hose and fit it over your rope before the loops are spliced in the ends. This rubber hose or canvas wrapping is what is known as chafing gear and saves the rope from being chafed through by rubbing against the edge of the deck, the bowsprit, or the bobstay.

Some people prefer a hundred per cent chain cable properly protected by rubber hose to a cable composed partly of chain and partly of rope. But if the rope is strong and new, the combination is better than straight chain, for the rope imparts a springiness which the chain alone lacks.

To make a boat fast to her mooring, lead the anchor rope over the bow and fasten it around a cleat or loggerhead in the bow of the boat. Examine the cleat or loggerhead very carefully to see that it is well built-in to the boat and not merely screwed down into some deckboards. Many a boat has gone ashore because the fastening on the deck has come loose. On many small boats, I have made it a practice to pass my mooring

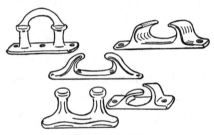

FIG. 7. Chocks

line securely around the mast. Then before leaving the boat, make sure that the mooring line will stay in its position directly over the bow. Either it must be laid in a chock (see Figure 7), or it must be tied with a length of rope at the headstay.

Let us assume, then, that you have the boat safely moored. Now we are ready to look her over.

CHAPTER IV

ACQUIRING A VOCABULARY

You cannot hope to learn to sail a boat unless you learn to call things by their proper names. Everything on a boat has a name, and it is very necessary to learn these names if you are to learn the functions of all parts of your boat. So let us sit down and memorize these strange words and their meanings.

We will begin with the body of the boat itself. It is called the hull. It is built on a long, heavy piece of timber running from end to end known as the keel. Fastened to the keel and extending down into the water is another timber or series of timbers known as the false keel. Above the keel is another timber called the keelson. Extending out from the keel to either side are curved timbers forming a framework. These are known as the ribs.

Over these ribs are fastened planks, and they are known as the planking. The planking on either side next to the keel is known as the garboards. The spaces where the edges of the planks come together are called the seams. They are filled with fibrous material such as cotton or oakum, called caulking. Where the ends of two planks come together, they are known as the butts.

The front end of the boat is known as the bow, and anything in the direction of the bow is known as forward, which is correctly pronounced "forrard."

Do not be ashamed of using the correct nautical pronunciation. Usage makes a word correct or incorrect, and it is not an affectation to call things by the pronunciation in common use.

The back of the boat is called the stern, and anything in the general direction of the stern is called "aft," "after," or "abaft." One may speak of the planking in the after part of the boat; and one may say of the mast of a catboat that it is just aft of the bow. The plank across the stern of the boat is known as the transom. Abaft the keel and under the boat is the rudder. The rudder is a movable board which swings about a vertical or almost vertical rod or post known as the rudder-post, which extends up into the boat. The upper end of the rudder-post is known as the rudder-head. Fastened to the rudder-head and extending forward, is the tiller, by means of which the rudder is moved from side to side. The principal function of the rudder is to control the direction of the boat. Sometimes the rudder is known as an outboard rudder and is fastened over the outside of the transom. Sometimes instead of a tiller, a wheel is used. Whether the rudder is moved by means of a tiller or a wheel, the means of steering the boat is called the helm. Inasmuch as most boats of the size we are contemplating sailing are steered by a tiller, we will confine all our

instructions to that form of helm. The part of the
keel just forward of the rudder is called the dead-
wood.

If you take your stand in the stern of the boat and
look forward, the right-hand side of your boat is the

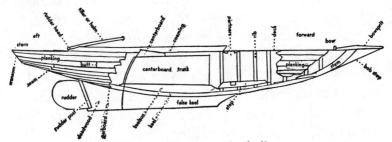

FIG. 8. The parts of a hull

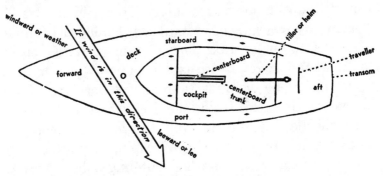

FIG. 9. Deck plan of a small half-decked boat

starboard. The left-hand side is the port. The port
side used to be known as the larboard side, but larboard and starboard sounded so much alike that there
was great confusion, and larboard has been changed
to port. Remember that the terms starboard and port

are not quite synonymous with right and left. If you are facing the stern of the boat, your right hand is to port and your left hand is to starboard. So that your right and left may change with your position on the boat; but starboard and port are fixed and immutable.

The part of a boat from which the wind is blowing is known as the windward (pronounced windard) side. The opposite side is the leeward (pronounced looard). If the boat is headed directly into the wind, the bow is to windward, the stern is to leeward. If the boat is headed away from the wind, the stern is to windward and the bow is to leeward. Synonymous with the term windward, is the term weather.

A lee shore, however, is a shore to your leeward. The wind is blowing on the lee shore. To get in the lee of a shore, however, is to seek shelter under that shore which is to windward. These terms are frequently confused and therefore are explained here.

On top of the planking is an almost horizontal floor known as the deck. Inside the deck where you sit and steer the boat is a little well, known as the cockpit. The boat may or may not have a cabin, but in this work we will consider that we are handling a boat with a deck and a cockpit, but no cabin.

Around the edge of the cockpit is a low fence known as the coaming; and around the outside of the deck there is usually a small strip known as the rail. So much for the hull.

Let us now consider the spars:

On a small boat of the type we are discussing, there

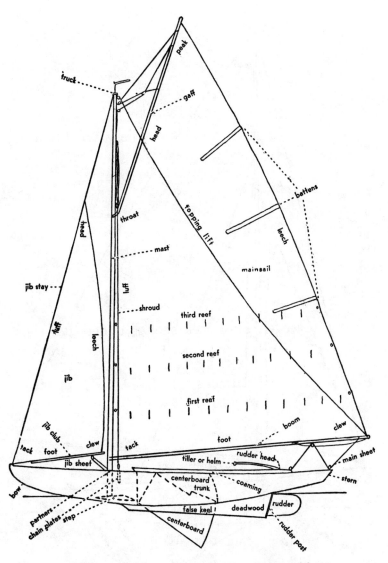

FIG. 10. The parts of a gaff-rigged centerboard boat

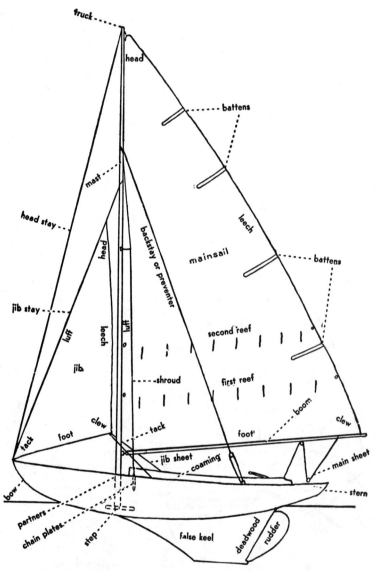

FIG. 11. The parts of a Marconi-rigged deep-keel boat

are at most six spars. First there is the mast. The mast is a vertical pole on which the sails are spread. The part where the mast enters the keel is known as the step. Where it passes through the deck it is called the partners. The very top of the mast is known as the truck.

The boom is the second largest spar on the boat. One end of the boom rests on the mast. The curved portion which bears against the mast is known as the jaws. Or it may be secured to the mast by means of a gooseneck. The other long spar to which the head of the mainsail is attached is known as the gaff. Sometimes there is a little, short spar laced to the bottom of the jib. This is known variously as the jib-boom or preferably as the jib-club. If the boat has a spinnaker, the pole which is used to spread it is known as the spinnaker-boom.

In some small sloops, a spar extends out from the bow and is known as the bowsprit.

Let us consider next the sails:

A small sloop usually has the following sails: a small triangular sail forward of the mast, called the jib. A large sail, abaft the mast, called the mainsail (pronounced mains'l). These are known as the working sails. Sometimes there are two jibs—the forward one called the jib, the other called the forestaysail (forestays'l). A huge, full-cut jib of light canvas used when sailing off the wind is known variously as the balloon jib, ballooner, or reaching jib. A huge triangular sail of light canvas set opposite the mainsail when running before the wind is called the spinnaker. The ballooner and the spinnaker are known as "light sails." They are not often found on small boats unless they have been used for racing.

The principal sail on a small boat is the mainsail. If the mainsail is of the gaff-headed type, it will be laced to the boom, and the gaff, and laced to hoops which slide along the mast. The top of the mainsail laced to the gaff is known as the head. The bottom of the mainsail laced to the boom is called the foot. The part that is laced to the hoops that slide on the mast is known as the luff. And the remaining edge extending from the outer part of the boom to the outer part of the gaff is known as the leech.

Just as the four sides of a sail have designating names, so the four corners also have names. The corner bounded by the luff and the head is known as the throat. The corner bounded by the head and the leech is known as the peak. The corner bounded by the luff and the foot is called the tack. And the corner bounded by the foot and the leech is called the clew. All four corners are known together as the clews of the sail.

In the clews are fastened little brass rings known as cringles.

A foot or two above the foot of the sail is a row of short cotton lines known as reefing points. Another row generally appears a foot or two above the first row, and sometimes there is another row above that. The lowest row is known as the first reef. The second row, the second reef; and the top row, the third reef.

There are cringles in the luff and leech of the sail in line with each of these reefs. They are called the reef cringles.

The sides of the jib bear the same nomenclature as the sides of the sail. The forward edge that is snapped on to the jib stay is the luff. The after edge that comes along the mast is the leech; and the bottom edge is the foot. Two of the clews bear the same nomenclature as in the mainsail. The tack is the corner bounded by the luff and the foot; the clew is the corner bounded by the leech and the foot; but the top corner is called neither the throat nor the peak, but the head.

The nomenclature of the parts of a Marconi mainsail are exactly like the nomenclature of the jib, and the same is true of a spinnaker. Some jibs have a single row of reefing points. Frequently small boats have an extra jib much smaller in size than the regular jib. This is known as a No. 2 jib or a storm jib, and it is used when the mainsail is reefed. Boats equipped with storm jibs rarely have reefing points in the big jib.

The jib is usually hoisted on the jib stay, a wire running from the forward edge of the mast to the bow of the boat. It is fastened to the stay by snap hooks. If there is a bowsprit, the jib stay runs to the outer end of the bowsprit instead of to the bow of the boat.

In the leech of the mainsail and in the leech of the jib are usually found a series of long, narrow pockets. The pockets are known as batten pockets; their function is to receive light, narrow strips of wood called battens which help hold the sail to its proper curvature.

The spinnaker is a light sail that is set flying. That is to say, fastened only at the three clews. We will discuss the spinnaker much later on in this book. If you find a spinnaker or a balloon jib on your boat, the best thing to do is to take it ashore, dry it thoroughly, and put it away until you have learned to sail.

We now come to the rigging.

There are two kinds of rigging; standing rigging and running rigging. The standing rigging consists of all those wires—or, in some cases, ropes—that hold the mast in place. The standing rigging is rarely altered after a boat is put in commission. It "stands" just as it is originally set up.

The running rigging consists of those lines, usually rope, which are constantly being hauled. They "run" through blocks or pulleys.

The standing rigging consists of the stays. They are used to "stay" or hold the mast in position. The stays on the sides of the mast are known as shrouds. You have starboard shrouds and port shrouds. In the case of a Marconi mast, there are generally two sets of shrouds—one set running to the top of the mast, and the other running part way to the top. They are known as upper shrouds and lower shrouds. The shrouds are kept away from the mast and given extra staying qualities by means of horizontal struts or spreaders. Sometimes there is a single set of spreaders and sometimes a double set—upper and lower spreaders. The shrouds are fastened at the deck to long metal bands that extend down the sides of the boat either outside or inside the planking. These bands are known as the chain plates. The stay which runs forward from the mast and carries the jib is called the jib stay. Sometimes, as in the case of a Marconi rig, a stay runs from the very truck of the mast to the bow of the boat forward of any other stay. This is known as the headstay.

If there is a bowsprit, there is usually a stay running from the water line or below up to the outer end of the bowsprit. This is known as the bobstay. Some boats are equipped with backstays or preventers. Backstays are of two varieties—permanent backstays (found only on Marconi rigs with very short booms extending from the truck of the mast to the stern of the boat), and running backstays which extend usually from about one-third of the distance of the mast below the truck to a point abaft the center of the boat on the rail. If your boat is equipped with running backstays, the windward backstay must always be kept taut and the leeward backstay must be slacked off.

Consider next the running rigging:

The ropes used to hoist the sails are called halliards, derived originally from "haul yards." On a gaff-rigged sloop you have three halliards—two on the mainsail and one on the jib. The jib halliard hoists the head of the jib. The throat halliard hoists that part of the gaff near the mast and thereby hoists the throat of the mainsail. The peak halliard is fastened out near the outer part of the gaff and hoists the peak of the mainsail. It is standard practice to have the throat halliard running down on the port side of the mast, and the peak halliard on the starboard side. In small boats, the halliards generally run through blocks on the deck and aft to cleats near or in the cockpit. They are fastened to the cleat by twisting them around, taking a turn alternately around either end of the cleat. This process is known as belaying.

The ropes that hold the sails in to the boat and enable the skipper to adjust them to the proper angle are called sheets. Never under any circumstances call a sail a sheet. A sheet is the name of a rope, not the name of a sail. It is equally landlubberly to call the sheet the "sheet *rope*" because that implies that sheet is the name of the sail, whereas it is and always has been the name of a rope. The main sheet hauls in the mainsail. The jib sheet hauls in the jib.

The main sheet runs through a series of blocks on the boom and on the deck. One of the blocks on the deck usually is fastened to a bronze rod called the "traveler." The jib sheet is usually double ended and each end is belayed to a cleat on the deck or coaming on either side of the helmsman. The middle of the sheet may run to the cringle in the clew of the jib or may run through a block on the club. The sheets and the halliards are the most essential lines in the running rigging.

There may, however, be certain other lines whose names and functions you should know. One of these is the topping lift. The topping lift runs from the truck of the mast to the outer end of the boom and is used to top up the boom to keep it out of water when sail is not hoisted.

Occasionally one finds even on a twenty-one footer a series of ropes which run from the sides of the boom up to the mast. They are called lazyjacks. They do nothing but gather in the sail when it is lowered, to keep it out of the water. Lazyjacks are more nuisance than they are worth on a small boat, but are very valuable in handling a sail of large area.

Another line seldom encountered in a boat of our dimensions but found in larger boats and particularly in boats with bowsprits, is a jib down haul. This line runs from the head of the jib down through the snap fastenings to the tack of the jib and is then headed inboard. It is extremely useful to pull the jib down after the halliard has been let go.

Three other ropes are worth mentioning, although they are not really part of the rigging. One is your anchor line, usually spoken of as the cable. The next is the line with which you make your boat fast to a dock; this is called the painter. The bow line of your rowboat or dinghy is also called the painter. The rope which pulls up your centerboard is called the centerboard pennant.

Sewn loosely into the leeches of the mainsail and the jib is a light cotton line known as a leechline. This line is used to help adjust the curvature of the sail. At the outset of your sailing, it is wise to see that the leechline is just as loose as possible. Do not even tie it down; just forget it is there and never by any chance use it to help tie in a reef. We will discuss the leech-line in a later chapter.

Examine your boat and see if you can identify all the parts that have been named in this chapter. It is quite likely that a good many of the parts will not be on your particular boat.

CHAPTER V

LOOKING HER OVER—PRELIMINARY WARNINGS

As soon as your boat is delivered to you, it is most necessary that you get fully acquainted with her. The temptation is to get under way at once and try your hand at sailing. This should always be postponed, even if the day is calm and you think you know what you are about. Take time to study out each line, cleat, and block. Try to understand the function of everything on board; see where the lines lead to and study out whether they are passing through the blocks in the right direction or whether they will be twisted up aloft when the sail is hoisted.

Every line has slight individual characteristics by which it may be recognized. Pull on the halliards and try to distinguish between the feel of the throat and the peak.

Now examine the ballast; see how much ballast you have. See just where it is placed. Find your pump and pump the boat dry. Your pump should be located so that water from any part of the boat will flow readily to the foot of the pump. If this is not the case, find the limber holes in the ribs and see that they are free and not clogged.

Your boat should be shipshape. The term "ship-shape" has gotten into the language because a ship must above all things be orderly. There must be a place for everything and everything must be kept in its place. Try to memorize not only what you have aboard but also its proper place.

Determine at once whether or not your inventory is complete. How about the anchor? If it is of the folding type, spread out the stock at right angles to the shank and see if you have the little iron wedge that will hold it in place. Go over your cable. Examine it for worn spots. Look into the pump. Pull out the plunger and examine it, and see that the valve at the bottom is in working order. Have you a sponge? Is there a stick on board with which to push down the centerboard? Have you a compass? Is it so located and hung that it will maintain a horizontal position for all motions of the boat? Are your charts on board? Have you an oar or settin' pole? Have you life preservers for all passengers? Have you a foghorn? Blow it and see how it sounds.

Now go over your lines. Are they cowtailed? Has the serving been pulled off during the rigging?

Is the mast properly stepped? Is it wedged tightly in the partners and is it wedged in the step so that it cannot roam forward or aft?

Put your tiller in the rudder and move it back and forth. With your boat at anchor it is not possible to tell exactly how the boat will react to the rudder. But it will be evident to you that when the tiller is moved to port the bow of the boat goes to starboard. When the tiller is moved to starboard, the bow of the boat goes to port.

At this point of your education, it is well to stress a number of "don'ts."

Don't think you know how to sail until you have actually had a great deal of experience.

Don't take instruction from anyone other than an expert.

Don't carry passengers until you are sure of yourself.

Don't put a strain on any line until you are sure of its function.

Don't stretch anything—line or sail or wire rigging—too tight.

Don't do things in a hurry.

Don't use anything on your boat until you know exactly what it is for.

Don't throw anything away. A block of wood or a rusty, twisted piece of iron may seem like junk; but it may have an important function which you will discover later.

Don't forget that there are rules of the road on the water just as there are on the highway. These rules of the road determine your right of way. Unless and until you definitely know that you have the right of way and unless it is perfectly apparent that the other fellow recognizes it, always assume that he has the right of way and give him plenty of room. The rules of the road will be discussed in a later chapter, but you will always be safe if you assume that the other fellow has the right to hold his course and that you must yield to him.

Remember your boat is safe when the wind is blowing on both sides of your sail at the same time. You can always parry an attack of the wind by heading the boat into the wind or by letting your sheets run so that your sails blow out like a flag. This is your safety valve.

CHAPTER VI

THREE USEFUL KNOTS

WE have left your boat tied to her mooring and have paused to study the nomenclature of the hull, spars, sails, and rigging. Before we proceed to bend and overhaul the sails, it is well to pause and study three knots which you will have to know and understand before it is safe or wise for you to begin your sailing. Marlinespike seamanship is frequently stressed to the point where it is very confusing to the beginner. I find that in my own sailing I make use of about forty-four knots, bends, and splices. But three knots will take care efficiently and safely of 90% of the work on a small boat. These three knots are the reef knot, the clove hitch, and the bowline (pronounced bo-lin). Knots are important for the following reasons:

First: an improperly tied knot, or a properly tied knot misapplied, may fail to hold, and you will lose your boat or otherwise get into trouble.

Second: a landlubber knot is quite likely to jam in such a way that it cannot be untied. The ability to untie a knot quickly and easily is just as important as to have that knot hold. If you cannot cast off a line at a time when it is imperative that you should cast it off quickly, the results may be disastrous. Furthermore, a knot that refuses to be untied and has to be cut may make it necessary for you to renew a sheet or a halliard, and that sport indulged in to any extent is likely to prove expensive.

There are three more terms which should be added to your vocabulary, for they apply particularly to knots and ropes:

The part of a rope that is attached to a sail or spar—in other words, the end that is not free—is known as the standing part. A loop that is formed in a rope is known as a bight. The end of a rope beyond a knot is called the fall.

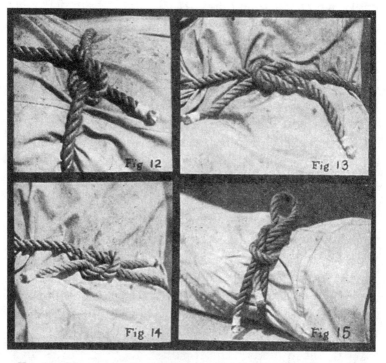

Fig. 12. The granny knot. Fig. 13. The reef knot which is also a square knot. Fig. 14. A square knot which isn't a reef knot. Fig. 15. A reef knot with one fall not pulled through.

Now get a piece of rope in your hands and tie these knots exactly in accordance with the instructions.

Consider first *the reef knot*. The principal uses of the reef knot are: 1, to tie in reefs; 2, to tie gaskets or canvass ropes around the sails for furling; 3, to join two ropes together. And in general it is a handy knot.

The easiest method to learn to tie a reef knot is to tie it the wrong way then correct the error. Pass your rope around your thigh, assuming that your thigh is the sail. Now tie the two ends of the rope together in the ordinary double knot. This knot, as tied by a landlubber, is known as a granny. Let us study that knot for a minute. You will notice that the standing parts which come around your thigh run transversely, but notice that the falls lead off from the knot up and down in the direction of your thigh and at right angles to the standing parts. (See Figure 12.)

Now carefully untie the second part of the knot and tie it in exactly backwards. (See Figure 13.) Now you will note that the falls lie parallel to the standing parts and you will notice, too, that the standing part and fall of each end of the rope are held by a bight formed by the other end of the rope. To cast off this knot, you can seize the two bights and pull them loose; or you can jerk either fall and the knot is loose. In case the knot is tied very stubbornly, you can pull one fall out straight so that it forms a line in continuation with the line of the standing part, and the other fall simply makes two half-hitches around it. These hitches can be slipped toward the end of the fall and easily released.

Now take the standing parts and pull them very tight. You will notice that the knot does not slip. The more you pull them, the tighter it gets. These are the chief advantages of any sailors' knot. Here is a simple rule for tying the reef knot: Pass the end of the rope in your right hand over the end in your left hand. Then pass the end in your left hand over the end in your right hand. Memorize it thus:

"First right over left
Then left over right."

Tie and retie that knot many times. You will gradually find that you do not have to tie the knot improperly first or to apply consciously the right-over-left-left-over-right rule.

There is another square knot, which is not a reef knot (see Figure 14), in which the standing parts are on opposite sides and the falls are on opposite sides. In other words, each side of the knot has one of the standing parts and one fall. Such a square knot is worse than a granny. The granny will jam and may possibly slip, but this false reef knot is certain to slip. It is listed here as a warning.

Always see to it that a fall and a standing part never get on the same side of a square knot.

A variation of the reef knot is shown in Figure 15. It is tied precisely like the reef knot, but one fall is not pulled through. This is a very handy knot for reefing the sails of a small boat because when it comes time to shake out the reef a quick jerk on the end of the looped fall will cast off the knot.

Fig. 16. The first movement in tying the clove hitch. Note that the fall is beneath the standing part. Fig. 17. The clove hitch completed—the fall again beneath the standing part. Fig. 18. The wrong way to tie a clove hitch: both half hitches through the same bight. Fig. 19. The clove hitch about its own standing part.

A reef knot can be depended upon only when two ends of the same rope or ends of two ropes of the same size are tied together. It is not safe to tie a small rope to a large one by means of the reef knot.

Next let us consider *the clove hitch*. This knot is called by a variety of names: clove hitch, half hitch, double hitch, two half hitches, etc. There is good authority for all of these names.

It is a very simple knot to tie yet perhaps it is improperly tied more often than any other knot. Like all good sailors' knots, it has the twin virtue of tightening under strain and of being very easy to cast off.

Turn a chair upside down so that you may tie the clove hitch around one of the legs. Assume that this leg is the piling of a dock. Secure one end of your rope so that you will imagine that it is attached to your boat. That end (and the part of the rope leading from it) is the standing part. The opposite or loose end is the fall. Now take a turn around the leg of the chair with the fall *underneath* the standing part. (Figure 16.) Let me repeat, the fall must come underneath the standing part. If the fall is above the standing part, the knot will be wrong. Now take the fall in your hand, pass another loop over the end of the chair leg with the fall underneath as before. Pull the ends tight and you have tied the knot. Now note the knot in the illustration. (Figure 17.) You will see that the standing part extends in one direction and the fall in the opposite direction. It is possible to tie two half hitches around the chair leg so that the standing part and the fall pass through the same bight. (Figure 18.) This is wrong and will not hold.

Do not take a turn around the chair leg with the fall above the standing part and then try to tie in the knot on top of that.

Two words of warning about the clove hitch:

First, it is not a safe knot to use unless there is a strain on the standing part, for it is only the strain on the standing part that keeps the knot tight. Beginners often tie a clove hitch around a sail where the strain is from the inside of the hitch and of course it will not hold. The lead of the standing part should be approximately at right angles to the timber around which the hitch is tied. If the strain comes lengthwise of the timber, the pull will loosen instead of tightening the hitch, and the line will be pulled off the end of the timber.

A variation of the clove hitch that is most useful is to pass the line around the timber and then take a clove hitch with the fall around its own standing part. (See Figure 19.) This hitch is particularly useful if you have a short line and a big pile to make fast to, as you may not have line enough to go twice around the pile but will have plenty of line to go once around the pile and twice around its own standing part.

The bowline. The bowline is a most useful knot and its purpose is to tie a loop or bight in the end of a rope. The bowline, for instance, can be used to make your cable fast to your anchor, to tie the outhaul or your reef tackle to the cringle in the leech of the sail; to make fast to a ring in a dock or in your deck. Most people who learn to tie the bowline from a book, tie it by a longer, slower, clumsy method. The following method is the way you will tie it eventually, so you may as well learn to do it correctly from the beginning.

Make one end of your practice rope fast, so that you will know it to be the standing part. Hold the standing part in your left hand, and the fall in your right. Now hit the standing part above your left hand with the fall you hold in your right (see Figure 20), and at the same time, without letting go the part held in your left hand, move your left hand higher up on the standing part and form a bight (see Figure 21). You will notice that you are holding the bight in your left hand and the fall in your right hand and that the fall passes *upward* through the bight. You will notice that the standing part is the under side of the bight. Practice this several times until you get this movement perfect. Do not attempt to complete the knot until you have mastered this part of it.

Now when you have mastered it, pass the fall under and around the standing part and down through the bight and pull tight. The resulting knot will be a large bight secured by two small bights (see Figure 22).

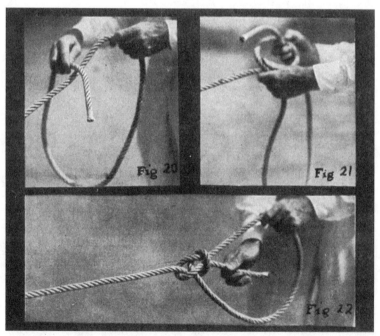

FIG. 20. The bowline—first movement. Fig. 21. The bowline—forming the first bight. Fig. 22. The bowline—completed

CHAPTER VII

BENDING AND HOISTING SAIL

Let us assume that you have a small sloop. Your sails may be bent to the spars when you get delivery of the boat or they may be given to you carefully folded and rolled in a sail bag. Make up your mind at the outset that a sail should be cared for as you would care for a sick baby; that it must always be kept clean, kept as dry as possible, and fastened to the spars as carefully as if you were making a fine painting. Fastening the sail to the spars is known as "bending the sail."

Do not carry your sails to your boat in the bottom of a leaky rowboat. Do not permit even the outside of the sail bag to get dirty. Do not throw your sails into the bottom of your sailboat until you are sure that the bottom is clean and dry. Pump out your boat before taking your sails out of the bag. It is a good idea, before you start any work on your sails, to inspect your boat thoroughly to see that it is dry and clean; to lift up some of the floor boards and place them across the cockpit or to place dry oars or boat hooks across the cockpit so that if the sail drops from your hand it will not fall into the bottom of the boat. Now we are ready to bend the mainsail.

Let us assume first that the mainsail is of the gaff type. You will find large brass-bound holes in the four

45

clews of the sail. These are called the cringles. Small
brass-bound holes along the head, the foot and the
luff are known as grommets. The two terms are interchangeable—but for the sake of clearness I will call
the large ones cringles and the small ones grommets.
The first clew of the sail to find is the throat. The
throat is generally seized to the jaws of the gaff by

Fig. 23. The gaff outhaul

passing a line through the throat cringle and either
through two holes in the jaws or through an eyelet
fastened on the under side of the gaff at the throat.
Use a short piece of cotton line for this purpose; pass
it through several times and tie it as tightly as possible
with a reef knot. Now find the peak of the sail. Tie
another short piece of cotton line into the cringle with
a bowline knot, pass it through a hole at the outer end
of the gaff from the underside to the upper side. Bring
the line back to the cringle, pass it through and pull
out the head of the sail until it is just hand tight.

Tie the end of the line with a clove hitch around both parts of itself between the cringle and the gaff. Do not pull the sail out more than hand tight and if it is a wet day or you are likely to get spray high up on the sail, draw the head a little less than hand tight. Stretching the sail is very disastrous, as it flattens out all the curves that give the sail its driving power.

In making the sail fast at the throat and the peak, do not use too long a line. This results in what the sailors call "Irish pennants"—little ends of lines all over the boat that do much to detract from its ship-shape appearance. Now take a cotton line one and one-half times the length of the gaff. Pass one end of this line around the mast and walk aft with both ends of the line. Pull hard on the line to stretch it as much as possible. It is important that the *line* should be stretched tight but that the sail should *not* be stretched tight. Put all your stretching into the line before you bend your sail. Stretching is particularly necessary with new line or with line that has not been stretched recently.

There are two kinds of line suitable for this work. One, a braided line; and the other laid line. The braided line is the sort used ordinarily for clothes line. The laid line consists of three strands and looks like regular rope. The laid line is much the better, as it stretches less. Both ends of this line should be served (see chapter on Marlinespike Seamanship). Now beginning at the throat, make one end of the line fast in the throat cringle by means of a bowline knot. Then take a half-hitch around the gaff at the first grommet.

Pass through the first grommet, lead the line to second grommet, take a half hitch around the gaff, pass through the second grommet, etc., until you reach the peak cringle. (See Figure 24.) Pass the line several times through the peak cringle and around the gaff, pulling the peak cringle snugly to the gaff, then make the line fast by a clove hitch around that part of the line that comes from the last grommet to the peak cringle.

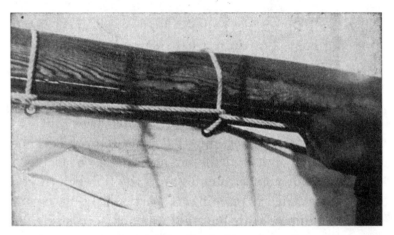

Fig. 24. Lacing the head to the gaff

Your sail is now bent to the gaff. Some sails when hoisted show deep wrinkles along the head when the lacing line is passed with a half hitch at each grommet. If this should prove to be the case with your sail, simply pass the lacing line over the gaff and through the grommets, omitting the half hitch at each turn. Next it is necessary to bend it to the mast hoops.

The standard material for this purpose is marline (pronounced marlin). Marline is heavy, double-stranded cord which is liberally tarred. Marline is the best material for this purpose because of its strength and its resistance to the weather, but it has the disadvantage of making brown, tarry marks on the sail. A heavy laid cotton cord about one-eighth inch in diameter is sufficiently strong for this purpose in a small boat and is rather cleaner to use than marline. A good grade of heavy fishing line is also suitable. The

FIG. 25. The hoop fastening

grommets are seized to the hoops by passing several turns through the grommet and around the hoop and wrapping several turns between the grommet and the hoop and tying the ends with a reef knot (Figure 25). You must be careful to seize only the grommets to the hoops, and to distinguish between the reef cringles and the grommets. The reef cringles are usually larger than the grommets and may be distinguished by their size. If in your particular sail they should be the same size as the grommets, you may distinguish them by the fact that they are always placed just a couple of inches higher than the grommet so that if two apparent grommets are placed within a couple of inches of one another, the lower one is the grommet to be seized to the hoop, and the upper one is the reef cringle which should not be seized to the hoop.

Some gaff-rigged sails are equipped with patent fastenings with a female member screwed on the hoops and a male member laced to the grommets. The female member properly belongs on the top edge of the hoop and not on the bottom edge and the male member is inserted into the female member by bending it vertically, passing it through the female member and then letting it fall to a horizontal plane. In bending the sail to the hoops by patent fastenings, do not try to force them or file them to a larger opening. The secret lies in turning the male member to the proper angle where it will slip into the female member very easily. Patent fastenings are strongly to be recommended, especially if you take proper care of your sails and remove them from your boat after each trip.

The sail is bent to the boom in precisely the same manner as it is to the gaff. First the tack is bent to a ring in the jaws or to the goose-neck, and tied down with a reef knot. Next a light line four or five feet long is made fast to the cringle in the clew, preferably by means of a bowline. This line is called the outhaul and is a very important line in determining the correct setting and proper care of your mainsail. The outhaul should be passed over the sheave (pronounced "shiv") or pulley at the very outer end of the boom. Some boats have a screw-eye for this purpose instead of a sheave. The outhaul is then led back into the boat where it can be readily reached by the helmsman and when the sail is drawn out to its proper tension it is usually belayed to a cleat on the boom.

Some boats have this cleat pretty well inboard. This has the advantage of being readily reached by the

FIG. 26. The boom outhaul

helmsman when the sail is trimmed at quite a wide angle from the boat. It has the disadvantage of using a long line which is apt to stretch or shrink more than a short one would. A good plan is to have the cleat about four feet from the end of the boom where stretching and shrinking will not be very annoying and yet where it may be reached without too much effort. (See Figure 26.) The outhaul should be stretched before making it fast to the clew. The foot of the sail should be pulled out on the outhaul until it is just hand-tight. Under no circumstances stretch it with all your strength. On a wet, rainy day it is better to err on the side of slackness rather than tautness, as the sail will shrink when it gets wet and will be stretched much more than it would on a dry day. If the wind is blowing at all hard, you may be pretty sure that the foot of your sail will be wet by flying spray. Most beginners attempt to stretch their sails out to the very ends of the spars. This should always be avoided. Spars are intentionally built longer than the sails because as sails get old and stretch they finally come out to the ends of the spars. Do not worry if a foot or so of spar extends beyond the clew of the sail. That is as it should be.

Now take another light line one and a half times the length of the boom, pass it around the mast and walk aft with both ends, stretching it in the same manner as you stretched the lacing for the head. After it is stretched, make fast one end to the gooseneck or tack cringle with a bowline, then lace it in the same manner as the gaff with a half hitch at each grommet and a clove hitch around itself at the clew cringle. It is well, also, to bind down the clew cringle to the boom by two or three turns of an extra line, which should be two or three feet long, and tie with a reef knot.

Now your mainsail is bent. The battens should next be put into the pockets. The battens are thin strips of wood which fit into pockets in the leech of the sail extending forward at right angles to the leech. The battens are of different lengths; corresponding to the length of their respective pockets. The longest pockets and battens are in the middle of the leech; the shorter ones toward the head and the foot. Battens should fit the pockets loosely. They should be tied through the grommets and through holes in the ends of the battens at the leech. The battens should be an inch or two shorter than the batten pockets so that the forward end of the batten never touches the forward end of the pocket. If your battens are too long and touch the ends of the pockets, do not hesitate to cut them off, as a tight-fitting batten makes a hard line in the sail and is apt to do permanent injury to its shape.

Bending a Marconi mainsail is rather easier than bending a gaff-rigged mainsail. Your mainsail halliard usually ends in a snaphook which you simply snap to a shackle in the headboard of the sail. There may be two or three holes for the shackle in the headboard, and a little experimentation will determine for you the hole which makes the sail set best. It is advisable at the start to use the hole nearest the luff, but if when you hoist the sail you find that when you have filled away and the sail is working, the leech is too loose and flaps, shift the shackle to the center hole. If that does not correct it, it may be well to shift the shackle to the after hole.

After you have snapped the halliard to the headboard, fit the slides onto the bottom end of the track on the after side of the mast. Make sure that the luff is straight and that none of the slides is twisted. When the bottom slide is on the track, hold it up by tying a light line beneath it around the mast. It is better practice to take a screw driver and back out the bottom screw on the track. Backing out this bottom screw one-quarter inch will be sufficient to keep the slides from dropping off the mast when you are lowering or hoisting sail. Now, beginning at the clew, fit the slides over the forward end of the track on the boom.

At the outboard end of the track on the boom, you will find a small bronze carriage usually fitted with a pin. The clew of the sail is placed in this carriage and the pin is driven through the two holes in the carriage and the clew cringle between them and secured in place by a cotter pin. With such a rig, the outhaul is generally made fast to the outer end of the boom, passed forward around the forward end of this carriage, back to the sheave at the outboard end of the boom, and forward again to a cleat. (Fig. 26.) Rig the outhaul in this manner and haul the sail out on the boom hand-tight, but bear in mind that the two ends of the outhaul act as a purchase, and unless you are careful you are apt to put more strain on the sail with this rig than in the rig described for the gaff-headed mainsail.

The track on a Marconi rig boom is generally of light material. The last foot or two at the outboard end of the boom, however, is usually made of heavy bronze bolted through the boom or secured with very long, heavy screws.

If the sail stretches far enough so that the carriage is running on this heavy part of the track, no other hold-down is necessary. But in the event that a boat is not equipped with this section of heavy track or in the event that the sail will not stretch far enough to permit the carriage to reach this section of track, the carriage and the clew cringle must be bound down to the boom by several turns of light cotton line as described in bending a gaff-headed mainsail.

Nowadays many gaff-rigged mainsails are equipped with a track and slides at the foot, and in that case the foot of such a gaff-rigged mainsail is bent to the boom precisely as has been described in the case of the Marconi sail.

The rig of the outhaul may vary on different boats, but in general you must bear in mind that the outhaul serves the purpose of pulling the foot of the sail out and another line or similar device is used to hold the clew of the sail down to the boom. Do not use one line for these double purposes, and do not hesitate to slack off the outhaul if your sail gets wet.

In the leech of the sail there is a light cotton line running from the head in Marconi mainsails and the peak in gaff-rigged mainsails to a point just above the clew. It is called the leechline. This line is sewed loosely into a pocket in the leech and leaves the pocket through a grommet just above the clew. It is used as a puckering string in the event that the leech is too loose. This rarely happens. Most leeches are too tight. They are seldom too loose. The best thing to do with the leech line is to leave it as loose as possible, coil it neatly, and secure it where it will not make an Irish pennant. If, when you get under way, the leech of the sail should flap or fall off to leeward, then you can tighten the leechline by drawing it in very gently. In no case should it be trimmed hard. The leechline must never be used for reefing, for tying down the clew or for an outhaul. Those are not its functions and if used for such purposes it will soon destroy the proper set of the sail.

Jibs on small boats are generally of two types: club-footed or loose-footed. In either event, they are fastened to the jib stay by simply snapping the snap hooks onto the stay, beginning with the head and running down to the foot. A snap hook on the halliard is generally snapped directly into the head cringle or in some cases snapped onto a shackle through the head cringle. Before bending the halliard, make sure that it leads fair; that is to say, that the halliard is not wrapped around its hoisting part or the jib stay and if there is a block (pulley) at the head of the jib make sure that the parts of the halliard running through the block are not twisted.

The tack of the jib must be snapped or seized to a ring in the deck at the bottom of the jib stay, or lacking that, to the very lowest part of the turnbuckle securing the jib stay. In some instances, the club is just as long as the jib. In most instances, however, it extends only from the clew, forward to the first grommet, which is usually larger than the other grommets. The forward end of the jib club is seized to this grommet by a short piece of line tied with a reef knot. The club is then laced in the same manner as the boom and gaff of the gaff-headed mainsail by a lacing line properly stretched and tied securely at the leech. The jib

sheet is rove through a block about one-third of the
length of the club forward from the leech. (Figure 27).
The position of this block cannot be determined
exactly, except by experiment. In general, the farther
forward the block is placed, the flatter the jib will
stand. But you should experiment moving the block
forward and aft on the club to get maximum efficiency

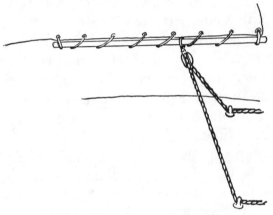

Fig. 27. The jib club and jib sheet block

from the jib. All this is explained in a later chapter
and is not particularly important when you are first
learning to sail.

If there are battens in the leech of the jib, you
should make sure that they are properly placed in the
batten pockets and that they do not touch the forward
ends of the pockets. Jib battens are so short that they
are generally left tied in place when the jib is housed.
The leech line of the jib is treated in the same manner
as the leechline of the mainsail. In the case of the
jib, it is even more important than in the case of the

mainsail that the leech should not be too tight. The reason for this is apparent because if the leech is curved it not only affects the efficiency of the jib but also backwinds the mainsail. That is to say, the wind blowing off the jib is changed in its direction by a hollow leech so that it blows directly onto the luff of the mainsail, thereby greatly affecting the mainsail's power to drive you to windward. All this will be explained at length in a later chapter.

If the jib is of the loose-footed type, there is no club and the middle of the jib sheet is snapped directly into the cringle at the clew and led through blocks or fairleaders on the side decks back to the helm.

With the sails now bent to the spars and stays, we are ready to hoist sail.

In a sloop you always hoist the mainsail first. If by any chance you should be sailing a yawl or ketch or schooner, begin with the aftermost sail. It is good practice never to hoist a jib until you are ready to cast off from dock or mooring or to break out your anchor. The reason for this is obvious when you consider that at anchor your boat should be a weather vane, always pointing directly into the wind. If you hoist a jib first, the wind catching in the jib is apt to carry the bow of the boat away from the wind; whereas if you get your aftermost sail hoisted first, the pressure of the wind on it simply makes you head into the wind so that you will not start sailing before you are ready.

To hoist a gaff-rigged mainsail, you begin by casting off the main sheet. Then raise your topping lift until the boom swings clear of the boom crutch. The boom crutch is the scissor-like hinged support which is placed under the after part of the boom to support it when the sail is lowered.

Belay your topping lift, take down the boom crutch, and stow it away safely. The topping lift now supports the boom and you are ready to hoist on the halliards. Remember that if your boat is properly rigged the peak halliard leads down on the starboard side of the mast, and the throat halliard on the port side of the mast. Pull evenly on both halliards so that the gaff rises horizontally. Do not let the peak go up faster or slower than the throat. Before starting to hoist, you will have planned the general direction in which you intend to sail. From this you can frequently determine whether you will have the wind most generally on your port or starboard hand. In hoisting the sail, it is wise to see to it that the peak ascends on what will be most generally the leeward side of your topping lift. If the boat is equipped with two topping lifts or with lazy-jacks, it is necessary, of course, that the peak should be hoisted between them. It should not be necessary to caution you against having any loose ends of line lying over the gaff before the hoisting process begins. Yet all too frequently novice skippers send the ends of their main sheet or other lines aloft for a ride on the gaff.

If the sail stalls on its way up so that you cannot hoist it readily. it is because one of the mast hoops is sticking on the varnished mast. A very slight coating of hard grease on the inner rim of the forward side of your mast hoops will prevent this occurrence; but if a hoop sticks in hoisting, it can generally be remedied at once by letting the throat drop suddenly for a foot or so. If this does not free the hoop, it will be necessary to belay both halliards on the cleats, go forward and lift up the forward side of the hoops that are sticking. There is comfort in the thought that when a hoop sticks so high up the mast that you cannot reach it, it is usually freed immediately by dropping the throat; and on the other hand when a hoop cannot be freed by dropping the throat it is generally at a point so far down the mast that it is readily reached by hand.

After freeing the hoop, return to your halliard fall and continue to hoist until the throat is stretched reasonably tight. Too much stretching on the throat has almost as bad an effect as too much stretching on the foot of the sail; but whereas most beginners stretch the foot of the sail too tight they usually fail to stretch the luff of the sail tight enough. On larger boats it is generally good practice to belay the peak halliard when the throat seems to be fully hoisted and the gaff is still in a horizontal position. Then put a little extra strength on the throat, make sure that the luff line is stretched tight, and then belay the throat halliard. If the boom swings about jaws instead of a gooseneck, it is wise to hoist the throat six or eight inches higher than the saddle on which the boom should rest. The reason for this is that when the peak is hoisted fully the angle of the gaff to the mast is changed, and the whole throat is therefore lowered a few inches. When the throat halliard is belayed, hoist the peak until deep, full wrinkles appear in the throat of the sail. The gen-

FIG. 28. Gaff-headed mainsail properly hoisted. Note the wrinkles parallel to a line from the peak to the tack

FIG. 29. Gaff-headed mainsail improperly hoisted. Note the wrinkles parallel to a line from the throat to the clew

eral direction of these wrinkles should be approximately parallel to a line drawn from the peak to the tack. (Figure 28.) Unless these wrinkles appear, the peak is not hoisted high enough. A sail that is headed into

the wind and stands perfectly flat without any apparent
wrinkles is improperly hoisted. If the wrinkles run in
a general direction parallel to a line from the throat
to the clew, the peak is very much too low and must
be hoisted higher. (Figure 29.)

After you have hoisted the sail to the proper position, belay the peak halliard and then study these
wrinkles. It must be borne in mind that the wrinkles

Fig. 30. Topping lift too tight. Note how it cuts the belly
of the sail

disappear as soon as you cast off, and the sail fills
with wind. But the sail cannot take its proper shape
unless it has the proper wrinkles when hoisted. If you
have done your hoisting properly, you will find that
the topping lift is now slack and the weight of the
boom is carried by the halliards. If this is not the case,
slack off the topping lift a foot or two. The topping
lift should be so slack that it does not cut into the belly
of the sail when it is to leeward. It is in its essence

a line for emergency use rather than for constant use and should be left slack unless some definite purpose can be served by having it taut. (Figure 30.) If your sail is equipped with lazyjacks, some similar adjustment will probably be necessary. As a rule, lazyjacks are too slack after the sail is hoisted. They should be just slack enough so that they do not cut into the belly of the sail and just taut enough so that they do not hang in loops below the boom where they are apt to catch in deck fittings when the boom swings back and forth over the boat.

Hoisting the Marconi mainsail consists merely in hoisting the halliard until the headboard is as high as it will go. The luff line should be stretched tight but not so tight that it flattens out the wrinkles formed in the luff just aft of the luff line. These wrinkles are vertical wrinkles parallel to the mast and they are as important in a Marconi mainsail as the proper wrinkles in a gaff-headed mainsail. Stretching the luff line too tight will flatten out these wrinkles and although most novice skippers err on the side of not stretching the luff tight enough, it is a less serious fault than stretching the luff too tight.

Corresponding to the difficulty of sticking hoops in the gaff-headed mainsail is the difficulty of sticking slides in the case of the Marconi mainsail. But in the Marconi mainsail the cause and the remedy are somewhat different. The slides in a Marconi mainsail generally stick at joints in the track. The track is seldom put on in one piece and where the ends of the pieces of track come together there is apt to be a little difference of alignment or a small gap on which the corners of a slide will stick. Occasionally, also, a screw pulls loose and gets in the way of the slides. Greasing the slides does not help very much and there is no weight of a gaff to free a stuck slide by suddenly slacking the halliard a foot or two. In the event of a stuck slide, you must go forward to the mast, seize the halliard with one hand and the luff of the sail with the other; then alternately raising the sail by the halliard and pulling it down by the luff, you can work the fractious slide over the inequality of the track. Defects in a track should be remedied as soon as possible because it is sometimes necessary to get sail down in a hurry, and that is usually the time when the track and the slide have a battle and the sail can neither be raised nor lowered.

In boisterous weather, great care should be taken to hoist the mainsail slowly and to look aloft throughout the hoisting. When partly hoisted, Marconi mainsails have a bad habit of flapping around so that they sometimes wrap themselves about the ends of the long spreaders that are almost invariably part of the rigging of a Marconi mast. To continue to hoist a sail when it has wrapped itself around a spreader is sure to result in a torn sail. A sail can usually be freed from the spreader by a gentle pull on the leech or it will probably free itself in a minute or two with a slight change in position of the boat. But there should be no pull on the luff or on the halliard while the mainsail and the spreaders are playing tag.

The jib is hoisted in the same manner as a Marconi

mainsail—luff line stretched taut but not so taut as to flatten out the wrinkles just aft.

With your sails hoisted, examine them for the following characteristics: first, the leech of the mainsail and the leech of the jib should stand perfectly flat. They should not be hollow. The luff of the mainsail and the luff of the jib should be full and should have the characteristic wrinkles. They should never be flat —always full. The leech of both jib and mainsail

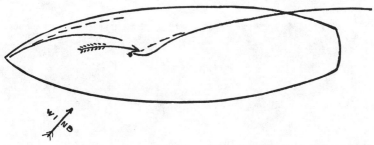

Fig. 31. The jib back-winding the mainsail. The dotted lines indicate the proper trim of the jib and the resulting proper hard fullness in the luff of the mainsail.

should be roached. That is to say, the curve described by the leech should be convex and should extend outward beyond a straight line drawn from the head to the clew in jib or Marconi mainsail or from the peak to the clew in a gaff-headed mainsail. The leech should not be niggerheeled. A niggerheeled leech shows a concave curve or a curve extending inward from a straight line between head and clew in the case of a jib or Marconi mainsail or from the peak to the clew in the case of a gaff-headed mainsail. The leech of the jib should particularly be examined to see that it stands flat and does not backwind the mainsail. (Figure 31.)

When sails are hoisted and before you cast off, always be sure that the halliards are carefully coiled down and capsized. The halliards on a small boat are usually coiled by taking the fall close to the cleat in both hands, separating the hands until enough rope is made to form a loop of the coil, placing both ends of the loop in your left hand and continuing the process. Do not coil a line over your hand and elbow. The coils

FIG. 32. Halliards properly coiled

are too small to be useful and the method is the mark of a landlubber. The coils should be laid down, preferably on the cockpit floor, but at any rate where they will not fall overboard and should be placed so that the top side of the coil leads directly to the cleat. (Figure 32.) That is what is meant by capsizing the coil. The coil not capsized has a fall or free end on the top, and the end leading to the cleat is at the bottom of the coil. This is incorrect because when the sail is lowered the rope runs out from the bottom of the coil instead of from the top and is quite likely to pull a loop of the coil along with it and jam it into a block.

Never place one coil on top of another. Never place a coil in such a position that it will be disturbed when the halliards are cast off the cleats and the sail is lowered.

On some boats it is necessary to hang up the coiled halliards or to tuck them in under the standing part of the halliard to prevent them from falling overboard. If this is necessary in your boat, you must bear in mind that before lowering sail the coiled halliards must be taken from their position and laid carefully on deck so that they will run off fairly and without fouling.

Personally I abhor coiled halliards and on one small boat which I owned I had drawers built under the forward deck. When I hoisted sail, I pulled open the drawers and let the falls drop into them just as they came from my hands. They lay thus naturally in such a way that they would pay out without kinking or fouling when the sail was lowered. The drawers were closed immediately after the sail was hoisted, and nothing could disturb the natural "lay" of the line. With this device I never experienced a fouled halliard; but lacking such accommodations halliards must be carefully coiled or they are certain to be disturbed by your feet or by the motion of the boat.

CHAPTER VIII

REEFING

THE sails are the power plant of your boat. They are designed to give maximum power for ordinary light winds known as a whole sail breeze. When it is blowing so hard that the boat, spars, sails or rigging are in danger, the sail is reduced by reefing. Some boats are better able to carry sail than other boats. A keel boat with plenty of outside ballast can carry whole sail when a centerboard boat with only a little ballast, all of it placed inside the boat, may well have to reef.

I recall staggering down the Sound in a small boat under close-cropped canvas in a terrible blow in which all the crew were wearing life preservers. It did not seem possible that we could sail through it, and right in the middle of the heaviest squall of all, we passed a big heavily-laden three-masted coasting schooner flying everything but the skipper's undershirt. A three-reef gale for a tiny boat was a whole sail breeze for the schooner.

You must judge the power of the wind in relation to the capacity of your boat. At the very outset of every sail you should determine the strength of the breeze and classify it as whole sail, one reef, two reef, or three reef breeze. Judge the power of the breeze by the condition of the water. If there are no whitecaps, it is probably a whole sail breeze. If there are small, occasional whitecaps, it means a one-reef breeze. If the whole surface of the water is as white as it is green, it is a two-reef breeze. If it is really blowing a gale, it is a three-reef breeze.

Judge the wind by its feeling on your body, by the things it does to your clothing. Judge it by the way other boats are behaving. If boats of the general characteristics of your boat are carrying two reefs and sailing properly, it is a two-reef breeze. If boats of the same characteristics as your boat are lugging full sail but are not carrying it comfortably; if they are obliged to luff up into the wind to let the wind blow on both sides of the sail; if they are staggering along with their lee rail buried, they are obviously carrying too much sail. Do not hesitate to ask more experienced sailors how many reefs to take in. On Great South Bay where racing boats are fairly tender, even the most experienced skippers do not hesitate to ask opinions of other experienced skippers as to their judgment of the power of the wind. They know that improper reefing will cost them the race.

Watch the wind for ten or fifteen minutes before you prepare to get under way. If it seems to be increasing in force, it is well to prepare for a heavier blow. If it is softening, the delay may save you the trouble of taking in a reef and shaking it out afterwards. I recall one race in which I double-reefed my mainsail and changed to a storm jib between the warning gun and the preparatory gun. I crossed the starting line nine minutes behind my class, but won the race by over ten minutes simply because I was properly reefed, while my competitors staggered along under a crush of canvas they could not carry. I recall another race in which I was carrying two reefs and a storm jib at the preparatory gun but crossed the starting line three minutes later with full sail and spent most of the afternoon bobbing around in a flat calm. You must reef to meet the conditions of the wind and the wind is nearly always fickle.

Most beginners overestimate the strength of an on-shore breeze and are almost certain to underestimate the strength of an off-shore breeze. Wind blowing on the shore kicks up a heavy sea. On the other hand, when the wind is blowing off-shore, the sea appears perfectly calm; but when you are out in it the story is vastly different. You can never judge the strength of an off-shore breeze by the appearance of the water. Land breezes are usually very puffy and squally. Sea breezes, on the other hand, are usually very steady. If they increase or decrease, the change in strength is generally gradual; but with a land breeze you may have no wind one minute and the next minute you may be dealt a knock-down blow of almost hurricane force. This is readily understood when you consider that land breezes travel over hills and mountains, forests and plains. Bunches of wind are caught and trapped behind obstacles while other bunches rush ahead over a terrain that is free from obstruction. When the wind strikes your boat it is mixed up of patches that have met obstacles and patches that have had a free course. So that you must be prepared to sail one minute with no wind at all and the next minute in half a gale.

In reefing for a land breeze, it is well to study not only the strength of the breeze but its other characteristics. Study the duration of the puffs and the relative duration of the calm spells between the puffs. If the puffs are strong but come at long intervals with relatively long spells of light airs between them, reef for the wind that blows between the puffs. If, on the other hand, the puffs are coming thick and fast, with only short spells of calm between them, then reef for the puffs. To make this clear, it must be explained that it is necessary at all time to keep way on your boat. If you have long spells of calm, your boat may lose all its headway if too closely reefed. Then when the puffs strike you, you are at their mercy. If, on the other hand, the calm spells are of short duration and you are properly reefed for the puffs, you can keep the boat moving by the momentum which you gain through carrying sail properly in the puffs.

Land breezes are always characterized by the dark spots or catspaws that scurry across the water beneath the puffs of wind. An alert skipper can always see a puff coming and can always be ready when it strikes. But he cannot parry a puff, however well prepared he may be, unless his boat is moving fast enough to allow a stream of water to flow past his rudder.

There is a bit more danger in over-reefing than in under-reefing. It is better to have slightly too much sail than a great deal too little sail. Therefore do not make the mistake of thinking that because you are a beginner it is better to reef at all times. This is a very common mistake and more beginners get into trouble from not having enough sail to work the boat than through carrying too much sail.

The reason so many boats are improperly reefed is not because the skipper knows no better but because he is too lazy. Reefing takes time and effort, and the lazy skipper would rather flirt with danger than bother with taking in a reef. Similarly, when the breeze has softened he will loaf along under too little canvas rather than bother shaking out a reef with the chance that he may have to reef again.

Each reef has a cringle in the luff, a cringle in the leech, and a row of short cords sewn at their middle points into grommets in the sail. These cords are called the "reefing points."

It is possible to reef under way; but in a small boat it is always easier and quicker to lower the sails, drop anchor or drift, and tie in the reefs properly. A boat is reefed in much the same manner in which the mainsail is bent to the boom. Just as you tied down the tack cringle in bending your mainsail to the boom, so you tie down the cringle in the luff at the first reef. It should be tied securely to the boom, using a reef knot. Then rig an outhaul through the cringle in the leech, pass it over a sheave or eyelet in the end of the boom, haul it out hand-tight, and make it fast to a cleat on the boom. The temptation in reefing is always to pull the reef tighter than you would stretch the foot of the sail. There is some justification for this as the reef brings your sail farther inboard; but if you value your sail, do not stretch it too tight. Now seize the middle of that part of the sail which lies between the foot and the first reef. Pull it out toward you and roll it carefully into a neat furl so as to bring the grommets of the reefing points down to the boom. Then beginning at the luff and working aft, tie in all the points tightly. To do this it will be necessary to pass one side of the point under the sail. Be sure that it passes under the sail only. Do not pass the point under the boom or under the lacing line. There is always danger that you may tie one side of a point to the opposite side of another point. This is due to the fact that you cannot see the points on the opposite side of the sail and you must be guided by feeling. You are quite apt to tie a point in the first reef, for instance, to a point in the third reef. To guard against this, take both ends of the point and pull them back and forth to make sure that you have both ends of the same rope. If a pull on a point which you have passed from the other side of the sail is not felt immediately by the hand that is holding the point on the near side of the sail, you will know that you have two different points and not two ends of the same point.

Smooth out the part of the sail that is reefed and make it as small and as free from wrinkles as possible. The points may be tied with a reef knot (see Fig 13 in Chapter V) or with a modified reef knot (see Fig. 15). If you use the modified reef knot, make sure that the bight of the end which is not pulled through is headed up. When all the points are tied down, take the leech of the part of the sail that is reefed, roll it up

Photo M. Rosenfeld

Fig. 33. Properly reefed

Fig. 34. Improperly reefed. Note slack hold-down at tack, lack of outhaul at clew, careless tying of hold-down at clew, foot of sail improperly furled, reefing points tied on opposite sides of the boom, and some reefing points tied around the boom. Reefing points near clew missing altogether. Note vertical wrinkles in sail, indicative of bad reefing.

tightly, place it upon the boom, and then, with another line, tie down the cringle in the leech to the boom. You will note that there are two lines through this cringle—the outhaul and the hold-down. Always use two lines for this work. Remember that while the reefing points are tied just around the sail, the cringles in the luff and the leech are tied down hard to the boom. If it is necessary to tie in a second reef, repeat the process but tie the second reef on the opposite side of the sail to the first one. If the first reef is tied on the port side of the sail, tie the second reef on the starboard side. Use separate lines for the luff cringles, separate outhauls, and separate hold-downs in the leech cringles. If you are tying in a third reef make sure it is tied on the opposite side to the second reef. It may be that the lowest batten in your sail will cut through the third reef. If that is the case, be sure you take out the batten from the pocket before tying in the reef.

If your sail is particularly flat, you will get better results by tying the reefing points in the following order: first tie the point nearest the luff, then the point nearest the leech, then the second point from the luff, then the second point from the leech, etc., until you meet in the middle. But for most sails it is better practice to begin at the luff and work aft. If you are in a hurry and two people are tying in a reef at the same time, have one work aft from the luff while the other works forward from the leech. Do not have one man start in the middle and work aft.

Most small boats do not reef the jib. They carry a full jib with a full mainsail or with a single reefed mainsail and a storm jib or No. 2 jib as it is sometimes called, of smaller dimensions than the standard jib when the mainsail is double or triple reefed. If the jib has reefing points, you proceed exactly the same way as in the case of reefing the mailsail, making sure that the clew is tied down, the outhaul stretched hand tight, the points tied in, the leech furled and laid on top of the club, and the leech cringle tied down to the club.

FIG. 35. A scandalized jib

Sometimes jibs are merely scandalized; that is to say, tied down at the luff and the leech but not otherwise reefed. If your boat has just a single jib without facilities for reefing it, it would be well to take it to the nearest hardware store and have them insert a cringle in the luff and another in the leech to enable you to scandalize it. Ask a more experienced sailor just how far above the foot these cringles should be placed.

In shaking out a reef, we reverse the order of tying it in. It is rarely necessary to lower sail in order to shake out a reef. Always begin with the middle reef point. Jerk the fall of the knot free, then jerk it in another direction and the knot is immediately untied. Work forward and aft from the middle reef point until all the points in that particular reef are untied. Then cast off the luff hold-down, then the leech outhaul, and finally the leech hold-down. This order must be preserved. If the luff and leech hold-downs are cast off before the reefing points, you are quite likely to tear your sail. If the leech hold-down is cast off before the leech outhaul, the whole weight of the boom will pull out on your leech and will not only stretch your sail badly but will also make it very difficult for you to cast off the outhaul while that strain is on it. This is the reason why you should always use two lines at the leech cringle. If the third reef has been tied in and a batten has been removed to make that possible, the batten should be reinserted before the leech outhaul and hold-down are cast off; unless, of course, the batten pocket is below the leech cringle. In a gaff-rigged mainsail, after you have shaken out a reef drop the peak to the horizontal position before attempting to hoist sail again. After you have reefed or after you have shaken out a reef, hoist sail very cautiously. When the sail above the topmost row of reefing points is hoisted, examine it carefully to see if all the points have been tied in or cast off as the case may be. Many a sail is torn through tying half a point on the port side of the first reef, for instance, to half of another point on the starboard side of the third reef. Then when the sail is hoisted, the entire weight of the sail and boom falls on the point in the third reef that should not have been tied in and a tear is almost inevitable.

Some day I hope to own a boat that will have three distinctive sets of reefing points. The first row of points could be of braided line; the second row of points of three-strand laid line; the third row of points of four-strand laid line. Then I could always be sure of tying in the proper reef and there would be no danger of tying half a point in one reef to half a point in another. They could be distinguished by their appearance or by their feel in the dark, but I have never seen a boat so equipped.

When reefing under way, it is always necessary to be sailing close hauled so the boom will be pretty well inboard. The sail should be lowered so that a little bit more than enough for the reef may be gathered along the boom. If the sail is not lowered quite far enough, it is impossible to tie in a neat reef. In a small boat, however, reefing under way is not advisable. In shaking out under way, the practice of cutting the leech outhaul and hold-down is strongly to be recommended. It not only saves time but saves a strain on the sail. The period when the sail is held only at the leech should be just as short as possible.

In reefing it is most important to preserve the fore and aft balance of rig. Very early in life I got into no end of trouble from carrying a double-reefed mainsail and a full jib set from a long bowsprit. The result was that there was too much sail forward of the center of resistance of the boat and too little sail aft. Consequently the boat carried a very pronounced lee helm and did not head up into the wind. When a mainsail is double or triple reefed, the jib must always be shortened and frequently with three reefs in the mainsail a small sloop can be sailed handily without any jib at all.

Some sails are not equipped with reefing points, but merely have a row of grommets through which a lacing line may be rove. To my mind it is much wiser to cut a cotton line into two-foot lengths, serve the ends and keep them as reefing points so that you may pass a point through each of the grommets and tie in each point separately.

CHAPTER IX

THEORY OF SAILING

GIVE a small boy a puddle of water, a chip of wood, a twig and a piece of paper and he will build himself a boat. All boats built out of such materials by small boys with a puddle as the inspiration are alike. A hole is gouged somewhere about the middle of the piece of wood, the twig or stick is thrust into it, the paper is roughly torn into a square and is set athwart the chip on the improvised mast. The boat is launched at the windward side of the puddle and sails to the leeward side. Then it is carried back to the windward side before it can sail again.

In ships as in other things the history of the individual is akin to the history of the race; and when primitive man first began to sail, his first crude boat was probably a raft of logs, his first sail a square sail supported by a mast somewhere about the middle, and his only sailing was dead before the wind.

In fact, the first sailboat of which we have any record is pictured on an Egyptian vase made somewhere in the Nile valley about 6,000 years before Christ. Although the hull of the boat had progressed somewhat from the raft stage, the sail was a square-rigged sail not dissimilar to the paper sail with which the small boy of to-day navigates a puddle. The conditions on

the Nile made such a vessel highly efficient. So efficient, in fact, that for centuries it prevented any further development. The Nile flows northward to the
Mediterranean, yet the prevailing wind blows from
the north, against the current of the stream. A vessel
with a large square sail can easily sail upstream against
the current. The same vessel with its sail furled can
just as readily drift down the stream with the current.
The early Egyptians hinged their masts near the deck
so that mast and all could be lowered for the trip
downstream. Oars, of course, were used; but the current and the sail did most of the work. It is rather
interesting to note that the Burmese junks which
to-day navigate the Irawadi are almost exact replicas
of the early Egyptian boats. For the conditions on the
Nile and the Irawadi are precisely the same, the current running against the prevailing wind. The old
square rig is by far the best rig ever devised for sailing
before the wind.

Long after the fore and aft rig was developed, the
square rig continued to be the favorite in ships that
made cross-seas voyages. We think of it as antiquated
to-day, but it must be borne in mind that most long-
distance voyages under sail have always been made in
the path of the Trade Winds; and that a fair wind,
that is to say, a wind blowing from abaft the beam
could usually be counted upon for the greater part of a
passage. A square-rigged ship behaves far better than
a fore-and-aft-rigged vessel when the wind is abaft the
beam. It took an enormous crew to handle the sails,
but sail was made or doused up on the yards where

the seamen were out of danger from seas that might sweep aboard. The yards could be braced to the proper angle and kept there; and all in all the square rig was ideally suited for the conditions governing cross-seas passages.

The first fore and aft rigs were developed by the Arabs. The Arab boats were rigged with sails known as lateen sails. They had short stubby masts and from them swung enormous yards so balanced that they raked high into the air aft of the masts. The Arabian dhow is very efficient before the wind, and the sails can be hauled nearly into a fore and aft position so that they are also effective on the wind. It was a long time before the lateen sail was converted into the present familiar fore and aft rig and it is interesting to note that the first fore and aft sails on square-rigged ships were lateen sails. The *Victory*, Admiral Nelson's famous flagship, was rigged with a lateen sail on her mizzen-mast and it was not until after the Battle of Trafalgar that the lateen yard was taken down and in its place was set a gaff-rigged spanker, the forerunner of the spankers which were so characteristic of the clipper ships.

The true fore and aft sail is a sail whose forward edge or luff is secured to a mast or a stay and whose surface pivots about that forward edge. When a fore-and-aft-rigged vessel is pointed into the wind, the sails lie directly amidships and flutter out like flags.

It was by very slow and easy stages that seafaring mankind weened itself from the square rig. Hundreds of years passed before seamen attempted to sail with the wind forward of the beam. When they got to the point of reaching, that is to say, of sailing with the wind blowing on the beam, they made almost as much leeway as headway. In other words, they slid off their course and moved through the water not only dead ahead but also sidewise. So that it was easier, especially in the days of galley slaves, to row the boat with a beam wind than to sail it. Gradually, however, boats changed their form. Keels were built to offer lateral resistance to the water. The high poops and forecastles which offered so much windage were gradually reduced, and at last it was discovered that it was possible to sail a boat against its propelling force—the wind. When you come to think of it, it is rather an astounding fact that a boat can make progress against the force that is driving it.

But, as a matter of fact, the wind does not drive a sailboat backwards. True, its force, exerted against a plane surface opposed to it, would be applied in the direction of the wind. But when that force is applied to the curved surface of a sail trimmed at a sharp angle to the wind, the force takes an entirely different direction.

It was formerly thought that the wind exerted all of its power on the windward side of the sail.

It was not until the Wright brothers began to fly and aviation became an actuality that we really discovered what made a vessel go to windward. And it must be borne in mind that man flew for many years without any real knowledge of what kept an airplane aloft. The discovery came about accidentally. An airplane was being prepared for a demonstration. There was not time properly to dope the wings. Therefore the engineer in charge of the test gave orders that the bottom surfaces of the wings only were to be doped, as it was believed that it was the bottom surface of an airplane wing that suspended the plane in the air. When the time came for the take-off it was found that the plane would not leave the ground. At about the same time, another plane met with an accident in the air and fell rapidly from a considerable height, putting an enormous strain upon the wings. It was found, to the astonishment of all who observed it, that the under surface of the wings was not damaged; but great strips were torn out of the upper surface. Meanwhile, the experimental plane had had the upper surface of the wings doped and had no difficulty at all in flying.

Aerodynamic experts immediately jumped to the conclusion that it was the upper surface of the wings that supported a plane in the air. The wind flowing over the curved surface of the plane creates a partial vacuum which lifts the plane against gravity. Similarly, the wind blowing past the leeward side of a sail imparts a lift, as it were, partially against the direction of the wind. It is this lift or suction that makes a boat go to windward. It is the leeward side of the sail that does most of the work.

Dr. Manfred Curry and numerous other experimenters have proved this in wind tunnel experiments and also in experiments with sails. The findings of these scientists are of absorbing interest to the advanced sailor.

But it will suffice for the novice to know that the wind blowing over the arched surface of an airplane wing exerts a negative pressure or upward lift as

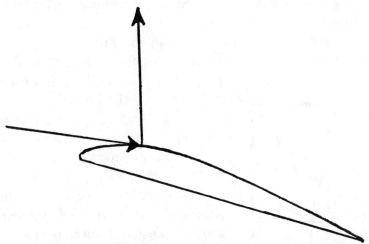

Fig. 36. The force of the wind applied to an airplane wing

shown in Figure 36. (The direction is approximate only. This book does not pretend to be scientific.)

Similarly, the wind blowing upon the arched surface of a sail imparts a forward lift. (See Figure 37.)

Now if we remember our physics, we will recall that any force may be

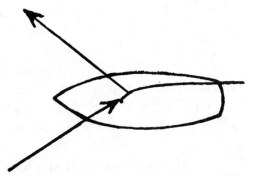

Fig. 37. The forward lift of the wind on the leeward side of the sail (boat is sailing to windward).

broken into its component parts by means of the old Parallelogram of Forces. In Figure 38, the line AB represents the force and direction of the forward lift given by the wind. If we draw a line BC parallel to the keel of the boat, its length will be proportional to the amount of forward drive in the line AB while the lines DB or AC drawn at right angles to BC will be proportional to the amount of leeward drive in the line AB.

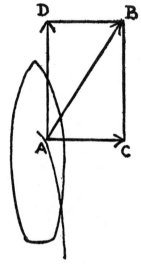

But the hull of the boat is so shaped as to offer the least possible resistance to that part of the wind's force represented by CB and AD. At the same time, the shape of the hull, and particularly the keel and the centerboard, are designed to offer the greatest possible resistance to that part of the wind's force represented by the lines DB or AC. The result is that the boat moves approximately along the line AD except in so far as the lateral resistance of the boat is overcome by that part of the force represented by AC or DB. This exception causes the boat to drift somewhat to leeward. It is known as leeway (pronounced, as it is spelled, lee-way).

FIG. 38. The parallelogram of forces

It is evident, however, that a boat will not go *directly* against its driving force. Therefore when a boat sails against the wind it is obliged to tack. That is to say, to sail as close to the wind as possible in one direction, then go about, head to wind, and sail off at an angle of almost 90° from its first course, thus zigzagging toward the direction from which the wind is blowing.

This is distinctly a layman's clumsy attempt to express a scientific explanation of a rather complicated phenomenon. But it should suffice for the beginner. It is more accurate than the most scientific explanation that was possible a few years ago—and sailors have been making their vessels go to windward for countless generations with no scientific theories at all.

CHAPTER X

BEFORE THE WIND

In many respects the easiest way to sail a boat is before the wind. This is known variously as "running," "scudding," "sailing free" and sometimes called "sailing downhill." If you were sailing an old square rigger it would be quite the easiest way to sail, for your sails would be bent to square yards which would be balanced on either side of the mast and would be braced by lines at the outer ends. A fore-and-aft-rigged vessel, however, is not so well adapted to running before the wind, and as a result this manner of sailing presents certain difficulties.

It is very important that you should be able at once to determine the direction of the wind. Your best indication is the fly or small flag balanced horizontally on the truck of the mast. The fly is the most accurate indicator of the wind but in very light airs the fly may droop and fail to show the wind's direction. Baby ribbon tied high up on the shrouds will sometimes indicate wind direction when the fly hangs limp. Cigarette smoke is also a valuable indication of wind direction. Wetting a finger in the mouth and holding it up so that the cool side shows the direction of the wind is the time-honored method but one which is rarely necessary. In general it is easy to develop a consciousness of wind direction. You feel the wind on one cheek more than another, you may feel it on the back of your neck, or on your hands, or your hair. Your true sailor is always conscious of the direction of the wind without making any determined effort to discover it. One of the most dependable and useful indicators of wind direction is the appearance of the waves. The waves come almost directly from the direction of the wind, and for the purpose of ordinary sailing the direction as determined by the waves is usually sufficient. It should be stated in passing, however, that waves do not roll exactly down wind. There is always a slight variation between the angle of the waves and the angle of the wind. Form the habit of watching the waves and judging the wind from them.

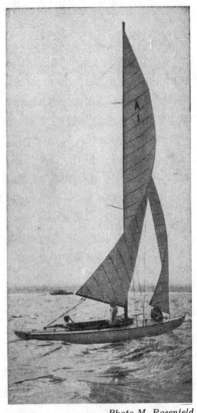

Photo M. Rosenfeld

FIG. 39. Before the wind

When you sail before the wind the main sheet is payed out until the mainsail is at right angles to the center line of the boat. This does not mean that the boom is at right angles to the center line of the boat. The top half of the sail always sags forward and if the boom were at right angles the gaff would sag off beyond a right-angle position. The sheet must be trimmed so that just as much of the sail as possible is at right angles to the boat without any part of the sail sagging forward of that line. If you are sailing dead before the wind the mainsail may be payed out to port or to starboard, but as a rule the wind is slightly over one quarter, and of course the sail must be on the opposite side. If the wind is coming slightly to starboard of a point dead aft, then the mainsail is set on the port side and vice versa. Before attempting to sail before the wind you should always put a strain on the topping lift to top the boom a little higher than in sailing any other course. If there are two topping lifts and the sail is set to port, hoist on the starboard lift. If the sail is set to starboard, hoist on the port lift. If you have but one lift and can plan your course beforehand and you know that your sail will be to port, hoist the gaff on the port side of the lift so that the lift will be on the starboard side of the sail.

The jib sheet should be trimmed so that the jib will be as nearly at right angles to the center line of the boat as will not interfere with its drawing. It will be found, however, that in running before the wind the jib is of but little use because the mainsail blankets it or cuts off the wind from reaching it. Therefore, as a general rule, the jib sheet is trimmed closer than the main sheet. After you have become proficient in sailing before the wind, it is sometimes wise to spread the jib on the opposite side to that on which the mainsail is set. A boat carrying its jib on one side and its mainsail on the other is said to be "wung-out," that is to say she is sailing wing and wing like a bird. The ordinary jib that is loose footed or bent to a club will not stay wung-out. If the jib has a sprit—a light spar running from the clew at right angles to the jib stay—it will remain wung-out reasonably well. Some boats are equipped with whisker poles. A whisker pole is a light boom with jaws on one end and a short spike on the other. The jaws rest against the mast, the spike is pushed through clew of the jib, holding the jib out at right angles to the fore and aft line of the boat.

Photo M. Rosenfeld

Fig. 40. "Wung out"—with whisker pole

A jib is a very effective sail before the wind when held out by a whisker pole. To make it stay in place, it is necessary to trim the jib sheet to put a strain upon the whisker pole and thus hold it against the mast.

If your boat is equipped with backstays or pre-venters, the backstay that is on the same side as the sail must be slacked off so that it does not cut into the full belly of the sail. The backstay on the other side of the boat must be trimmed up taut.

It is very important to maintain the proper trim of the boat while running. The full weight of the sail is forward; the full pressure of the wind on the sails tends to drive the bow of the boat down and raise the stern up. Therefore, when you are running before the wind always move your passengers or crew farther aft to counteract this forward thrust of the sails.

If your boat is a centerboard boat you will sail before the wind much faster with your centerboard raised up. Most centerboard boats can be sailed well before the wind with the board raised entirely. But if the boat shows a tendency to yaw or swing off her course in either direction it is wise to lower the board about one quarter way.

There are three dangers in sailing before the wind: the accidental jibe, broaching to, and rolling. The accidental jibe is by far the most dangerous. When the wind is dead aft, your boat will not jibe. When the wind is a point or two on the side opposite to that on which the sail is carried, the danger is decreased. But if the wind should blow only slightly over the quarter on which the sail is carried, it gets behind the sail and slams it over to the other side very violently. The accidental jibe is one of the most dangerous things in sailing. The boom gathers a terrific momentum. If it should hit you on the head on a windy day, it would probably kill you. It is almost certain to carry away your backstay. It is quite likely to break your mast or gaff, to part your main sheet and even to capsize your boat. Therefore, the accidental jibe must be avoided by every sailor and at all costs. You will never jibe accidentally as long as the wind blows slightly from the quarter opposite that on which your sail is set. When the wind passes the center line of the boat and blows from the side on which the sail is set, you are said to be sailing "by the lee." If your jib is not wung-out, it always gives warning of sailing by the lee by flopping over to the opposite side. Therefore it is advisable for the beginner not to wing out his jib, as by so doing he destroys a wonderful warning signal. The minute the jib lifts to the side opposite to your mainsail put your helm down, that is to say, toward the mainsail, and you will bring the boat out of danger instantly. When you are sailing in very puffy weather, the wind may change sufficiently to get on the wrong side of the sail without giving you warning. In such a case it is wise to keep the wind well over the quarter even though it may be necessary to sail off your course to keep it there. In other words you will "tack downwind." In sailing in a seaway there is danger of accidental jibe in that your boat, coasting down the back of a wave, may get momentarily out of control and allow the wind to come over the wrong quarter. It is always wise therefore until you become an experienced helmsman to make sure that the wind is blowing slightly over the quarter opposite the sail to give you a sufficient margin of safety.

The second danger in sailing before the wind is the danger of broaching to. This danger is particularly great in a seaway or in sailing a catboat, or in sailing a boat with too small a rudder or with a rudder of faulty design. You will be going along perfectly well when suddenly the boat seems to make up her mind that she will sail herself and will start to nose around to bring her bow into the wind with her boom broad off. This is very dangerous, as the boom immediately dips down into the water and starts to pull the boat over after it. The moment the boom is in the water the rudder becomes useless because the boom and the big area of sail which it drags in after it exerts a more powerful influence than does the rudder. The only safeguard against broaching to is to be alert for the very first tendency of the boat to turn away from the side on which the sail is set. Check that tendency firmly and instantly with the rudder. It is easy to check at the beginning; it is hard to check after the broaching to has gathered momentum. If the boat continually shows a tendency to broach to, lower the peak of the mainsail, or if the boat is Marconi rigged, stop and reef.

The third danger is the danger of rolling. A boat that rolls while running before the wind is apt to get her boom into the water with the same bad consequences as when she broaches to. Your defenses against a rolling boat are as follows: First, if the boat has a centerboard, lower it. Second, trim in the main sheet a few feet. Third, try to check the roll with the rudder. You will soon get the hang of this by pushing your tiller alternately up and down (away from the sail and toward it) in unison with the rolling of the boat. Trimming on the topping lift is most necessary when a boat starts to roll, as that is one of the best ways to keep the boom out of the water. Catboats are the worst offenders when it comes to rolling. The sloop shows much less tendency to roll than the catboat, and inasmuch as its boom is shorter in relation to the length of the boat, the danger is greatly diminished. Boats of broad beam roll much more easily than boats of narrow beam when running before the wind.

Whereas the accidental jibe is very dangerous, the intentional jibe is not dangerous at all if it is performed correctly. Most sailors, however, will live a lifetime on the water and never learn how to jibe. That is why the jibe has such a bad name with sailors. And yet the jibe can be performed in a gale of wind without causing the slightest damage. When you jibe, the boat is turned so that the wind passes from one quarter to the opposite quarter past a point directly astern. The jibe is distinguished from the tack or "coming about" by the fact that when you tack the wind passes from one bow to the opposite bow through a point directly ahead. In other words, you tack with the bow to the wind; you jibe with the stern to the wind. When the wind is directly ahead, the sails flap out from the mast or jib stay exactly like flags. But when you jibe, the sails are full of wind on one side and the next instant they are full of wind on the opposite side, so that they generally move violently from one side to the other. When you tack, the luffs of the sails, which are fast, are first presented to the wind. When you jibe, on the other hand, the leeches of the sails which are not fast to anything are first presented to the wind.

This is the correct way to jibe: First let us assume

that both jib and mainsail are being carried on the port side. Head your boat so that the wind is blowing over the starboard quarter, that is to say, on the starboard side of a line directly aft. Now trim the main sheet until the boom is brought directly amidships and hold the sheet fast. After the boom is brought amidships push the helm up, or to starboard. Do this very gently and slowly until the wind is brought directly aft. The sail will flop gently over to the starboard side. Then, watching the helm to see that the boat does not turn too much to port, pay out the sheet gently, a little bit at a time, until it is in the proper position on the starboard side. The jib will take care of itself. Remember that the boom must be brought to the center of the boat while the wind is on the opposite quarter. Do not let the wind get directly aft until the boom is brought amidships. If you are careless and wind gets aft before the boom is amidships, or gets slightly to port, the sail will slam over violently and may do some damage. Many sailors let the sheet run rapidly after the boom has passed amidships. This is wrong. For the sail gathers momentum as it goes and it is bound to bring up with great violence, probably parting the sheet or a shroud, or breaking the gaff or the mast.

If the boat has backstays, the stay that is behind the sail must be trimmed together with the sheet and should be made fast before the boom passes the point amidships. The other backstay must be cast off so that it will run freely out before the sail. Never jibe in a stiff wind until you are absolutely sure that you have mastered this technique. It is wise to practice jibing many times in light airs, because then if the wind gets aft before the boom is brought amidships the jibe will not be technically correct, but very little damage will be done.

One point must be borne in mind. A boat is jibed by the wind blowing from the same quarter as the sail; and it is accomplished by the relation of the wind direction to the direction of the boat, not by the relation of the wind direction to the position of the sail. This is a very important point to remember. If the sail is broad off to port and the wind blows over the port quarter you will jibe. If the sail is trimmed almost amidships or even flat amidships and the wind is blowing slightly over the starboard quarter you will not jibe even though the angle presented by the sail to the wind is much narrower than with the sail broad off and the wind over the same quarter. Careless yachtsmen often jibe without trimming the sail amidships, simply by letting the wind blow from the same quarter as the sail. This is known as a flying jibe or a "North River" jibe. It is always the mark of a careless sailor and should not be indulged in even in light airs. Jibing is dangerous only when the wind is allowed to blow from the same quarter as the sail, before the sail is brought amidships, or when the sheet is payed out too fast; otherwise the jibe is perfectly safe.

One of the accidents that may attend a flying jibe is known as a goose wing. In the case of the goose wing the boom jibes but the gaff does not. In that event the boom and the gaff go right up in the air on opposite sides of the mast exactly like a pair of goose's wings. Do not try to goose wing your boat, as broken gaff

jaws almost inevitably result. But if you should accidentally goose wing your boat, the only way out of
the difficulty is to put the helm down toward where
the sail was before the jibe and jibe the boom back
to its original position. It is impossible to pull the
gaff over and impossible to do anything with the aid
of the sheet. Jibe the boom back to its original position and then, if your gaff jaws have survived, you can
make another jibe to the position to which you originally intended to go.

Sailing with a quartering wind is very similar to sailing before the wind. Both the jib and the mainsail are
trimmed a little closer, so that the wind blows squarely
against the sail. The only danger in sailing with a
quartering wind is the danger of broaching to. This
may be guarded against by being alert to check with
the rudder any tendency of the boat to nose around
into the wind. If the boat demands excessive rudder,
this may usually be counteracted by trimming the jib
sheet a little closer, and by moving the passengers a
little farther aft. It is wise in a centerboard boat to
carry between a quarter and a half of your board when
sailing with a quartering wind. If the rudder is still
excessive, it is sometimes wise to rig a line from the side
of the boat, taking a turn around the tiller, and hold
the fall of the line as well as the tiller. If the strain
is too great and the boat still shows a tendency to nose
up into the wind the safest thing to do is to drop the
peak if the boat is gaff rigged. With the peak dropped
the sail is scandalized and the tendency to broach to is
immediately cured. If further reduction of the sail

area is necessary pass a line through the highest reef cringle you can reach, or if you are already reefed, pass it over a mast hoop six or seven feet above the deck. Lift up your boom at the tack and tie it up. This will quickly reduce the sail area aft of the center of resistance and thus enable you to sail in safety.

This procedure, of course, is impossible if the boom is secured to the mast by means of a gooseneck, but it

FIG. 41. Mainsail scandalized by dropping peak

is very effective if the boom has jaws. It is not wise to raise the tack unless the peak has previously been lowered.

It must be borne in mind that lowering the peak reduces the sail area that is aft of the center of resistance of the boat and when you change your course to sail the boat to windward, it is always necessary to hoist the peak first.

CHAPTER XI

SAILING TO WINDWARD

IF you will refer to the chapter on the theory of sailing you will see that it is possible to drive a boat against the force that propels it, because the vacuum created on the leeward side of the sail creates a force, which may be broken down into two component forces, one of which imparts a forward motion in a direction approximately 45° from the direction of the wind. To sail to windward, therefore, it is necessary to sail about 45° away from the direction of the wind, then change the direction of the boat so that you will sail approximately at right angles to the course you have been sailing and thus progress in the direction of the wind by zigzagging toward it. This method of zigzagging toward the wind is known as "tacking." A boat with her sails on the port side and the wind on the starboard side is said to be on the starboard tack. A boat with her sails on the starboard side and the wind on the port side is said to be on the port tack. If you are sailing a centerboard boat, your centerboard should be lowered to a point where the after end of the top of the board is just above the lowest point in the centerboard trunk. The centerboard should not be lowered below this point. To do so puts the center of resistance of the boat too far forward.

It also makes an unnecessary drag and puts too great a strain on the bolt which supports the centerboard at the forward end. Many beginners drop their center-

Photo M. Rosenfeld

FIG. 42. The trim of the sheets when sailing to windward

board too low. The main sheet should be trimmed just as flat as practicable. A main sheet may be trimmed too flat and you can tell when the sheet is too flat by the fact that the boat has no life. The proper trim for most boats is when the boom is hauled in over the point where the side joins the stern. The main sheet will lead almost vertically over the end of the traveler. The jib sheet should be trimmed until the jib is practically parallel with the mainsail. But if the jib is too flat it will back-wind the mainsail, that is to say, the wind blowing off the jib will blow directly on to the luff of the mainsail, so that it will seem as though you were sailing your course too close to the wind and were getting the wind on both sides of the sail. The best way to determine the trim of the jib sheet is to slack it off until the jib is practically a flag. Now point the boat slightly into the wind until she is luffing and you see wrinkles forming in the luff and know that the wind is blowing on both sides of the sail. Then head her just far enough away from the wind to stop the luffing. Then holding her directly on this course, trim the jib sheet until the back-wind from the jib makes the mainsail luff. Then slack off the jib sheet until the jib begins to luff. Then trim the jib sheet to a point midway between these two points. I will discuss the finer points of trimming the jib sheet later, but this will do for a beginning.

A boat that is sailing to windward, whether she is tacking or merely sailing in one direction as close to the wind as she can get, is said to be close hauled. That term is very descriptive, because the sheet is trimmed as flat as possible. There is a point in the sails known as the center of pressure. The pressure of the wind on all parts of the sails forward of this point is equal to the pressure of the wind on all parts of the sails abaft this point. Similarly, there is a point in the hull known as the center of resistance. The boat's general shape and keel offer resistance to a sidewise movement through the water. The total resistance of all parts of the boat forward of the center of resistance is equal to the total resistance of all parts of the boat aft of the center of resistance. A boat that is properly

Photo M. Rosenfeld

Fig. 43. Luffing

designed and properly "hung" and properly reefed will have its center of pressure slightly aft of a line passing through the center of resistance. As a result, a boat sailing to windward will tend at all times to point directly into the wind so that the wind blows on both sides of the sails. The helmsman must counteract this tendency by moving his tiller gently toward the high side of the boat. This is known as putting his helm up.

Of course when you are working your boat to windward, it is your object to sail just as close to the wind as possible. This is known as pointing high. A slow boat that will point high will often beat to windward a faster boat that will not point so high. The other boat may move through the water faster, but the boat that points high will sail closer to the wind, and will therefore sail the shorter distance. Your object then is to point the boat just as close to the wind as possible and still keep her "footing." You determine this by watching the luff of the sail. When the wind blows on the back of the sail, the sail will wrinkle at the luff. When this occurs, push the helm up slightly until the wrinkles disappear. Then the boat will be sailing as close to the wind as possible and still traveling along fast. A good helmsman always glues his eye to the luff up near the throat of a gaff-rigged boat and approximately at the same point in a Marconi-rigged boat, because there the wrinkles first appear.

In sailing to windward it is very important that the proper trim of the hull should be maintained. If you carry passengers, move them forward and aft in the boat until you are able to keep on her course with the helm amidships. The importance of correct hull trim cannot be over-emphasized. It is especially important in a very small boat where a single passenger will make great differences in the boat's performance. The passengers also should be moved from side to side to get the correct lateral trim. The boat should be sailing with the lee deck just a few inches out of the water. If the deck shows a tendency to go beneath the water, by all means move your passengers high up on the windward side. If the wind is very light it might be well to have more of the passengers to leeward than to windward. Most beginners pile all their passengers on the windward side even in very light airs so that the boat leans slightly to windward. It is impossible to sail a boat well in this position. With the passengers placed so that the boat is down to her sailing lines with the water a few inches below the lee deck and the least possible pressure on the rudder, experiment with the trim of the jib, trimming it in a few inches until you feel the rudder directly in the center of the boat and are able to steer her with slight pressure by the thumb and first finger. If you are able to sail your course as close to the wind as possible without luffing, and with minimum pressure on the tiller and if at the same time the jib is neither luffing nor back-winding the mainsail, your jib-sheet trim is correct.

On all courses to windward the topping lift should be slack. If the topping lift is on the leeward side of the sail it is most important that it should be so slack that it does not cut into the belly of the sail but allows the sail to take its full rounded shape.

If you are obliged to sail with the tiller at a sharp angle to the boat, the boat is said to carry a heavy weather helm. A weather helm slows down the performance of the boat and is rather burdensome to sail. But a boat with a heavy weather helm is always a safe boat, as she is always anxious to fly up into the wind and stop sailing. If in order to hold your course, you are obliged to hold the helm down or toward the sail, the boat is said to carry a lee helm, and a boat with a lee helm is a dangerous boat. Her center of pressure is forward of the center of resistance and she tends to head away from the wind. Fortunately boats with lee helms are very rare. Lee helm arises from improper reefing, carrying too much sail forward and too little sail aft.

When you are sailing, it should be your object to head up to windward at every possible moment. When a stronger puff than usual comes along, it is wise to push your head up into the wind and maintain the same speed. Your good sailor watches his puffs and utilizes them to work his boat closer to the wind. A poor sailor pulls his helm up and enjoys the thrill of the boat's leaning, but does not make the progress of the skipper who heads up to windward at every possible moment.

On the other hand, the good skipper avoids "pinching" his boat by pointing too close to the wind and thereby losing headway. The minute the luff starts shaking, he pulls her back gently and just enough and thus keeps as close to the wind as possible without luffing.

A boat always heels more sharply when sailing to windward than on sailing any other course. And for that reason sailing to windward is perhaps the most dangerous course to sail. At the same time it is the safest course, for the skipper can always luff and let the wind blow on both sides of his sails at the same time. When the sails present their luffs to the wind, they flutter out from the jib stay and from the mast and in that position the boat cannot be knocked down. Therefore when there is too much wind for safety, always put your helm down, point the nose of the boat into the wind, and luff her.

When you are sailing on a squally day, the puffs may strike so suddenly that the boat will not respond quickly enough for safety. In that event, be prepared to slack off the main sheet sharply. This will have the same effect as pointing the bow of the boat into the wind because it lets the wind blow on both sides of the sail at the same time. It is always better to luff than to slack off the sheet unless the wind is of such sudden violence that slacking off the sheet is necessary. "Starting" or slacking the sheet is in a measure a safety valve. It acts much more quickly than luffing because in luffing, the boat must respond to its helm and must change its course and it is much quicker to let out a few feet of sheet than to make the boat travel through the necessary arc, to bring her bow to the wind. But unless the puff is of unusual violence and suddenness, luffing is a sufficient parry and it has the double effect of keeping the boat footing and at the same time pointing nearer to the wind.

Some skippers always coil down the sheet in anticipation of having to start it suddenly. This is not good practice. It is seldom necessary to pay out more than a few feet of sheet and you can always keep four or five feet clear in the cockpit. If the sheet is coiled, there is always the danger of the coil being picked up and jammed into the sheet block as the sheet is being payed out. Therefore it is my recommendation that you never coil the sheet but always keep four or five feet of it absolutely clear in anticipation of having to start it quickly. In the same manner many helmsmen hesitate to make fast the main sheet on any small boat. It is wearisome business holding both the sheet and the tiller, and a turn or two around a cleat should not delay you very much in letting the sheet run. Therefore I recommend a middle course. Make your sheet fast with just a turn and hold the end. But under no circumstances wind the sheet back and forth and in and out around the cleet or put a half hitch around the last turn.

In letting the sheet run, a foot or two is all that is necessary. Many beginners pay out so much sheet that the boom gets into the water. With the boom overboard the rudder is useless and this must be guarded against at all costs. One point that must be stressed in connection with luffing or starting the sheet is the necessity at all times for keeping under way. As long as the boat is moving through the water at a fair rate of speed the skipper has her under control. A boat can be steered only because there is a stream of water slipping past the rudder. And the rudder bracing against the stream of water will direct the boat. When the boat has lost her way, the stream of water stops flowing past the rudder and immediately the rudder becomes a useless piece of wood with nothing to work against. When your boat is at anchor, try moving the rudder back and forth. You will see that it has practically no effect upon the direction of the boat. But when the boat is moving it responds immediately. Every time you luff, you kill the boat's headway so that you must be careful to sail away from the wind again before headway is lost or dangerously diminished. Even if there is too much wind for you to fill away safely it is better for you to take a chance by filling away than to run the risk of losing your headway by luffing for too long a period. In the same way, starting the sheet immediately kills the boat's headway and the sheet must be trimmed again promptly and sharply before you lose steerage way.

After you have been sailing a sufficiently long distance on one tack, you go about and sail on the other tack. As previously stated, going about consists in bringing the boat's head into the wind and then sailing with the wind on the bow opposite to the bow from which it has been blowing. Going about is distinguished from jibing by the fact that you go about with the bow to the wind whereas you jibe with the stern to the wind. Let us assume you are sailing on the port tack and wish to go about on to the starboard tack. A half minute or so before you go about, notify the passengers of your intention. The usual sea-going hail is "Ready about!" Then just as you are starting to perform the evolution, you should cry once more "Hard alee!" and at the same time ease the helm gently, then push it down hard to the leeward side, bringing the bow of the boat into and past the wind. If your jib has double sheets and is trimmed to leeward, it is necessary to let go the sheet on the starboard side and later trim the sheet on the port side. Many boats regardless of the rig of the jib sheet will not go about unless the jib sheet is cast off just as the helm is put down.

As in every other phase of sailing, there is a right and a wrong way to go about. The wrong way is to jam the helm down suddenly, spin the boat around on her heel and start immediately sailing on the other tack. The right way is to ease the boat gently up into the wind so that she will "fetch" as far as possible to windward before she loses her headway and then, while she still has steerage way, push the helm down sufficiently hard to carry the wind to the proper quarter to fill the sails on the other side. In this way, you lose no time in going about, but actually gain something in that you have carried your boat a long way into the wind. In going about, you must be careful not to take your boat so far off the wind on the other tack that you cannot readily luff. The sails should fill when they are over the port side, trimmed to the same angle as they were when they were over the starboard side when you were sailing on the port tack. It is very bad practice to carry the boat way off the wind and then bring her back to her course.

If your tacking is not skillfully done you are quite likely to be caught "in stays"; that is to say, the boat will hang directly in the wind, with the wind blowing on both sides of the sails so that you will lose headway and you will not be able to complete the tack. In this situation, nine beginners out of ten try to push the sail to its proper position. This maneuver is worse than useless. Let us assume that you are sailing on the port tack and wish to go about and sail on the starboard tack. You cry "ready about" and push the helm down and the boat goes up into the wind but does not go past the wind. It hangs there for a moment, then begins very slowly to drift backward. What do you do? First trim the jib as flat as possible. Second put your helm to port—not to starboard. Reach up with your hand to the boom and hold it amidships, or move it slightly

Fig. 44. In stays. The boat was hung up in trying to go from port to starboard tack. Note the jib sheet is trimmed flat; helm is held to port, not starboard; and main boom is held to starboard. This picture was posed to illustrate the maneuver for single-handed sailing, under circumstances where the jib could not readily be held out to starboard.

to starboard. In just a minute you will swing past the dead center of the wind and will get the wind over the starboard bow just where you want it. Then you can pull up the tiller to starboard and in a moment you will have steerage way. Let us see just what has happened. While you were hanging in stays, your boat was not moving ahead. If it were moving ahead you would have had sufficient steerage way to swing past the dead center over to the starboard tack. Just for a moment the boat stood still, then it started to drift backward. Now the minute the boat starts to go back it is moving stern-first through the water; the action of your rudder is reversed; the water is flowing from the aft end of the rudder toward its forward end. Therefore to make the bow of the boat turn to port you push the tiller to port, bringing the rudder to starboard. On the other hand if the boat were going ahead, to make the bow turn to port you would push the tiller to starboard. Similarly, by trimming your jib sheet and holding the boom over to starboard you give the wind a chance to drive the bow to port. Always bear in mind that the minute your boat is not going ahead it is going backwards. And when it is sailing backwards your rudder action and everything else must be reversed.

We now have the boat sailing on the starboard tack. Somewhere to windward is the point you desire to reach. As we sail on the starboard tack that point creeps along on our beam until we wonder whether or not we could reach it if we went back on the port tack. How do we determine when we have sailed far enough on the one tack to be sure of reaching our objective on the opposite tack? For the beginner sailing an ordinary boat, a pretty good rule is as follows: With the boat sailing as close to the wind as she can head without luffing, look out directly over the boat's side. If possible, sight along the after edge of the cockpit. If the point is directly abeam the chances are that you can reach it on the next tack. After you become

more proficient and are getting the utmost out of your
boat, it may be possible to sail a little closer to the
wind. If you carry a compass it would be easy to
determine the number of points on the compass between the two tacks. And when your objective bears
at the proper point according to the compass, you can
go about and reach it. It is generally good practice to
sail long tacks until you approach fairly near your

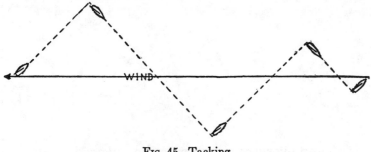

Fig. 45. Tacking

objective. Then sail shorter tacks so as not to sail
beyond it.

One question always arises in the mind of any
skipper who is sailing a boat with which he is not
familiar. How far can he let out her heel with safety?
As a rule every boat is pretty safe as long as her deck
is out of water. Some boats are safe with the water
clear up to the cockpit coaming but most boats do
not perform efficiently when heeled down so far, not
only because of the water on the deck but also because
her underbody is dragging the bilge at the beam
through the water. There is a critical point in the heel
of a boat at which it usually is easier for the boat to

keep on going over than to return to an even keel. This critical point is especially noticeable in shoal draft centerboard boats. They are very stable to begin with. It takes a great deal of wind to make them lean much, but after the critical point has been reached they want to go all the way over.

Photo M. Rosenfeld

FIG. 46. Jib trimmed flat, mainsail started and luffing

The action of a keel boat is different. A boat with a deep, heavy keel relies for its stability upon the weight of the keel and its location deep down in the water. Such boats present little resistance in the shape of a flat floor and hard bilge. They will heel much more readily than the centerboard boats in light airs, but after they have reached a certain point it takes a perfect gale to make them go over any farther because the wind must lift the keel against gravity and the farther the boat heels the greater the leverage of the keel, and therefore the greater the stability of the boat. You must learn to know your boat; but you will soon learn her ways and be able to trust her at various angles of heel for varying strength of wind.

If you are sailing to windward and the wind freshens and becomes too much for your sail, it is always wisest to reef. If reefing is impracticable for any reason, it is still possible to sail safely and efficiently by means of the following stunt.

Trim the jib sheet very flat. Start the main sheet until nearly half the sail is luffing. Then, do not try to pinch the boat by pointing too close to the wind, but try to make her foot instead. It is astonishing how fast and how safely a boat will travel when trimmed this way.

The sailor must always be alert for the sudden puff that may result in a knockdown. Luffing and letting the sheet run are his two greatest safeguards. But at all times he must be ready for emergency by keeping his boat moving as swiftly as possible through the water and never losing steerage way.

CHAPTER XII

REACHING

WHEN a boat is under way and neither beating to windward nor running before the wind, she is said to be reaching. A reach is any course sailed with started sheets that is not directly before the wind. When the sheets are trimmed almost flat and the boat is sailing just a point or two off close-hauled, she is said to be on a close reach. When the wind is abaft the beam, she is said to be on a broad reach. On a close reach the sheets would be started a little more than if she were close-hauled, and the boat should be sailed in the same manner as you sail her close-hauled; that is to say, the sheet should be out just so far that by pointing a trifle closer to the wind, you will cause the sails to luff. On a broad reach you trim your sails so that the wind will blow directly on them, in other words, so that the sails (not the booms) will be as nearly as possible at right angles to the wind. The hull should be trimmed by moving your passengers forward or aft so that neither the bow nor the stern will be too low in the water.

Now, when you are sailing before the wind, you are always guided by the wind's direction, you watch the fly and the waves and avoid sailing by the lee at all costs. When you are sailing close-hauled you sail as close to the wind as possible, watching the luff, pre-

venting it from wrinkling and yet keeping it at the
point where it just does not wrinkle. When you sail
on a reach, it is usually advisable to select a landmark, or if no land is in sight, to sail by compass bear-

Photo M. Rosenfeld

FIG. 47. *Left*, a close reach. *Right*, a broad reach. Note the trim
of the sheets

ing so that you hold the boat steadily to a particular
course. You will find that it is very hard to keep a
boat heading exactly on a course, especially if there
is a heavy sea running. But the way to steer is to aver-

age your course. If for a moment you find that you are pointing higher than your landmark steer for the next moment on the other side of it. If you are steering due west by compass and you find yourself sailing west by north steer for a moment on a course west by south. In that way you will average your course and steady the boat.

The only danger from reaching is from a beam sea which may cause the boat to roll a bit and may slop over the windward side. But serious rolling is unusual unless the seas are very high because in this position the sails have a wonderful steadying influence. If you are sailing a centerboard boat it is wise to carry about three-fourths of your board. It need not be down quite so far as in going to windward. The topping lift need not be trimmed except in a broad reach and unless the sail is very low. If possible it should be trimmed on the windward side of the sail.

As a rule reaching is the finest course to sail and it is the course on which the beginner ought to do most of his practicing until he gets perfectly familiar with his boat. It is easy for the beginner to plan his after-noon's sail so that he can start on a reach with the wind directly abeam until he has sailed far enough to suit him, then trim sheets and go about, start sheets again and sail back over the same course to his starting point. This can be repeated over and over again until the beginner has enough confidence to try beating to windward.

In changing your course from a reach to close-hauled, it is well to trim the sheets slowly, ease the tiller down gently and do everything gradually and deliberately. It is not advisable to go about from a reach. Trim your sheets until your boat is close-hauled and then go about. The movement may be made smoothly and without delay but you should definitely sail close-hauled before you attempt to put your boat about. To attempt to tack a boat from a reach often has the same consequences as broaching to. The boat gets out of control and the boom goes overboard. Another danger in attempting to tack while sailing a reach is that you will not have sufficient steerage way to carry the boat past the wind and as a consequence you will hang in stays. To change your course from a reach to a run you put the helm up gradually and pay out the sheets. If you bear in mind the three courses, running, beating and reaching, and change from one course to another gradually, doing nothing suddenly or in a hurry, you will rapidly master the art of sailing. It is sometimes necessary so to turn your boat when you are beating or reaching that the wind will be brought aft and then you will jibe. This evolution is known as wearing. If you intend to wear your boat, it is not necessary to start your sheets because you will only have to trim them again for the jibe. Keep them trimmed, put your helm up, but be sure that the sheets are trimmed flat amidships when the wind comes dead aft. Then, when your boat is jibed, pay out your main sheet gradually as described in the chapter "Before the Wind."

CHAPTER XIII

MAKING AND CLEARING A DOCK OR MOORING

To sail your boat to a dock, or to your mooring it is necessary to stop the boat from going ahead. That is the problem in its essence. And if there are no complicating circumstances, it is an easy thing to do. But it must be done correctly. It has been explained how a boat ceases to go ahead when hanging in stays with the bow to the wind and the wind blowing on both sides of the sails. When you try to make a landing at a dock you do just that. You put your boat in stays. And when she has lost her momentum she will stop going ahead. It is evident that a dock or mooring must always be approached from the leeward, that its location must always be to the windward of the boat, and that you must shoot your boat up into the wind from such a direction and in such a manner that the boat will lose all its headway and come to a standstill just before you reach the dock. This is known as shooting up into the wind.

You approach the dock preferably on a close reach, and at least three or four boat lengths away. Then, timing yourself so that the boat will be heading into the wind when she is directly to leeward of the dock, you trim your sheets gradually, push down the helm gently, bring your bow into the wind and head directly up wind toward the dock. Shooting up into the wind is just like fifty per cent of going about. In other words you go halfway about and then stop. This means that the helm must not be pushed down so violently or so far.

It is very bad practice to try to make a dock with a strange boat until you know how far she will shoot. A broad, flat, lightly-built boat may shoot less than her length. A deep, narrow, heavy boat may shoot five times her length, and the distance of the shooting depends very largely upon the smoothness with which she is brought into the wind. A boat that is traveling fast will shoot farther than a boat that is traveling slowly. So it is always wise before attempting to shoot up to a dock in a boat you do not know, to throw overboard a piece of wood or a crumpled newspaper or anything that will float, and practice shooting up to that mark, rather than to a dock or buoy.

In shoal water the centerboard is sometimes useful as a brake. Have a stick ready to push it down as far as it will go and lean your weight on top of it. The rudder too will act as a brake by pushing it hard over to one side and then the other. But, to use many brakes is the sign that you have underestimated the distance of the shoot and a confession of bad seamanship.

You should always aim to fetch short of a dock and long of a mooring. Never try to make your boat go beyond the dock. Be sure that it stops before you reach it. Similiarly, be sure that your boat will carry far enough to make you reach the mooring and perhaps a little beyond, because you can always pick up the mooring and carry it a few feet, but docks do not behave in that amiable manner.

If the wind is blowing on the side of a dock and you intend to shoot up into the opposite side, try, if possible, to shoot into the end of the dock rather than the side. Then if you are going too fast it is easy enough to steer the boat past the end of the dock without damaging either the dock or your boat. If this evolution is smoothly executed and your boat will carry just to the right distance, do not permit any of your passengers to run forward until just before the dock is reached. This always throws a small boat off her balance and stops the way of the boat. If you are going just a little too fast, of course it is a good idea to send someone forward as that will help to kill the boat's way.

If you are coming in a little too fast the dock must be held off with foot or boat hook. There is a right and wrong way to use a boat hook. Never hold it directly in front of you, with the butt held in line with the stomach. This is the surest way to get a severe injury or to be knocked overboard. Always hold the boat hook out to the side so that if you are coming in at all fast and you do not have strength to hold the boat off, at least you will not be damaged by your own boat hook.

Similarly there is a right and a wrong way to use your feet in stopping a boat. Most people attempt to hold the boat off by standing on the left foot and holding out the right foot. If the boat is moving fast your legs will come together like the two blades of a pair of scissors, and the boat will receive a severe blow.

Even a strong man has very little strength in his legs
when they are used this way.

Fig. 48. The wrong way to fend with a boathook

Fig. 49. The right way to fend with a boathook

The proper way to fend off a boat with your feet is
to sit down on the bow and hold both feet out, balanc-
ing yourself with your hands on the jib stay. In this

manner your legs are straight and you are firmly set
and braced with your hands on the stay. The shock

Fig. 50. Wrong way to fend with the feet

Fig. 51. Right way to fend with the feet

of fending off the boat may bend your knees but you
still have ample strength to stop the headway of even
a fast moving boat. Furthermore, when you are thus

seated the jib is not likely to push you overboard if it fills away.

If you are shooting up to a dock and have not quite enough way to make the necessary distance, you can generally retrieve your error by throwing a heaving line to a person on the dock. A light line should be coiled ready for this purpose. Make sure that you have one end fast before you heave the other. I have seen

Fig. 52. The heaving line. Note how high it is thrown

many a good line thrown away without an end retained on the boat. Be sure to throw the line high enough. If the line reaches the dock, request anyone on the dock to take a turn around a piling and hold it. Then you do the trimming from the boat. Do not let the man on the dock pull your boat in. Pull slowly and carefully and remember that if you trim too fast you will give the boat a fresh momentum and she may hit the dock harder than if you had sailed right up to it.

If your heaving line misses the dock and you start to drift backward, remember that the situation is just exactly the same as if you were caught in stays. The action of the rudder is reversed. If you can get your boat off the wind you may be able to gather enough momentum to get back to the dock; but probably your dignity will suffer less if you sail well away from the dock and then go back and make a clean fresh attempt. If you get a line to the dock be sure that your body is not part of the line. In other words, do not hold onto the line with one hand and the mast with the other, and try to pull both ends together. Do not jump on to a neighboring boat holding your headstay with one hand and pulling the painter of the boat with the other. That is about the worst strain a man can undergo and it usually results in failure. If you put yourself on one end of the line and the other end is fastened, you can handle it, but if your own body is part of the line it is a very different story.

Such is the solution to the simple problem of making a dock or mooring. Of course the problem is not always simple. It is frequently complicated by the wind, the neighboring boats and by circumstances.

Suppose there is not room for the long, graceful swing. Suppose you are sailing down on the dock before the wind. There is a T on the end of the dock and you can shoot up in the lee of that T, but there are rocks and vessels that are in the way and you cannot make the long, graceful swing. The shore is too close to permit your shooting four or five times your length.

What do you do? In that event a short, hard swing may be needed to kill the way of the boat. The longer and slower you swing the greater distance your boat will carry into the wind. The shorter and sharper you turn the less distance your boat will carry. It is possible to sail almost before the wind, swing the boat suddenly and hard, and stop her way within her own

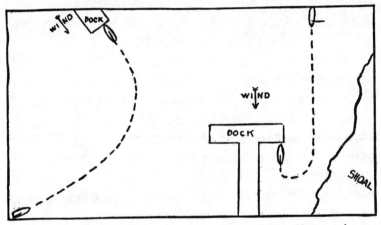

Fig. 53. *Left,* Gradual swing, long shoot. *Right,* Sharp swing, short shoot (made necessary by lack of sea-room)

length. The short swing is necessary when there is not room for a long swing.

Suppose there is no lee side to the dock. In other words, the only way you can approach the dock is from the windward. What can you do? The only safe course of action in such a case is to sail as close to the dock as possible, shoot up into the wind, heading away from the dock, and when you have lost your way drop anchor. Then with your sails lowered, you can pay out your anchor line until your stern is almost touching the dock. A stern line can then be thrown to the dock and your boat is safe from chafing.

Suppose the wind is blowing lengthwise of the dock so that while the dock is not directly to leeward, it is not directly to windward either. In that case, plan your swing so that you will be headed directly into the wind when one side of the boat is about a foot from the dock. Shoot up alongside the dock until your boat has lost her way; then, reaching over with line or boat hook, make fast to the dock and lower your sails.

Sometimes tides complicate things. When the tide and the wind are blowing from the same direction the problem is simple enough. You merely plan to shoot up wind harder because the tide will kill your way more quickly than if the wind alone were against you. But when wind and tide are from opposite directions and of about equal force, the problem is complicated once more. In that event it is possible to come up into the wind just as if there were no tide, but plan to stop your boat about a boat's length from the dock. The tide will then carry you into the dock. If the tide gets working too hard, you can hold your jib across the boat and thus make the wind help to keep you from the dock. The tide, however, will gradually take you into the dock and once having made fast, lower sails as quickly as possible before the tide swings your stern around and makes you lower your sails over the water.

A boat should behave well at a dock or mooring with the sail raised provided the bow is pointed into the wind, but it is always well to lower sails as quickly as possible at a dock. A shoal draft boat with the center-board up will act as a weather vane pointing directly into the wind. But no boat will behave well if there are other boats crowding it, and it is always wisest to lower sails as quickly as possible.

If the wind is driving your boat against the dock always put out fenders. If you are to be tied to the dock for any length of time and there is considerable rise or fall of tide, the fenders must be tied to the boat. If there is very little change of tide during your proposed stay it is better to tie the fenders to the dock. A boat will move somewhat along a dock and fenders tied to her sides may protect her from chafing against the piling at one moment and at the next moment bear against nothing but air. If they are fast to the dock, however, they will fend any part of the boat that may rub along the dock. There is always the possibility, of course, that you may sail away and leave perfectly good fenders tied to a strange dock.

When you are leaving your mooring, it is well to plan in advance in which direction you intend to sail. Let us say that you plan to sail off on the port tack with the sails over the starboard side. Untie your mooring line, but before casting off, walk back with it along the port deck. This will throw the boat's bow to starboard and bring the wind over the port side. Your sails will fill and you will start off at once in the direction you intended. If you merely cast the mooring overboard from the bow you will start drifting backward and may go off either to port or starboard without very much power or control as to direction.

Sometimes it is difficult to get clear of a mooring, especially if there are boats on either hand and you know that you cannot gather steerage way before you crash into another boat. Sometimes this may be avoided by pulling up on your mooring line until you are well over your anchor, thus changing your position forty or fifty feet before you are ready to cast off. At other times it is well to drift astern until you are clear of other boats, then anchor and hoist sail. To get under way in such a manner as to endanger other boats is an unforgivable sin and a sure mark of the land-lubber. Sailors must above all be good neighbors, especially in a crowded anchorage.

To cast off from a dock is rather more difficult than clearing from a mooring, especially if there are other boats on either hand. This is a technique that must be acquired, especially at such places where many boats sail to a bathing beach and are tied up in long rows to a dock. The beginner is advised to back his boat out and make fast with a long double-ended line to the traveler of the farthest boat out from the dock. Then if he makes sail he can cast off one end of his line, pull it through the traveler and be twenty or thirty feet clear of the neighboring boats before he starts to sail.

The proper method of getting clear is a bit more complicated. A boat may be backed out from a dock by remembering the axiom that when a boat is going backward the action of the rudder is reversed and that other axiom that if a boat's sails are trimmed absolutely flat amidships she will not start sailing ahead. Let us assume that you are tied up to a dock with the wind blowing across it and a large boat tied up on either side of you. On your port hand lies the shore; on your starboard hand is open water. If there is a little clear water between your boat and the boats that are beside you, hoist your sails, trim the main sheet and jib sheet flat amidships, raise your centerboard if you have one, place your tiller one inch to

FIG. 54. Backing out from a dock. Jib and mainsail trimmed flat. Action of helm reversed

starboard and hold it there. If you are sailing alone and have no companion, lash the tiller firmly in that position. Then go to the dock, cast off the painter, and hold the boat's head steady until you are sure that she is looking right into the eye of the wind with her sails perfectly flat amidships. Now give the boat a tremendous shove straight aft, jump aboard, tread lightly down the middle of the boat, undo the tiller by casting off the lashings, holding the tiller just one inch to starboard of amidships. The boat will move straight aft and you will begin to feel the strain on the rudder. As you start to clear the stern of the boat that is to starboard, let your tiller go over to the starboard side. It will want to do so anyway because of the strain that is on it. The stern will go off to the port, the bow will swing to starboard. Hang on to your sheets. By no means start them. When you have reached this point you will get a perfect shower of advice from the dock and neighboring boats. Everyone will tell you to put your tiller the other way and to let your sheet run. Pay no attention to the advice. The wind will now strike the sails, but since they are trimmed flat and your boat is still going backward, the boat will continue to sail backward and the bow will swing perfectly clear of the neighboring boats. When you are well clear, put the tiller to port, start the sheets, and you will be sailing. The essence of this maneuver is to have the tiller just to starboard of amidships, to have the sheets flat, to be looking directly into the point of the wind and to push straight down wind. If, by any chance, the sails should take charge, or the tiller should fail to go to starboard, or you should push the bow to port instead of straight back, you may come to grief. This maneuver calls for courage and faith. Not one amateur sailor in a thousand can pull it off successfully and most of the people who will offer advice from the dock are not aware of the principle underlying it. They are accustomed to sailing boats forward and never realize what happens when a boat is moving backward.

In a similar situation, if the wind is blowing more from the shore it will be necessary to wear out from the dock. In this case the maneuver is reversed. The tiller is placed slightly to port of the amidships line and the boat, when shoved off, swings her head toward the shore instead of toward the open water. When you are clear of the neighboring boats, keep the sheets trimmed flat, put the helm up to starboard, swing

Fig. 55. Pushing out with the boom from the windward side of a dock

around in a three-quarter circle, jibing as the wind passes the stern.

If you have room and have a spritted jib, it is possible to fan your way out from the dock by moving the jib first to starboard, then to port, and letting the wind on the jib drive you backward. If you feel the bow of the boat going off to port the jib must be placed to port to drive the bow back to the line of the wind, and similarly if you feel the bow falling off to starboard, you must move the jib to starboard to drive her back into the line of the wind.

One of the most difficult situations that arise when leaving a dock is the result of a change of wind. You may tie up to the leeward side of the dock on a northwest wind, leave your boat, and when you return find that the wind has shifted to the southeast, so that you are now on the windward side of the dock. What do you do in such a case? If you hoist your sail it will blow out over the dock, and there would seem to be no other way of getting clear. The solution is simple if the dock is not so high but that the sail can be made to swing above it. Hoist the sail and let it blow over the dock, get the passengers on board, and cast off the painter. Then, while standing on the dock, take the end of the boom and push with it against the mast until the bow of the boat is brought into and past the direction of the wind. Give one final mighty shove and, holding on to the boom, swing yourself aboard your boat, trim the sheets and you are off. The boom acting as a lever against the mast enables you to get out of this awkward situation.

CHAPTER XIV

HELMSMANSHIP

AFTER the beginner has learned to maneuver his boat with a fair degree of confidence, he is quite certain to slump and become careless. If at this point he could understand that he has just mastered the very rudiments of sailing and that the finer touches are still to be acquired, he would progress rapidly. As a rule, however, the beginner continues as a beginner until he starts to enter races. Then with the other boats passing him as if he were standing still, it begins to dawn on him that he has not mastered the fine art of helmsmanship.

A sailboat is the most alive creation ever made by man. She has her whims and moods and there must be a sympathy and understanding between the helmsman and the boat. The helmsman must develop "good hands" just as the horseman must. So close is the relationship between the arts of horsemanship and helmsmanship that I make it a rule whenever possible to ride a horse with a good mouth on the morning of a race. The horse somehow compels the necessary fine adjustments of the hands and wrists and the habit carries over to the afternoon so that I find myself sailing an infinitely better race. Just as the horseman must feel his mount in every part of his body—in his seat, his balance, his knee grip—so the helmsman must feel the boat and the wind with every part of his body. Instinctively you will feel the angle of heel with your seat, with the bracing of your legs. You will sense whether or not the boat is going through the waters at her best speed or laboring and fighting against some unseen force.

It is wise to let the boat do most of the sailing. It is surprising how beautifully a well-hung boat will take care of herself and how much better she can sail herself than be sailed by the helmsman. If the helm is heavy on a course to windward, it means that something is wrong somewhere. The helm should be right in the middle of a boat and you should be able to guide her by the thumb and forefinger resting lightly on the tiller.

With a heavy weather helm, examine your boat to see if the helm can be remedied. One of the most important items to consider is the fore and aft trim. Move your passengers or your sandbags forward or aft and see if this relieves the pressure of the water on the rudder. Take into account the trim of your sheets, particularly the jib sheet. Trimming the jib a trifle flatter will often relieve tremendous pressure on the rudder. Only the helmsman can determine the proper trim of the jib. Look to your reefing. If you are sailing with a small jib and a single reefed mainsail, the center of pressure of the sails is probably too far aft of the center of resistance of the hull, and a heavy weather helm will result. If you have double-reefed your mainsail and are carrying a full jib, the center of resistance has probably moved aft of the center of pressure and a lee helm results. Look to the rake of the mast. A gaff-rigged mast should rake slightly forward; a Marconi-rigged mast should stand perfectly straight or perhaps rake slightly aft. An inch or two in the rake of the mast will make a vast difference in the performance of the boat. So true is this that many small racing boats are equipped with movable mast steps so that the most efficient position of the mast can be determined by the trial and error method and the boat hung exactly at the point where she will be most lively. The whole problem of a light helm may be summarized as follows:

The center of pressure of the sails must be kept just slightly abaft a vertical line extending through the center of resistance of the hull. Anything that disturbs the relationship between the center of effort and the center of resistance will be reflected in the helm.

In the case of a heavy weather helm where the tiller must be held at quite an angle, it is wise to ease the helm to the center of the boat every minute or two and thus spill the water that is behind the rudder. This will not appreciably set the boat off the course and yet it will have a wonderful effect upon her liveliness and speed through the water.

If the boat suddenly seems logy, it is well to suspect an accumulation of seaweed on the rudder or the keel. The star boat skippers on Great South Bay where there is much seaweed, are constantly annoyed by vast accumulations of weed on the keel and on the rudder. These boats are all provided with hooks or forks with

which the crew pushes off the accumulation of seaweed
from time to time. Seaweed does not cause much
annoyance on a centerboard boat, but if it does it is an
easy matter to lift the centerboard from time to time
and let the seaweed wash away. It is a good idea when
sailing a keel boat regularly through seaweed-infested
waters, to have the bottom of the boat and the keel
painted white. With white paint a glance over the side
will immediately reveal the presence of seaweed.

In sailing as in all other sports, too much emphasis
cannot be placed on correct timing. Your motions of
the tiller should be timed to the movements of the
boat and to the action of the waves. The timing of
most good helmsmen is perfectly automatic. They
adjust themselves subconsciously and immediately to
every slight variation in the boat's performance. To
the beginner the timing must be conscious. He must
make an effort to get in tune with the boat.

The final problem of helmsmanship is to "stay with"
the boat. Many helmsmen start their sailing beautifully. Their timing will be perfect. Their hands good.
Their kinæsthetic perception of the boat's performance will be beyond criticism. Their sense of wind
direction will be accurate. But after they have sailed
for half an hour or so, their attention lags, they become
sloppy, they relax and are bored, and the boat immediately slows down. Staying with the boat is more a
matter of habit than of anything else. But it should
be part of the beginner's effort to acquire that habit of
staying with the boat at all times while he is sailing

CHAPTER XV

BALLAST AND TRIM

THE performance of any boat can be improved by proper ballast. Ballast is necessary in any boat; and most boats, especially small boats, do not carry enough. I have known boats only eighteen feet long that were not really seaworthy until they had eighteen hundred pounds of ballast placed inside of them. Most shoal-draft racing boats of twenty or twenty-one feet over all carry from two hundred to six hundred pounds of ballast. The standard weight of the iron keel of the star boat is eight hundred and sixty pounds with a limit of nine hundred pounds.

Ballast is of two types: inside and outside. The outside ballast is built into the keel, the inside ballast is laid on the planking. The average shoal-draft boat with a centerboard and a flat floor should be ballasted with inside ballast. In such boats ballast built into the keel is only slightly more effective than ballast laid inside. The deep draft boats with narrow hulls have their ballast built into the keel at the lowest possible point. If by any chance such a boat loses its keel the loss may be made up by inside ballast. But at best the substitution of inside ballast in a boat that was originally designed for outside ballast is a poor makeshift and the boat is apt to be tender at all times. Inside bal-

139

last has only one merit over outside ballast—it is apt to make the boat steadier in a seaway, especially after a storm when there is a heavy sea and light wind. In such conditions the boat with the deep keel and the heavy weight at the bottom is apt to roll and pitch violently. Many cruising boats compromise by placing about half the ballast on the keel and the other half inside, the outside ballast giving the necessary stability for carrying sail and the ballast inside making for steadiness in a seaway.

It is safer to assume that a boat is improperly ballasted than that the original ballast is correct. Sometimes the addition of just a little weight will make all the difference in the world. I remember once ballasting a catboat with bricks, the only available material. The bricks were not good ballast because they were too light and the boat was very tender. She leaked badly, however, and after a few days the bricks became thoroughly water-soaked and thereby gained in weight. After that the boat was very stiff and able, the weight of water in the bricks making a noticeable difference in her performance. If your boat is slow and logy, if she seems to be sunk too deep into the water, if it takes a gale of wind to heel her over to her sailing lines, it is probable you have too much ballast. If, on the other hand, your boat is over-lively, and tender; if she seems to want to put her deck under water; if you are forced to reef while other boats of the same general characteristics can carry full sail, then she is inadequately ballasted and would show great improvement with a few hundred pounds of additional weight.

Ballast can be supplied in several forms. Perhaps the easiest and most convenient are cheap iron sash weights, which are very heavy for their bulk, and which stow snugly; elevator weights are even better. If you can stand the expense, lead cast in molds to fit the spaces between the ribs is just about the best ballast available. If you use pigs of lead it will probably be easier on the boat to rest them on the ribs instead of on the planking. Many authorities maintain that ballast should never rest upon the planking and this is certainly true when the boat is hauled out of water. When the boat is afloat, however, those parts of the planking on which the ballast rests are practically always water-borne and the amount of ballast carried is not particularly burdensome to planking that is floating in the water.

The sand bag is a very good and cheap form of ballast. It has the unhappy faculty of leaking if punctured and for that reason many skippers prefer bags filled with pebbles. Sand will leak out of a small hole, whereas pebbles will not. For experimental purposes it is often useful to pick up some handy wooden boxes and fill them with stones or pebbles. You can start out with too many stones and throw them overboard until the weight is just right, finally putting the remaining stones into the canvass bags. Small stones weigh more for their total bulk than large ones because the large ones have a bad habit of leaving air spaces between them.

Ballast should be stowed as low as possible and as close to the center line as possible. One must always make a decision as to whether to bunch the ballast amidships or to string it out to the ends of the boat. Be guided by these considerations: A boat with ballast amidships is livelier in response to the helm. She will come about more rapidly, be less apt to hang in stays, and be more easily steered. On the other hand a boat with ballast in the ends is apt to be steadier on the helm, pound less in a sea, and be generally more sedate in her behavior. You must study the characteristics of your boat and decide which way of stowing ballast will appeal to you more. Remember this: A boat with her ballast amidships may pound more violently in waves, but the spray is likely to be thrown off to the sides. A boat with ballast in the ends will cleave through the waves with less pounding, but what spray she throws is apt to travel the entire length of her and she will probably be a wetter boat.

Great care must be exercised to keep the ballast where you put it. Ballast that shifts to leeward when the boat heels sharply is more of a danger than a help. Battens should be fastened to the planking on either side of the ballast and they should be high enough so that the ballast cannot shift regardless of the angle of the heel. Iron ballast should be red-leaded and varnished. Rust increases the weight of iron ballast slightly but it is not nice to have around a boat.

In stowing ballast you must be careful to preserve the proper fore and aft trim. The principles stated in previous chapters must be borne in mind so that the center of pressure of the sail area must be kept slightly abaft a vertical line through the center of resistance of the hull. A naval architect can figure out accurately from his plans just where the center of pressure and the center of resistance will occur. But the only way the skipper can determine it is by the feel of the helm when the boat is going to windward, as described in the chapter on helmsmanship.

Inside ballast is often very useful in preserving the windward and leeward trim of a boat. The old boats known as sand-baggers carried an enormous spread of sail. A numerous crew with each man selected for his avoirdupois perched on the weather rail and each man carried with him the heaviest sand bag he could handle. The skipper of a small boat will do well to have a few sand bags which he can lift up to the weather deck as occasion may demand. If you are making a long tack it is wise to lift a bag from the lee side of the boat for this purpose. If you find that your boat is stiff and able when you carry one or two passengers but tender and unreliable when you are sailing alone it is well to replace the weight of the passengers with a couple of extra sand bags. Keep them on shore for this purpose and take them along when you are sailing alone.

Too much stress cannot be placed upon the difference in performance in a small boat with proper and improper trim. I recall particularly one race in which I was leading by a small margin. I moved one man of my crew just four inches abaft of his position in the boat and immediately I began to pull away from my competitors. I won that race by the widest margin in my experience and attribute it to the fact that I managed to have my weight stowed exactly right.

Two friends of mine were sailing catboats of practically identical design side by side one day, on a broad reach. Each carried four or five passengers. The two boats were sailing side by side at exactly equal speed, and the occupants of both boats were actively engaged in kidding one another. Presently one of the men on the *Majesty* walked forward and sat on the boom right at the tack of the sail. Immediately the *Majesty* pulled away from the *Modesty* and left her far astern. Thereafter the skipper of the *Majesty* always placed a man in exactly that position whenever he was sailing that course. He had an enviable record for winning races.

CHAPTER XVI

SEVENTEEN WAYS TO GET INTO TROUBLE

THERE are seventeen major ways in which the skipper can get into trouble. There are probably seventeen hundred minor ways. But these seventeen seem to cover the difficulties which are happening all the time. The first source of trouble is carrying passengers before you have learned to sail. Nearly every beginner delights in showing off his new-found art. If he would confine his passenger list to experienced sailors and strong swimmers he would keep out of difficulty. But it always seems as if the beginner carries children, timid girls, or trusting but badly scared old people, who aggravate every difficulty, getting in the budding sailor's way and making tragedies out of minor incidents. A sailor has not learned to sail until he has had his boat out in all weathers, under all conditions of reefing, is intimately acquainted with the water, and knows what to do in an emergency.

The second major cause of difficulty is the overloaded boat. Small boats should not carry more than two or three persons at any time; when they carry six or eight or ten they are loaded down beyond the sailing lines. The skipper has no room to let go his halliards, to let go an anchor, or to handle his backstays. Passengers get their feet tangled up in the sheet, bump one another at the cry "hard alee," invariably put their fingers down into the centerboard trunk at the moment the skipper is jerking frantically on the pennant to raise the centerboard, and if the boat should happen to leak, they weigh it down dangerously and seriously interfere with the necessary pumping and bailing.

The third major cause of difficulty is running aground. Even the old-timers do this occasionally when they make an error in their position or meet with fog and a shifting wind or trust to the buoy that is out of position. But the beginner seems to be aground more than he is afloat. Running aground is usually not very serious but it can become an expensive pastime.

Carrying too much sail is the fourth major difficulty. It is generally due to laziness in the matter of reefing. It causes many knockdowns and frequent loss of spars, sails and rigging. It is often inevitable in sudden squalls and is frequently caused by silly bravado.

Carrying too little sail may be listed as the fifth major cause of trouble. It is quite as important a failing as carrying too much sail, especially in a squally land breeze. The boat must always have enough sail to work her, and reefing down to the point where the boat loses steerage way between puffs is quite as dangerous as having too much sail in the puffs.

Collision may be listed as the sixth cause of trouble. Collisions occur frequently. In racing they are sometimes unavoidable. But there are far too many collisions from failure to observe right of way rules, from boats running through a busy anchorage, and from boats getting out of control at the wrong moment.

Fog may be listed as the seventh cause of trouble. If more small boats carried compasses, the trouble from fog would be largely eliminated. Of course cruising boats making long passages are always subject to collision and running aground through fog, but there is little excuse for the skipper of a small boat out merely for an afternoon sail failing to find his way home if he is alert and carries a compass.

The eighth major difficulty comes from carrying away sails, spars or rigging. More parts of a boat are carried away in light, moderate winds than in heavy gales because most of our boats are not properly equipped and more sailing is done in light airs than in heavy blows. The time to change a halliard is before it parts—not afterward.

Jamming the centerboard rates ninth. Boards are jammed principally through their striking an obstruction while the boat is turning or making leeway. Parting the pennant has almost the same effect as jamming the board.

The tenth major difficulty may be listed as losing the rudder. A boat without a rudder is not entirely crippled, but the complications that ensue may be serious.

The eleventh source of trouble comes from failure of wind. Being becalmed is not a very trying experience, but being becalmed in a tideway has been known to cause the loss of many a boat. And people do such silly things when they are becalmed, such as jumping overboard and trying to swim to shore—a shore that is more distant than it looks.

Shifting ballast has upset many a boat. It is the twelfth major cause of trouble.

Insufficient ballast may be listed as the unlucky thirteenth.

Leaks rank as the fourteenth. Nearly every boat leaks somewhat. But when the water comes in faster than you can bail it out, you may be sure you are in trouble.

Losing a man overboard is the fifteenth way to get into trouble and a serious trouble it is. As a rule people fall overboard at the worst possible time—in a black night and a heavy sea, or in shoal water with sticky muddy bottom, where they can neither swim nor walk and where the boat cannot maneuver back to them. Or they may be knocked unconscious and overboard at the same moment by a blow on the head in an accidental jibe. Or the skipper sailing alone with his boat boiling along and the helm lashed may trip on a cleat and go overboard.

The sixteenth cause of trouble is the fouled anchor. Anchors foul in two ways. In one way you cannot get it up. In the other way you cannot keep it down. Either way is bad.

The seventeenth cause of trouble lies in sticking slides and hoops on the mast. Hoops stick less than the slides on the track of a Marconi mast. When you just must get your sail down but no power on earth will free that sticking slide, when the halliard cannot move the sail either up or down, and it is blowing blue blazes in a thunder squall, you may well rate this difficulty as one of the major ways to get into trouble. A similar difficulty results from using too small a halliard or too big a block so that the halliard will roll off the sheeve and jam way up aloft. These are the seventeen major ways to get into trouble. Guard well against their happening, but if they do happen let us see what we can do about it.

CHAPTER XVII

SEVENTEEN OR MORE WAYS TO GET OUT OF TROUBLE

THE degree of self-confidence of the skipper has a direct bearing on the amount of trouble he encounters. The over-confident skipper is nearly always in trouble; the under-confident, almost as frequently. It is well to begin your sailing with little confidence in your own ability and to have that confidence increase at the same pace as your progress. It is also most necessary that you should maintain absolute discipline on board. There can be only one skipper, and his authority must be absolute. I have a very keen recollection of some sailing that I did in my early youth with my mother as my passenger. She knew nothing whatever about sailing but insisted upon taking command and exercising her parental authority over her son. The results were nearly disastrous.

Listen to advice if it comes from reliable sources but make your own decisions, abide by them, and see that your passengers obey your orders promptly and without question. Social amenities should never interfere with seamanship. If your boat is overloaded with six passengers, but can comfortably carry five, do not make an exception and carry six even if it breaks up a party. If you warn your passengers repeatedly not to put their hands down the centerboard trunk when they duck their heads when the boat goes about and they continue to do so, inform them frankly that you will never ask them again. Also, try not to feel guilty if a necessary jerk on the centerboard pennant bruises a finger or two that, despite your warning, may be thrust down the trunk. If your prospective passengers are dressed in shore finery and embark with you with the persistent idea that they are not going to get wet, whereas you know that they will, be bold enough to leave them ashore. They will spoil your sail (and their clothes) if they should go with you, and there is no use making yourself miserable.

Except in thick fog, there is no reason for ever running aground, and for most part running aground even in a thick fog is inexcusable in the short distances a small boat ever sails. There are two ways to keep from running aground. The first rule is at all times to know exactly where you are. The second rule is always to presume that you haven't enough water unless you positively know that you have.

Except for very abrupt shoals, if you are sailing a centerboard boat the centerboard always gives ample warning. You feel it strike bottom, you see it rise up in the trunk; and that is always a signal for going about unless you are prepared to take the consequences of running aground. If a boat goes aground, do not try to bump her or push her over the shoal. Go out the way you came in. On most boats, the deepest part is aft of the center, so if you can turn the boat about to point over your reverse course you will have just a little way to go before you are in deep enough water to float the boat.

Every small boat should be provided with a "settin' " pole. There is a right and a wrong way to everything about a boat. A pole is better than an oar for pushing purposes. It gets a better purchase on the bottom and is much less likely to break. The wrong way to push is to face the pole with the end of the pole sticking

Fig. 56. Wrong way to use a settin' pole

out behind your back. If you push this way, you have no strength in your arms, a poor grip on the pole, a poor grip with your feet on the deck and, on the whole, you exert very little power. Turn around with your back to the pole and your body nearer to the water than your hands. This gives you a wonderful grip both on the pole and on the deck. All the strong muscles of your body are put into play—the muscles of your forearm, your biceps, muscles of your back, and the very powerful muscles in your legs. In this position, too, it is easy to get your foot against a shroud or the coaming and thus exert extra power. A light, weak man using a settin' pole properly can move a boat under circumstances where a strong, heavy man using the same pole improperly cannot budge it. Always make sure that the pole is straight. A pole that bends under pressure is very dangerous to use;

Fig. 57. Right way to use a settin' pole

for if it breaks, the man who is using it may tumble overboard and impale himself on the sharp splinters of the break. The illustrations show the right and the wrong way to use a settin' pole.

The sails can be made to help in getting off a shoal. If there is plenty of wind and you trim the sails flat, the boat will heel over, draw less water in consequence, and move off without much pushing. If there is not enough wind for this purpose, a boat can be hove down by a couple of men getting overboard with both ends of a halliard and pulling down on the mast. The enormous leverage of the mast will make this work much easier than it seems, and a boat that is not too hard aground will generally slide off easily after she is hove down a few inches.

It is standard practice to warp a boat off with her anchors. Take the anchors out in a rowboat or, if the water is shoal enough, wade with them in the direction of the deep water. Get them down firmly and heave on the cable. If your boat has a winch, it will be most effective for this purpose. Otherwise it may be necessary to rig a tackle to the cable and trim on that. It has been my experience with warping that the anchor moves through the bottom considerably faster than the boat moves off the shoal; but warping has been known to free many a stranded vessel.

Towing off with a motor boat is often very effective. After a line is made fast, the slack should be taken up gradually until the line is tautened and then the boat is pulled free. If the boat is hard aground it may be necessary to start the motorboat at fair speed with the line slack so that the shock of the tightening line will pull the boat out. This practice should not be resorted to until other means fail because the shock of the tautening line is a great strain not only to the stranded sailboat but also to the towing motorboat and is very likely to part the cable or to pull out cleats, ring-bolts, or Samson posts to which the line may be made fast. If the boat is on the edge of a shoal and may be towed sidewise into deeper water, the use of a parbuckle is often helpful. To rig the parbuckle, pass the towing line from the motor boat over the deck of the stranded boat, then under her bottom, up on the near side, and make fast on the deck. When the strain tightens, it will not only pull the boat sidewise but will also roll her down. This exerts a tremendous leverage and is quite likely to free a boat that is otherwise stranded hard.

The use of a heavy spar as a lever is sometimes very helpful. With the power boat in which I used to nose around shoal waters, I often made it a practice to unstep the signal mast, get overboard with it,

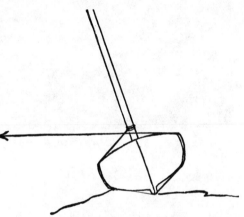

Fig. 58. The parbuckle

worm it under the keel, and lift the other end. It is surprising how much power a man can exert on the end of a decently long spar.

If the water is sufficiently shoal, you can do more by getting overboard and pushing than by any other method, for two reasons: first, you lighten the boat by your own weight; second, you can exert more power. Of course, a deep keel boat will run aground in water that is too deep to permit this practice. The art of pushing is very similar to the art of using a settin' pole. Get your back under the counter with your legs bent. Then straighten up. Do not face the boat and do not push with your hands or chest.

Fig. 59. Wrong way to push

Fig. 60. Right way to push

Merely changing the trim will frequently get a boat off. Send your passengers forward if you are aground astern, and vice versa. Movable ballast shifted forward or aft will also help.

The problem of getting out of soft mud presents difficulties peculiar to itself. In soft mud you cannot get overboard nor can you effectively use a settin' pole. The pole merely sinks in the mud, and although you may push the boat a little forward, you pull it back again when you pull the pole out. In soft mud, however, a boat can be made to wallow. Jump from one side to the other and try to rock the boat. The keel will excavate a little hole so that the boat can be backed out. The flat side of an oar is very useful in soft mud. If you can turn the boat so as to use the oar over the stern, sink it as deeply as you can with the blade of the oar perpendicular to the center line of the boat. Then pull back on the handle of the oar, thus forcing the boat ahead.

All these directions have been made without reference to tide. When there is no tide, the skipper must help himself; but where there is a considerable rise and fall of tide, it may be depended upon to help unless you are so unfortunate as to run aground at dead high tide. If the tide is ebbing, you will, of course, try to resort to some of these means rather than wait until the flood comes again. If, however, the tide should be ebbing and you should decide to wait for the flood, try to support your boat so that she will ride on an even keel. If your boat has a self-bailing cockpit, you should take pains to plug the scupper holes. If you fail to do this, and the boat settles down on her side, the rising tide may fill the boat through her scuppers before the boat herself has a chance to float and the water will not only have to be pumped out but may do considerable damage. It must be borne in mind that the tide does not rise steadily. It seems to flood in three stages. First it rises until it is about one-third high. Then it stands still, and in some places may even recede a little. The second stage of the flood follows until it is about two-thirds high, when it again seems to stand still or may even recede a little. Then it will continue to flow until maximum high tide is reached. Therefore do not give up hope of getting your boat off by means of the tide until you are certain that the actual high tide has been reached. Many a stranded boat is left absolutely bare at low water. If that should happen to your boat, you can frequently dig a hole under her keel and a trench from the hole to deep water so that when the tide returns you can float again.

So much for running aground.

Collisions of any sort are always inexcusable except in dense fog. One way to avoid collision is to keep a sharp lookout. If you are sailing from the windward side of the boat, make one of your passengers responsible for any boats that may approach to leeward, for from your position you may find it impossible to see under the boom. When you are sailing before the wind and have a spinnaker set, keep a lookout in a position where he can see ahead. Until you have learned the rules of the road and know whether or not you have the right of way, always presume that the other fellow has it and get out of his way. It is usually a safe presumption that the skipper of the other boat does not know his right-of-way rules.

In the summer of 1930 the schooner yacht *Varuna* was sailing on Long Island Sound close-hauled on the starboard tack. Her skipper saw the power yacht *Shadow K* bearing down upon her. He assumed that the *Shadow K* would recognize his right of way. He did not know that the *Shadow K* was being steered by her Metal Mike or gyroscopic automatic pilot. He did not know that the lookout had left the bridge. The *Varuna* was cut in half and sunk, a total loss.

When you see another boat sailing toward you or about to cross your course, note her bearing. In a few minutes observe the bearing again. If the bearing has changed, there is no danger of a collision unless one of the two boats alters her course. If the bearing does not change between the two observations, you will know that there is danger of a collision. If you should get close to another boat, be careful how you alter your course. Suppose you are sailing on the starboard tack and the other boat is sailing on her port tack. The two boats come close together. Then suddenly the other boat goes about. You must go about, too, to avoid collision. Do not bear away, as by so doing your bow would strike her stern. If, on the other hand, the other boat bears away to pass under your stern, you should bear away too, so that your bow will move to leeward and as a result your stern will move to windward. If you should luff at the same time the other boat bears away, your stern may collide with her bow.

The law requires that motor boats shall be equipped

with foghorn and bell, yet very few sailboats are so equipped. The horn should be blown with a prolonged blast once every minute if you are under way in a fog, on the starboard tack and two long blasts on the port tack and three long blasts if the wind is abaft the beam. The bell should be rung for five seconds out of every minute if you are at anchor. If you are sailing in waters like Long Island Sound where large vessels pass regularly, the horn and the bell are very necessary parts of your equipment.

There are various government aids to guide you in a fog; the submarine fog signal is supposed to be detected by microphones placed in the sides of a large vessel for that purpose, but occasionally they can be heard by an observer with his ear down to the planking below the waterline. If they sound more clearly on one side of the boat than on the other, the submarine fog signal is in the direction of greater clarity and the source of the signal may be determined from the chart. Foghorns are blown at lighthouses and listed on the chart and are a great help to navigation in a fog. Buoys as indicated on the chart frequently have bells, gongs, or whistles. The bell and the gong may be distinguished as follows: The bell sounds a single note; the gong consists of a number of gongs set one above the other, and the action of the waves swings the clappers of the gongs at different rates so that you hear several notes—some high, some low. If a gong buoy and a bell buoy are in close proximity, they may be distingushed by whether you hear one note or more than one.

Sounds act peculiarly in a fog. There seem to be dead areas into which no sound of a horn will penetrate. You may hear a horn perfectly at a distance of three miles and not hear it at a distance of two miles. In the event of a fog, try to keep out of steamship lanes. There are certain definite paths which steamships usually follow, and if you will observe them carefully in clear weather you should be able to avoid them in a fog.

The skipper should, however, be apprised of the advent of a fog. It can usually be observed at a distance before it reaches your boat. The little feathers of spindrift that do not particularly affect visability can generally be seen for some minutes before a fog closes in. At the first warning of fog, be sure to get a fix; that is to say, determine exactly where you are. Then set your course for a near objective. Remember, it is better to feel your way along in a fog, sailing from buoy to buoy and from point to point rather than to try to steer a long, straight course for home. If you have no compass, the direction of the wind makes a pretty good substitute. Wind does not often change direction in a fog. If the wind changes, the fog probably is lifting. The trouble, however, is that the direction of the wind seems to change at all times when you cannot see beyond the length of your boat. Remember that the wind is apt to remain fixed, whereas your sense of direction is apt to be very unreliable. So trust to the wind blowing from the same point at all times during a fog unless you have a compass and know definitely that it has changed.

The loss of spars and shrouds is a frequent cause of trouble and there is very little that can be done if they should go overboard. If your mast goes by the board it may be possible to step the boom, make a jury rig with a reefed sail, and get along somehow. If your step should give way, you should proceed with utmost caution. If you are not careful, the mast may poke a hole through the bottom of the boat. You can generally worm your way along with greatly reduced sail by wedging the foot of the mast and the broken step in place by means of your cockpit benches, your ballast, boom crutch and other loose junk. But be sure to carry just as little sail as you possibly can if anything should happen to your step.

The part of a shroud that generally gives way is the turnbuckle. Most turnbuckles are too light and are under such strain that they snap rather easily. Turn-buckles carry away on jibes or by striking them against another boat or a dock. It is easy to rig lanyards through the end of a shroud and a chain-plate. Several turns of light line first made fast to the shroud, then passed through the hole in the chain-plate, back through the bight of the shroud, back to the chain-plate, etc., drawn up while the boat is under sail and the shroud with the broken turnbuckle to leeward, will do duty for the turnbuckle. Remember, this is the way the shrouds on the old ships were fastened, with deadeyes and lanyards for centuries before turn-buckles were invented. If a break in a shroud should come anywhere within reach it can be repaired tem-porarily by tying the ends in large bowlines and reeving lanyards through the two bowlines. They must be set up while the broken shroud is to leeward.

If a spreader should break, it is sometimes possible to use the boom crutch, the boathook handle, or other loose wood on board, placing the emergency spreader as high off the deck as you can reach. If a sheet should part, it may be spliced with a long splice and re-rove through the blocks. Or the sheet may be shortened by reeving it through fewer blocks. But in order to get the boat into the wind so as to bring the boom into the boat to reeve the sheet, it will probably be necessary to anchor. The topping lift serves admirably to replace a broken halliard. If the halliard blocks should pull out at the masthead, it is sometimes possible to throw a weight with a cord attached over a spreader, make the halliard fast to the cord, and pulling it up over the spreader it is possible to hoist sail sufficiently to get home. If the jaws of the gaff should break, an emergency rig can be made with a parrel; that is to say, a rope loop with little wooden rollers placed upon it. An excellent parrel can be made with wire and a wooden bundle handle cut into short lengths. If ladies are on board with their sewing, spools will serve excellently for this purpose.

If a severe accident should happen to a mainsail— if it should be badly torn or blown out—the spinnaker can be rigged as a trisail hoisted from the topmost peak halliard block and hauled out loosefooted on the main boom.

One frequent cause of trouble on a centerboard boat is a jammed centerboard. If the board is down and

you strike a shoal, the board may be bent in such a way
that you cannot get it up. Also, if the pennant should
part you will have nothing to lift it with. Sometimes
it can be pulled up by means of a boathook thrust
down the trunk. Another method of lifting it is to
pass a line under the boat, make it fast amidships on
one side of the boat, and pull on the line on the other
side. It is very wise always to have a large screweye
in the very top of the centerboard which can be engaged
by a boathook or a piece of iron bent in the form of a
hook whereby you can lift it. If all else fails, you can
run your boat ashore cautiously until the board comes
up again into the boat.

The loss of a rudder is not always serious. I remember sailing a small boat for eight miles without a
rudder, steering her by the trim of the jib. An oar
out over the leeward quarter makes a pretty good
emergency rudder and if there is not an oar on board,
a floorboard may be used for the purpose.

It is possible to make progress even in a calm if you
observe the following rules:

First, do not disturb the set of the sails. Sails will
hold a certain amount of wind and impart something
of a drive to the boat even if no wind is perceptible.
But if your passengers run all over the boat and shake
the sail, they will kill what little headway you have.
It is very hard to preserve headway in a calm nowadays because of the swells kicked up by motor boats;
but if you are sailing at night and no motor boats are
around, it will pay you to keep perfectly still when
attempting to sail in a calm. If the tide is with you,

stay out in the middle; if it is against you, stay near shore where the adverse tide will run less strongly and where you may possibly have the benefit of back eddies.

The time to see that your ballast is properly battened in is before it starts to shift, not afterward. But once the ballast has started to shift, counteract it immediately with a sand bag up to windward. Head into the wind as quickly as possible and get the ballast back into place. One of the worst forms of shifting ballast is a passenger or a member of your crew who cannot stay perched up on the windward deck but loses his balance and falls to leeward. I have had them fall right into the sail on occasion. Water makes good ballast if it could be kept to windward, but inasmuch as it always flows to the place where you do not want it, it makes the worst possible ballast.

There are more ways to fight a leak than by using a pump. The first thing to do is to find the leak. If your boat has a cabin or plumbing fixtures, suspect the plumbing fixtures first of all. If your boat leaks more on one tack than on another, look for the leaks high up on the side that is to leeward when the leaking is most noticeable. If the boat leaks equally on either tack, look for a leak near the bottom. A centerboard boat leaks most frequently at the trunk or at the point where the trunk enters the keelson. An old boat is apt to leak in the wake of the mast or the chain plates. A boat that has been anchored in the hot sun and has not been sailed recently is most apt to leak high up on the sides near or at the deck line. Examine the rudder post. If you have had any collisions or have run into a dock fairly hard, look for leaks around the bow. If you have an auxiliary motor, look for leaks in the exhaust line and at all places around the cooling water system and especially at the stuffing box of your propeller shaft. If you leak much more on one tack than on another, change your tack and stay on it until you get the leak plugged. It is astonishing how many things a resourceful man may use to stop a leak. A piece of a shirt tail; match sticks; chewing gum; a lock of hair or rope yarn will sometimes fix the most stubborn leaks.

Leaks in plumbing can be patched temporarily with white lead and tape. Leaks in a lead pipe can be peaned with a hammer. If a pipe has rusted away badly, whittle a plug out of the handle of a deck mop or boat hook, smash the pipe completely, and drive the plug into the hole.

One of the most frequent causes of plumbing leaks is the installation of a brass elbow or union in an iron pipe line. Study your pump and make sure you understand its action. The simplest form of pump consists of a galvanized iron pipe with small feet on the bottom to raise it $\frac{1}{4}''$ or so above the floor. This pipe has a one-way valve usually made of leather or rubber at the bottom. The plunger is equipped with a small leather bucket which also acts as a valve. The bucket descends through the water in the pump and folds up slightly to let the water flow past it. When you lift the plunger, however, the bucket expands, filling the entire cross-section of the pump and lifting out the water that is above it. This forms a partial vacuum beneath the bucket so that water is sucked up through the lower valve. When the plunger is again pushed down, the valve at the bottom of the pump closes, holding the water in the pump. Most pumps must be partly filled with water before they will work. If a pebble, a piece of rope or other foreign matter gets jammed in the lower valve, the downward motion of the plunger simply presses the water out of the bottom of the pump into the boat. Therefore if your pump will not work, examine the lower valve to see if it is propped open.

There are many small and comparatively expensive brass pumps on the market with a ball check valve. These valves are supposed to operate on both the upward and downward stroke of the plunger. But they throw so small a stream and get out of order so frequently that they are usually not worth the space they occupy. A simple, cheap pump made by your local tinsmith out of galvanized leader pipe is the best pump for all practical purposes.

Many centerboard boats are equipped with pumps that operate into the centerboard trunk. These work very well when a boat is on an even keel but they should be so rigged that they can readily be removed from their fasteners and put down into the bilge when the boat is heeled over so that you can pump directly overboard from the lowest part of the bottom.

Picking up the man who has fallen overboard calls for prompt and cool action. The first thing to do is to throw a life preserver. The racing rules of the Yacht

Racing Association of Long Island Sound require that two serviceable life preservers shall be kept on deck or in the cockpit at all times during a race, and a boat failing to comply with this rule is promptly disqualified. When a man is overboard, the situation should never be treated as a joke. The chances are more than even that he has hurt himself in falling or he may have received a severe blow from the boom in a jibe which has not only knocked him overboard but may also have caused severe injuries. In turning to pick up a man who has fallen overboard, be sure that you do not attempt to swing the boat in a shorter circle than her normal turning radius. If you try to turn too short, you will sail past the man and not be able to reach him as quickly as if you took a long, gentle, natural swing. Try to reach the man when you are headed into the wind and have lost all way, even though it may take five or six seconds longer to do so. I know of one case where a man was knocked overboard by being struck a violent blow from a boom in an accidental jibe. He was not hurt by the blow from the boom but had three ribs broken when he was yanked forcibly into the rescuing boat.

The question of man overboard becomes more serious when the lone sailor falls overboard many miles from shore. If the helm should be lashed and the boat proceeding steadily on her course, his situation is serious indeed. If you should ever lash your helm and leave it to go forward, proceed with great circumspection and with a full consciousness that falling overboard almost certainly means drowning.

If you are alone and should fall overboard with your helm free, do not swim after the boat. Sooner or later the boat will come into the wind, will hang there a moment, drift back to leeward, fall off the wind, fill away again, and once more come up into the wind. Her path will be a series of short semicircles. Try to figure out the point at which the boat will come into the wind and swim for that point across the chord of the arc which the boat is describing. If you are lucky, you may catch her.

If your anchor is fouled on the bottom and you cannot get it up, there are several tricks which may prove helpful. In the first place, if you know the bottom to be foul—full of rocks, piling, or other obstacles—make fast a tripping line to the anchor before you let it go. A tripping line consists of a light line made fast to the fluke of the anchor that will be uppermost when your anchor is down. The upper end of the tripping line should be buoyed so that it can be picked up in case the cable will not lift the anchor. The pull on the tripping line comes directly above the fluke that is fouled and is likely to pull it free from the obstruction, whereas the pull on the cable merely imbeds the fluke deeper. In the absence of a tripping line, it is sometimes possible to work a turn of the cable around the fluke. If you have a rowboat, tow the cable as slackly as you can several times in wide circles around the spot where you know the anchor to be. This may work a turn or two of the cable around the fluke, and the pull will come on the fluke instead of on the stock, and thus your cable will act as a tripping line. If it is at all possible, you should pull on the anchor from the opposite direction to that in which the flukes are known to be pointed. For example, if your boat is directly south of the anchor, and the anchor cannot be lifted, try to get a turn around the fluke and then do your pulling if possible from the north side of the anchor.

Sticking mast hoops are a nuisance in hoisting sail and a positive danger in lowering sail. The remedy for sticking hoops is grease. It is rarely necessary to slush the mast, but slush or grease should be applied to the inner edges of the forward part of the hoops. Hard grease is best for this purpose. A time-honored product, now seldom seen, is grease known as Mastene, but any hard, water-proof engine grease will work well. Do not use the black, sticky kind of grease. It will walk all over your boat. I remember once using rancid butter for this purpose, but the butter was so strong and disagreeable that it was almost impossible to live on the boat. A guest inscribed the following poem on the wall of my cabin to commemorate the strength of that dead butter:

> I ran my boat upon a bar
> And thought all night I'd have to stay;
> But the blessèd butter on the spar
> Pushed her off right away.

A sticking slide on a Marconi mast is a much more serious problem. The slide sticks only where two sections of the mast come together. When you get a single strip of metal thirty or forty feet long, it is bound to expand considerably in the heat of the sun and contract in cooler weather. Unless the track is in several pieces, the expansion and contraction of the metal is bound to cause buckling. On the other hand, when the track is installed in several pieces, the ends of the sections may not come fairly together, and it is at these points that slides stick. Proceed gently when a slide sticks on a Marconi track. Do not try to force it through. Take the halliard in one hand and the luff rope in the other and work the sail alternately up and down until the slide gets over the obstruction.

An added difficulty to the sticking slide is that a Marconi mast is almost impossible to climb with the sail set. The track prevents your hands getting a grip for the purpose of shinnying, and the sail affords no foothold. If a hoop sticks on a gaff-rigged mast, it is an easy matter to climb up the mast on the hoops to free the hoop that is stuck. Make sure, however, that both throat and peak halliards are firmly belayed with no slack before you climb your hoops, otherwise you and the sail may come down together in a heap.

CHAPTER XVIII

CAPSIZING

Boats capsize far less frequently than most people imagine. Certain types of boats are practically non-capsizable. Even if they should be knocked down flat, the keel will bring them back as soon as the sail is over at such an angle that it spills the wind out of the head. The danger in a keel boat is somewhat different from the danger in a centerboard boat. The keel boat may lie down so far that her cockpit will fill, and unless it is of the self-draining variety or the boat is equipped with water-tight bulkheads or air tanks, the weight of the keel may cause the boat to sink. In a centerboard boat, the danger is somewhat different. There is no deep keel to bring the boat back to its sailing lines. A centerboard boat does not heel so readily as a keel boat because she has a broad, flat floor and hard bilges. The farther over she goes, the greater her bearing surface on the water.

But there comes a point in the heel of a centerboard boat where it is easier for the boat to continue to go over than to return to an upright position. That is known as the critical angle of heel and once it is passed nothing will return the boat to the upright position. The plain, ordinary knock-down comes when the pressure of the wind against the sail is greater than the weight of the boat, her ballast, and other stabilizing influences. But such a plain, unvarnished knock-down is very rare indeed, and occurs only in very heavy and very sudden squalls. The more common knock-down comes as a result of loss of way while sailing. Boats are capsized in puffy weather simply because they lose their way between the puffs. Then when an extra-strong puff comes, there is no water flowing past the rudder and the helmsman has lost his ability to parry the puff by pointing the boat into the wind. If a boat has way on her, it is seldom capsized. I have seen dozens of boats capsized in Shinnecock Bay from one single cause: the bay was thickly planted with eel-pot stakes, and small boats carelessly sailed would foul the stakes with their main sheets. A boat thus anchored by its sheet loses all its way and is at the mercy of the wind. Boats blanketed, or having their wind cut off by other boats, by sailing under the lee of a high bluff or through a bridge or in the lee of a building lose their way and are often knocked down by the wind sweeping around the corner. If you have steerage way, you can always parry the attack of wind. If you lose steerage way, you are at its mercy.

The accidental jibe is a frequent cause of capsizing and so is broaching to with a boom broad off. For as heretofore stated, the sail in the water trips the boat and asserts a more powerful influence than does the rudder.

The dangers of drowning as a result of capsizing are very greatly exaggerated. I have seen many boats capsize with their passengers and crew dressed in white flannels and perishable summer frocks and not a single person aboard has so much as suffered wet feet. Boats capsize slowly, not quickly. There is plenty of time to climb to the high side and to sit there dry and comfortable until rescued. There is a popular superstition that the people in a capsized boat are apt to fall under the sail. That is practically impossible. If you fall out of a boat at all, the sail will be in the water before you are. The danger lies not in getting under the sail but in getting on top of it with the loose, wet canvas wrapping itself about you and hindering your movements. With small boats there is a certain danger of the boat recapsizing—swinging up to the vertical and over on the other side.

The method of righting a capsized boat is as follows:

First: Cast off all the halliards and pull the sails down on to the booms. Then put all your weight up on the windward side. If this does not lift her, get help from another boat and tow on the halliards in the direction opposite to that in which the mast lies. Then when you get her vertical, bail her out, slack the head and foot lacings, hoist sail, and be on your way again.

In the event of capsizing, stick to the boat. You are certain to be seen before very long, and a rescue boat will come to your aid. Even if the shore seems near enough to swim to, do not try to make it. The shore is always farther away than it seems from a capsized boat, and the head of the swimmer is a very small object not likely to be seen from shore. If, after capsizing, your boat drifts in the wrong direction, get an anchor over promptly.

CHAPTER XIX

WHAT TO DO IN A THUNDERSTORM

THUNDERSTORMS always give warning, and there is very little excuse for ever being caught unprepared. The best warnings are the weather reports. Look at the newspaper before starting out. If it says thunderstorms, you may be pretty sure that you will have a dose of them during the day.

The radio weather reports are usually more recent and therefore more dependable than the newspaper reports. Weather reports are broadcast at certain hours over certain stations every day. It is an easy matter to take the precaution to tune in on the days you plan to sail.

Even if you miss the broadcast weather reports, the radio is one of the best thunderstorm forecasters. If there is a great deal of static in the air, watch out for a thunderstorm. It is always well to listen for static for a few minutes before starting to sail. So reliable is this indication that the large power companies trace the approach of thunderstorms by means of radio static and anticipate the sudden peak loads that are imposed upon their plants when the darkness of a storm comes and a whole city turns on the electric lights. It takes about twenty minutes to get the large generators working at capacity, but the power companies are always ready because radio static warns them of the approach of the storms and their accompanying darkness.

There is an intimate relation between thunderstorms and heat. If the day is hot and muggy, look out for a thunderstorm.

Low cumulus clouds that hang close to the horizon, black underneath and hard edged are usually an indication of thunderstorms. High, cumulus clouds are generally an indication of fair weather. Thunderstorms move generally up from the leeward, working partially against the wind. They do not often work directly against the wind, but they never come down from the windward. In the neighborhood of New York and generally along the north Atlantic coast, thunderstorms seem to have adopted a standard practice. They arrive usually on a southwest wind and approach from the north northwest. Their action, however, is considerably affected by tide. A thunderstorm is carried in the direction of the tide and may pass out with the ebb and return again on the flood. When you see a thunderstorm approaching, try to get in the lee of a shore or rather hide behind the shore that will be to windward when the thunderstorm breaks. It is easy to forecast the exact direction of the wind of the storm by watching the movement of the approaching clouds. Rest assured that the wind will not be blowing from the pre-storm direction when the storm breaks. Just before the storm comes, it irons out the wind and you find yourself left in a flat, ominous calm. The longer and more pronounced the calm, the more violent the storm will be when it breaks. As soon as the calm sets in, be sure to have everything snug on your boat. Lower all sail. Furl it, and put on the gaskets. Rest your boom on your boom crutch and flatten down your main sheet. Tie everything that is loose and apt to go overboard. Then if you can possibly reach bottom, get out an anchor. It is surprising how comfortably you will ride out a thunderstorm if you are anchored. If your anchor will not reach bottom, plan to scud before the storm with your stern to the wind. A storm jib which you may have ready to bend in case the blow is not too strong may be used to give steerage way. In severe storms, small boats make excellent targets for the lightning, but lightning need not necessarily be dangerous so long as you keep away from the mast and the shrouds. It is a comfort to think that if your boat should be struck by lightning it probably will not be sunk. Lightning always leaves a boat above the water line. I have never known but one boat to be struck by lightning and she was snugly tucked away in a boathouse. The lightning cut a series of symmetrical chips out of the mast and, true to form, left the boat a foot and a half above water line.

Do not fear waves in a thunderstorm. The storm rarely lasts long enough to raise waves of dangerous height. There is an old adage which is worth remembering:

> If the wind before the rain,
>   You may soon make sail again;
> If the rain before the wind,
>   Topsails lower and halliards mind.

Beware of a storm where the rain comes first, followed by the wind. When the wind comes before the rain, the worst of the blow is over before the rain starts. Beware of the return engagement of the storm. You may predict a return engagement under the following conditions:

If there seems to be more than one storm—two separate cloud banks converging toward one another—the second storm may bring back the first one. If the tide is about to turn, look for a return of the storm. If the wind comes before the rain and the storm does not seem to be too severe, it is generally safe to get under way before the storm has completely passed.

Thunderstorms frequently iron out all the wind so that if you do not get under way promptly, you may be becalmed for a long time; and slopping about in a calm with the air chilled by the storm and all your clothing wringing wet from rain is not a comfortable experience. Salt water is seldom chilling; rain water always makes you cold.

CHAPTER XX

SAILING IN A TIDEWAY

So far, most of the instructions for sailing have paid little attention to the tide. Unless the tidal current is very strong, sailing in a tide is precisely the same as sailing without a tide in so far as your course through the water is concerned. But inasmuch as the water is moving, your progress over the bottom will be affected by the tide. Where the tide is very strong, however, it may have a pronounced effect upon the management of your boat.

Let us review once more the action of the rudder. Remember the rudder is enabled to steer the boat because a stream of water is flowing past it. In normal still-water sailing, the stream of water is caused by the boat's forward motion. In sailing in a tide, however, the stream of water may take a different direction owing to the tide. If the tide is foul—that is, directly against the boat—the effect on the rudder will be just the same as sailing in still water. If there is a cross-tide, the stream of water flowing past the rudder will be a component of the direction of the tide and the forward motion of the boat. If the tide is strong and fair, however, it may flow past your rudder at such speed as to nullify the stream going the other way caused by the forward motion of the boat. In that case, the action of the rudder is reversed, just as it is reversed when the boat is hung in stays or when you are backing out from a dock. Although in relation to the shore the boat may be going ahead, in relation to the water that is around it, the boat in such circumstances is sailing backward. With such a tide you put your helm down, when in ordinary circumstances you would put it up and vice versa.

There is a trick of sailing known as lee-bowing the tide. If you are going to windward and can set your course so as to take the tide on your lee bow, your progress will be fast and your actual course to windward will be higher—or closer to the wind—than your apparent course. The tide on your lee bow keeps setting your boat to windward. Bearing this in mind, it is often possible to start your sheets and make your boat foot faster than she otherwise would. When you are lee-bowing the tide, it may be advisable to try to sail to leeward of your objective rather than to windward of it, because the tide will more than offset your leeway and will carry you up to windward.

There is much controversy as to the depth to which to carry your centerboard when sailing a centerboard boat in a tideway. It has been my experience with centerboard boats that no more board should ever be carried than is necessary to stop leeway or to steady the boat, or to preserve the proper trim. The wetted surface of the immersed board offers considerable resistance to forward motion, and for that reason no more board than is necessary should ever be used. With a tide on the lee bow or a strong fair tide, the

greater the depth of the centerboard the more the tide
will help you. If the tide is against you, however, the
deeper the board is carried the more surface will be
exposed to the adverse action of the tide. Many
authorities maintain that this is not the case and that
the board should be carried in a tideway precisely as
it is carried in sailing still waters. In deference to their
opinion, it is only fair to state their case: Their claim
is that a boat sailing in a tide must go through the
water just as it must go through the water if there is
no tide. The fact that the water is moving has nothing
to do with the way the boat is sailed. With this school
of thought I heartily disagree.

The trouble with this conception is this: it is based
upon the idea that a boat is sailing through one fluid
medium—water. The theory is that if that medium is
moving, it will move anything floating in that medium;
and medium, boat and all will move equally over the
bottom. Therefore the boat must be handled just as if
the medium were standing still.

The opposite theory is that a boat is not sailing
through one fluid medium but through two—water and
air. And since it derives its propulsive force from the
air, the effect of the tide must be considered in the
handling of the boat.

In the middle of a body of water the tide is stronger
than at the edges. It is stronger in a deep channel than
over shallow places. It may be impossible to make
progress against the tide in the middle of a race and
yet quite easy to work against it along the shore. The
reason for this is that the friction of the shore slows

down the tide and the rushing of the tide through the middle of the race is quite apt to cause certain little back eddies along the shore that help you more than hinder you. Eddies are particularly noticeable near points that make out from the shore. If you know of their presence it should be an easy matter to study the effect of tides in the waters in which you sail.

Tide tables and current tables are published by the U. S. Coast and Geodetic Survey and all the tides and all the currents are predicted for a year for every part of the Atlantic coast. Both tables may be purchased for 25 cents. The tables are made up with exact predictions for every day of the year for certain reference points such as Boston Harbor, Willets Point, etc., and the tide and the current for other parts are referred to the nearest reference point with a time and a height of tide difference. Current tables are just as necessary as tide tables because the currents do not change their direction consistently with high and low water. In places where tidal current is strong the time of slack water is predicted in the tide and current tables and also in the Coast Pilot. It is easy to plan to sail through a tidal race at slack water when you will encounter no difficulty, and yet at maximum strength of current it might be totally impossible for you to make any progress against the tide.

The direction of the current is also indicated in the current tables and by little arrows on the charts. Direction of the current is most important to know. The north shore of Vineyard Sound is known as The Graveyard because so many vessels have been wrecked there.

The cause for this is probably found in the fact that both the flood and the ebb currents set somewhat toward the shore. It is not always true, you will see, that the ebb runs in exactly the opposite direction to the flood.

Even in light tideways it is possible to read the force and the direction of the current from buoys, stakes, dock pilings, and other fixtures. A buoy, for instance, will develop little rings in the water that make it seem as if the buoy is being towed toward the direction from which the current is coming. The current flowing past the buoy has the same effect as if the buoy were being moved in the opposite direction through the water. Thus the water jumps up on the tideward side of the buoy and streams off, leaving a wake in the direction toward which it is flowing.

Making allowance for tidal currents will be discussed in the chapter on "Coastwise Navigation."

CHAPTER XXI

LAYING TO

THE idea of laying a boat to is to make her stop sailing and maintain her approximate position without the use of an anchor. You know you can stop a boat from going ahead by pointing her into the wind. You know, too, that if she lies in the wind as when she is caught in stays in going about that she begins to drift backward until she falls off the wind and fills away, at which time she will start sailing again. Now if you can put the boat into the wind and so arrange the tiller and the sheets so that she will not fall away to the point of sailing, she will stay approximately right there, drifting slightly to leeward. The helm is lashed down or to the leeward side of the boat. The sheets are trimmed to the point where she will not sail, and the boat goes to sleep. The way it works out is as follows:

The boat is headed into the wind and the helm is down. Now the boat starts moving backward. With the helm down, the bow falls off until the boat starts to sail again. With the helm still down, she rounds up into the wind again, then falls off again and sails a little bit. Now, by trimming the sheet the action of the boat can be controlled to the point where every time the boat starts to fall off in the slightest degree she will immediately head up into the wind and stop sailing, and the cycle of falling off, sailing, and luffing into the wind can be reduced bit by bit until the boat stays absolutely where you want her. The sails will flutter along the luff. The sheet will not be trimmed flat. The boom will be approximately out over the quarter or possibly beyond that point. The trick of it is to get the boat into her groove, which must be determined individually for each boat. The effect of trim is very important. A small boat that will lie to perfectly with the helmsman at the tiller may start to sail again if he should walk forward.

CHAPTER XXII

WAVES

BOATS are built to go either through waves or over them and the shape of the boat has much to do with the comfort of its passengers in a seaway. The old-fashioned straight-stem boat went through the waves, not over them. It pounded very little, but when a sea struck a straight-stem boat the spray traveled straight aft and struck hard. To-day, with practically all sail-boats built with a spoon bow, the bow goes over the waves and not through them. The spray is thrown low and off to the sides, but the spoon bow pounds where the straight-stem boat does not and this pounding may be very disagreeable and even dangerous.

When the *Shamrock V* sailed back to England after her races against the *Enterprise*, she was nearly broken in two by the heavy pounding of her long overhangs in the seas. I have known a boat with a long forward overhang to break three ribs in an afternoon's beat to windward.

The easiest way to take a sea is just slightly off the bow. If you are headed directly into it, you will not only lose steerage way but the whole boat will be thrown backward. Even a power boat is more comfortable cutting through the waves at a slight diagonal than heading directly into them.

Running before a sea is one of the most comfortable ways to sail and yet if the seas are high there is always the danger of pooping. A boat sliding down the back of a wave that has passed under her, lowers her stern so that if the following wave breaks, it may come right aboard. A sea striking the quarter opposite that on which the sail is set may cause the boat to broach to. On the other hand, a sea striking on the same quarter as the sail may cause an accidental jibe. A comfortable and easy way to run before a heavy sea is under the jib alone. If the wind is not too strong, the dangers of the following seas may be avoided by carrying a whole press of canvas, with the mainsail out on one side and the spinnaker on the other. The spinnaker exerts a steadying effect against the thrust of the main boom and it is often possible to tear along comfortably under both mainsail and spinnaker when the boat would yaw and roll dangerously under mainsail alone.

A beam sea is perhaps the most dangerous in that it causes the vessel to roll badly. But the effect of a beam sea is offset by the steadying effect of sail. The most dangerous rolls are the rolls to leeward and back again to windward. A sailboat does not roll nearly so badly as a power boat under the circumstances, and a power boat may be in genuine danger from a beam sea, whereas a sailboat which is prevented from rolling to windward by the pressure of the wind against its sails will ride a beam sea in comfort and security.

Small-boat sailors rarely have recourse to the use of oil to calm the waves. But no chapter on waves would be complete without some mention of oil. Although oil may not flatten out the waves to any appreciable extent it does prevent them from breaking in the vicinity of the boat. It is generally put into canvas bags pierced with holes, but a sponge soaked with engine oil will make an excellent oil bag and any means that may be used to get the oil on the water is acceptable. Oil is frequently pumped out through the toilet and waste pipes of boats that have cabins.

If you are running before the wind, spread the oil from both bows. You will thus sail through your own slick and be safeguarded from following seas and from quartering seas as well. If you are sailing with a beam sea, put your oil bag over your windward bow. Another bag on the lee quarter will help. If you are lying to or at anchor, put oil bags forward and out on both sides of the boat. An oil bag pulled out on a pulley attached to your anchor line will be of great service when you are at anchor.

CHAPTER XXIII

COASTWISE NAVIGATION

COASTWISE navigation or "piloting" as it is sometimes called is the art of safely guiding your boat from point to point without danger of wrecking. The essence of coastwise navigation may be summed up in three sentences:

1. Always know precisely where you are.

2. Lay down the course from where you are to where you want to go.

3. Always presume your course to be foul unless you know it to be clear.

The foremost aids to navigation are government charts. A government chart is an actual picture of the waters, the land under the water and the land around the water. They are made by the U. S. Coast and Geodetic Survey of the Department of Commerce. Charts are made by actual surveys and by actual soundings. Not every sounding that is made is placed upon a chart, but no figure is ever put on a chart unless an actual sounding has been made at that precise point. There are little inaccuracies in charts due to the fact that conditions change, that there is always the possibility of human error and that the paper on which the charts are printed must be wet

189

before the printing is done and the contraction and expansion of the paper may make small inaccuracies.

The government charts are about the most perfect things that have ever been humanly made and you should trust to them implicitly. If any of your experience should be contrary to the information shown on the chart, it is usually wise to trust the chart rather than your experience.

Charts are made in several scales. There is a single chart, for instance, that covers the whole of Long Island Sound. The same information is also shown on two other charts, one of which covers the Sound west of Stratford Shoal and the other covers it east of Stratford Shoal. It is apparent at once that these two charts contain much more detailed information than the single chart because they have twice the space in which to show it. The section of the Sound west of Stratford Shoal is further covered by a dozen smaller charts. One of these charts, for instance, covers the north shore of the Sound only, from New Rochelle to Greenwich Point. What is merely a dot on the chart of the whole Sound covers many square inches on a chart of this small section. Therefore it is always wisest to sail with the largest scale chart available, that is to say, the chart that shows the least territory on the same size sheet of paper. Figure 61 shows how various charts cover the coast of Long Island.

All charts are marked in several places with compass roses. You will note that these compass roses are double. The outer rose marked in degrees indicates true north and all other true directions. The inner

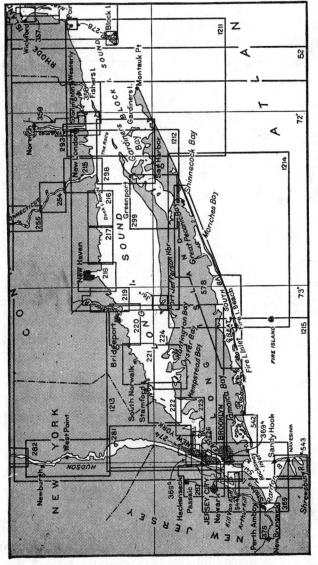

FIG. 61. Showing how the Government charts cover the coast of Long Island. Note that almost this entire area is covered by Chart 52 which is therefore on the smallest scale. Compare the area covered with that of Chart 222 which is printed on the same size sheet of paper. It is evident that the smaller the area covered, the larger the scale and the more detailed and useful will be the chart. (Reproduced by permission U. S. Coast and Geodetic Survey.)

rose marked in points indicates magnetic north and other magnetic directions.

Prominent landmarks—such as docks, towers, cupolos, flagstaffs, houses—are clearly shown. High

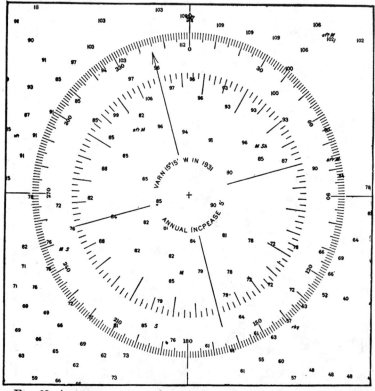

Fig. 62. A compass rose as it appears on a Government chart. The outer rose marked in degrees gives true directions. The inner rose marked in points gives magnetic directions. The numbers, except in the outer scale, are soundings. (Reproduced by permission of the U. S. Coast and Geodetic Survey.)

hills are indicated by the conformation lines. The soundings are shown by figures. On small-scale charts the soundings are shown in fathoms. On large-scale charts the soundings are shown in feet. And in most charts, soundings are given for mean or average low tide. It is possible, of course, to have a tide lower than the charted depth shows, but for most part the depths will be higher at all times except at dead low tide. In connection with the tide tables, it is easy to figure the exact depth at any sounding at any time. Curves of dotted lines are drawn along the shore at one fathom, two fathoms, five fathoms, ten fathoms, etc. A fathom is six feet. All aids to navigation such as buoys, lighthouses, spindles, are clearly shown and printed in their correct colors. Red buoys are always printed in red, and black buoys in black.

Light buoys are indicated by a little star; lighthouses by a big star; bell buoys are indicated by the word "bell," etc.

A chart is of but little use unless it is used in connection with a compass. A compass, unfortunately, is a most unreliable instrument. The bigger the compass card, the better the compass. The mariner's compass consists of one or more needles so pivoted that they will swing to the magnetic north. Fastened to the needles is a compass card that has the points of the compass marked upon it. The whole card swings around inside a receptacle known as the bowl. On the inside of the bowl are four vertical lines known as lubber lines. The compass must be placed in the boat in such a position that one of these lubber lines points toward the bow; another to the stern; and the other two to either beam.

The compass is suspended in rings or gimbals

—pronounced "jimbals"—so that no matter how the boat rolls or pitches the compass card remains level.

The circumference of a modern compass card is marked in degrees of which zero and 360 are north and

Fig. 63. A compass card

the marks progress from North around by way of East, South and West. The compass is also marked into thirty-two divisions or "points." The four principal points are North, East, South and West. These are known as the cardinals. The points midway between the cardinals, namely, Northeast, Southeast, Southwest and Northwest, are known as the intercardinals. The cardinal points are eight points apart. The intercardinals are four points from the cardinals and eight points from one another. The spaces between the cardinals are subdivided and then subdivided again. The point midway between Northeast and North, for instance, being North Northeast; and the point between Northeast and East being East Northeast. Midway between these latter points and the cardinals or intercardinals, the points are designated by the nearest cardinal or intercardinal, the word "by" and the cardinal on whose side it is placed. For instance, the point between North Northeast and North would be North by East. The point between Southeast and East Southeast would be Southeast by East. The thirty-two points are abbreviated as follows and called in the following order. This is known as boxing the compass:

N—North
N x E—North by East
NNE—North Northeast
NExN—Northeast by North
NE—Northeast
NE x E—Northeast by East
ENE—East Northeast
E x N—East by North
E—East
E x S—East by South
ESE—East Southeast
SE x E—Southeast by East
SE—Southeast
SE x S—Southeast by South
SSE—South Southeast
S x E—South by East

S—South
S x W—South by West
SSW—South Southwest
SW x S—Southwest by South
SW—Southwest
SW x W—Southwest by West
WSW—West Southwest
W x S—West by South
W—West
W x N—West by North
WNW—West Northwest
NWx W—Northwest by West
NW—Northwest
NWxN—Northwest by North
NNW—North Northwest
N x W—North by West

To steer a boat by compass you so maneuver the boat so that the point to which you wish to sail comes in line with the lubber line. It must be borne in mind that the compass does not point to the true North Pole. The true North Pole is the northern extreme of the axis of the earth and all charts are laid out in relation to it. The magnetic North Pole is the point of the earth which attracts the compass needle. It is located in the northern part of Canada. Explorers in the far north have often gone past the magnetic North Pole so that their compass needles pointed due south. The difference between true North and magnetic North is known as the variation of the compass. It is different in different parts of the earth and does not stay put because the magnetic North Pole is constantly moving. The movement is predictable, however, and the chart bears the variation at the time the chart was printed and the correction for the change in variation for every year after the printing of the chart. Since change in variation is only slight, it is not necessary for the small-boat navigator to take it into consideration if the chart he uses is only a few years old, as the errors in helmsmanship are so great that change in variation would be only a minor matter. It is important, however, that he shall take his courses from the inner or magnetic rose on the chart and for purposes of small-boat navigation disregard the true compass rose on the chart entirely.

A compass is very much affected by magnetic influences in the boat herself. These attractions in the boat are what is known as compass deviation as distinguished from compass variation. Your iron ballast, your iron keel, your motor if you have one, the generator and magneto if your motor is so equipped, all affect compass deviation. On a large boat a compass is compensated by regular compass compensators who come aboard, swing ship, as they call it, sailing the boat on different courses and bringing the compass to its proper bearing by the installation of small magnets. Lacking a compass compensator, it is a good plan to make a deviation chart. Draw two concentric circles marking all the points of the compass on the inner and outer circle. Then sail your boat over several courses on which the directions are absolutely known. If, for instance, you are sailing Northeast magnetic by chart and your compass reads Northeast by North, draw a line from the Northeast point in the outer circle of your deviation chart to Northeast by North on the inner circle. Then when your magnetic course calls for Northeast, a glance at your deviation chart will tell you that when your compass reads Northeast by North you will be sailing due Northeast.

Sail various courses and then backtrack on them, noting the deviation in at least a dozen places all around the compass.

Another source of compass error is known as "heeling error." If you have a deep iron keel your compass will be deviated when the boat heels over and the keel moves out to one side. You may correct for heeling error by noting your course with allowance for deviation when the boat is headed on the course and the sheets are slacked off. Then trim your sheets until the boat is down to her sailing lines and read the compass again. The compass thus corrected for variation, deviation and heeling error will give you your correct compass course.

Thus you have several types of courses—the true course which is your actual course over the earth. The magnetic course, which is your course in relation to the magnetic North pole and is the true course corrected for compass variation and taken from the magnetic compass rose on the chart. Third, you have the compass course which is the magnetic course corrected for deviation and heeling error.

In addition to charts and a compass, the Coast Pilot is a most valuable aid to navigation. The Coast Pilot is published in several sections for different parts of the coast and sells for a fraction of a dollar. It is a most complete and informative book. It tells you everything that you have to deal with in sailing, outlines your courses, describes prominent landmarks, warns you of dangers, tells you where you may buy food and gas, tells you where to anchor, and in short has all the information that any navigator responsible for the care of a large or a small vessel could desire to have in sailing strange waters.

It is important that you should be able to recognize the navigational aids when you see them in the life as well as understand them on the charts. The most important aids are the red and black buoys. Nowadays most of the buoys are of the nun or can type. The black buoys are cans—great cylinders of iron. The red buoys are all nuns, made of iron with conical tops so that at a distance they resemble a nun with her veil. Every buoy bears a number. Red buoys have even numbers. Black buoys have odd numbers. Along the coast and in exposed waterways, tall nuns and tall cans are used. In harbors, short nuns and short cans. The difference is one of size only. Sometimes spar buoys are substituted for nuns or cans. Spar buoys are very tall spars generally made of steel that stick high out

FIG. 64. A red nun buoy and, beyond, a light buoy

FIG. 65. A black can buoy

of the water and may be recognized at a distance. The only difference between red and black spar buoys is their color. Now why are buoys painted black and red? It is because they are placed on opposite sides of a channel. When you enter a harbor from the sea or whenever you proceed from a larger, more seaward body of water into a smaller, more landward body of water, you leave the red buoys to starboard and the black buoys to port. Whenever you leave a harbor or proceed toward the sea or go from a smaller body of water into a larger body, you leave the black buoys to starboard and the red buoys to port. There is only one way in which you can memorize these buoys. Go to a point that is familiar to you where there are both red and black buoys and remember which side you leave those buoys in entering and leaving that particular harbor. Then you will know that all other buoys are placed in accordance with this scheme.

Two other forms of buoys should be familiar to you. A buoy that is striped horizontally with red and black stripes is an obstruction buoy. It means that underneath that buoy and usually on the landward side of it or up-channel from it is a rock or other obstruction. Give such buoys a wide berth. You can remember that the horizontally striped buoys mean "Keep away" by picturing how a man would look if he were waving you off with his arms. His arms would extend horizontally in the direction of those stripes. Similarly, buoys striped vertically black and white are channel buoys and indicate the center of the channel. You can remember that the vertically striped buoys

Fig. 66. A red and black horizontally striped buoy means "keep away"

mean the center of the fairway by picturing a man who would be beckoning you to come. His arms would move in a vertical position parallel to the striping of the buoy.

Some buoys have bells, gongs, lights, or whistles. The difference between the bell buoy and the gong buoy has been explained. The lights deserve a word of explanation. There are three types of lights: fixed, flashing, and occulting. A fixed light needs no explanation. It burns at all times. A flashing light differs from an occulting light in that the flash is only momentary, whereas the occulting light stays burning for an appreciable length of time, generally

Fig. 67. A black and white vertically striped buoy means a channel.

eight or ten seconds. In most instances but not in all, the occulting light burns for a longer period than the period of darkness. In other words, it is like a fixed light that blinks out; whereas a flashing light is a light that is principally out but flashes momentarily.

Spindles, usually triangular in shape and mounted on poles or iron pipes, are frequently placed on the shore in the neighborhood of dangers so that bearings may be taken from them.

As stated above, one of the elements in piloting is always carefully to lay down a course from where you are to where you want to go. You do this on the chart, then translate it into the terms of your compass course. The first thing that is necessary is to take a departure. A departure may be taken from any fix or any known position. It is most essential that the departure shall be accurate. A channel buoy or a known position off a dock or yacht club is a good point for a departure. We will discuss later the methods for determining a fix.

Let us assume that you are taking your departure from a red nun buoy. Locate the buoy on the chart. Then locate another buoy which we will say is ten miles away, also on the chart. Then take a pair of parallel rulers and lay one edge on the chart between the two buoys. Parallel rulers may be bought from any ship chandler or any store that sells navigating equipment. They consist of two rulers fastened together with two arms of equal length so that the rulers may be pulled apart or pushed close together and yet the outer edges of both rulers will always remain parallel. Walk the rulers across the chart by opening them out and squeezing them together until one edge passes through the middle of the compass rose. Make a small pencil mark at the place where the edge of the ruler passes through the circumference of the magnetic compass rose. Read off the direction in points. That will give you your magnetic course. In using the parallel rules you must be careful that they do not slip. This is done by pressing down hard on the ruler which is not being moved and moving the other very lightly.

If you do not have a pair of parallel rulers, a draftsman's triangle and a straight edge will make an excellent substitute. I have often made a triangle out of cardboard for this purpose, determining the edges with an ordinary ruler. Thus an ordinary ruler and a piece of cardboard cut to the shape of a triangle will make an excellent substitute for parallel rules.

To use the triangle and straight edge, place one edge of the triangle on the line on the chart between the point of departure and the destination. Place the ruler along one of the other edges of the triangle and, holding the ruler still, slide the triangle along the edge of the ruler to the compass rose. It may be necessary to move the triangle in two directions, placing the ruler along one edge of the triangle for one direction and along the remaining edge of the triangle for the second direction.

A very simple and effective method of determining your course is to take it from the meridian on the chart instead of from the compass rose. To do this you will need a protractor. Protractors come in several forms, but perhaps the simplest and the most useful is merely a circle of transparent material on which a compass rose marked in degrees and points is printed.

The central part of such a protractor is marked with numerous vertical lines running parallel to the north and south marks of the compass rose. To use the protractor proceed as follows.

With lead pencil draw a line on the chart from where you are to where you want to go. Place the center of the protractor over your point of departure and hold it there by sticking one of the points of your dividers through the center of the protractor into the point of departure on the chart. Revolve the protractor until one of the north and south lines coincides with a meridian line (north and south) on the chart. Be sure the zero point of the protractor points north and not south. Now read off in degrees the point at which your pencil line on the chart crosses the edge of the protractor. This is your true course. Turn to the nearest compass rose on the chart and translate the true course

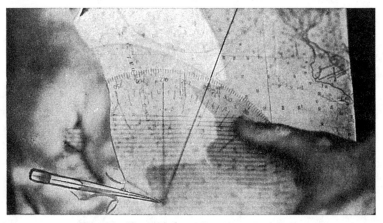

FIG. 68. Showing how to use a protractor

into the magnetic course by reading the magnetic point that falls opposite the degree mark corresponding to that which you have just read off the protractor. Do not be confused by the fact that the protractor is marked both in degrees and in points, for both of these systems of markings when referred to the meridian are true bearings and not magnetic. To get the magnetic bearing it is necessary to refer to the inner rose on the chart. (See Fig. 68.)

Of course, it may be necessary in case the chart is old and the annual variation is considerable, to correct the magnetic course for variation. But after the magnetic course has been determined, change it to the compass course by allowing for deviation and heeling error, and you will have your compass course. The compass course thus obtained would be very accurate for a power boat where the tide is a negligible factor; but in a sailboat two other factors must be taken into consideration: one is your allowance for leeway and the other is your allowance for current. To determine the allowance for leeway, sail your compass course for a short distance and glance back at your wake. Try to estimate from the angle which the wake makes with the angle of the boat the difference between the course steered and the course made good. If your leeway shows that you are being set down a half point or a point to leeward, it will be necessary for you to point a half point or a point higher on the wind in order to attain your objective. We now have a new compass course which is corrected for leeway. A further correction may be made for current.

If the current is fair, driving in the same direction as you are sailing, it will merely get you to your objective faster. If the current is a foul current, going in just the opposite direction, it will merely slow down your progress without making any appreciable difference in your course. But if the current is a cross-current straight on your beam or at an angle on your bow or stern, you will have to resort to a little diagram to determine the allowance for current in your course.

Let us suppose you are sailing a course from A to B as shown in the accompanying diagram (see Fig. 69). At any point of that diagram such as M, let us draw another line MO representing the direction of the current. The arrowhead shows the current's direction and it must be borne in mind that the line MO must be set down opposite to the direction of the current. Now it will be necessary for you to make a guess at the speed of your boat through the water.

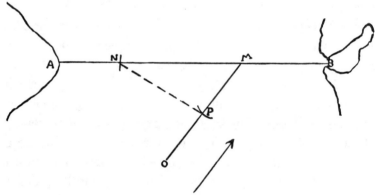

Fig. 69. How to correct your course for a cross current

This can be fairly accurately determined by means of a taffrail log, but without a log you will soon learn to make fairly accurate estimates of speed. Assume that you are sailing at a speed of four knots—that is to say, traveling at the rate of four nautical miles per hour. You should have on your boat as well as the chart, compass and parallel rules, a pair of dividers or compasses which will enable you to lay off distances on the chart. With these dividers, take the measure of four nautical miles from the latitude scale on the side of the chart. Always use the latitude scale for distance; never use the longitude scale. A nautical mile is equal to one minute of latitude. But a minute of longitude differs in all parts of the earth of unequal latitude. It is equal to a nautical mile only at the equator. Take this measurement of four nautical miles and lay it off on the line AB from M in the direction of A. Let us say that the dividers fall at the point N. Now let us assume that the current as taken from the current tables is two knots. Measure off two nautical miles from the latitude scale with the dividers and lay it off along MO from M in the direction of O. We will mark this point as P. Join NP. With the parallel rules, carry NP over to the magnetic rose on the chart, and that will give you your magnetic course corrected for current. It will be evident that if you sail in the direction NP, the current will be driving you in the direction of OM so that actually, although you may be pointed in the direction NP, you will be making good a course along the line AB and at any minute of your sailing you will be somewhere along the line AB.

It must be evident from this that the tide and current tables mentioned in the chapter "Sailing in a Tideway" are a very necessary part of your navigating equipment. Another essential is a taffrail log, but unfortunately they are not often found on small boats. The taffrail log consists of an instrument like the odometer in an automobile speedometer. It is operated by a little device like a propeller known as a rotator which is thrown overboard and towed behind the boat.

The rotator turns a heavy cord known as the log line which in turn revolves the log and shows on a dial the distance run. The only caution to be observed in the use of the log is that great care must be exercised in throwing the rotator overboard and pulling it back, for if it strikes against any part of the boat, the blades of the rotator are apt to be bent and the reading of the log will be incorrect. The log, unfortunately, does not give you the distance traveled over the bottom. All that it gives you is distance through the water, but since the water itself may be moving due to tidal current, there is a difference between distance run as shown by the log and distance made good which is the distance not through the water but over the bottom. In the case of a fair current, you must add to the log reading the distance you would have been carried by the tidal current if you had been standing still. In the case of a foul current, you must subtract that difference. In the case of a cross-current, you must refer to the diagram for course, and having projected your distance on the course NP prick it off and from that point draw a line parallel to OM and its intersection with line AB will give you your distance made good.

Your distance made good, laid off along the course made good, gives you your dead-reckoning position. In other words, you know where you were when you took your departure. You know by these various calculations the actual course you have been sailing, and you know from your log how far you have traveled along the course. When that distance has been corrected for tidal current, you may make a mark on your chart and know fairly accurately that that is where you are.

But no dead-reckoning position is ever very reliable. You may make a mistake in estimating your deviation or the strength of the current or the amount of leeway. Your log may be over-reading because of the speed of your boat or under-reading because of the lack of speed. Your steering is apt to be a bit wild as it is almost impossible to hold a course steadily in a small boat. So, although a dead-reckoning position has its value, it should not be relied upon if it is at all possible to attain a fix—that is to know definitely exactly where you are.

The first method of obtaining a fix is by bearings. If you pass a lighthouse or a prominent flagpole or other clearly defined and identifiable object and that is directly abeam while you are sailing a due east course, you will know that the object is directly south of you and that therefore you are directly north of the object. A line drawn directly north from the object will indicate a line of position. In other words, you may be sure that your boat is located somewhere along that line. Where that line crosses your course by dead reckoning, it will give you a more dependable fix than a position determined by your dead-reckoning course made good plus your distance made good. It is sometimes difficult to take a bearing accurately in a small boat. An azimuth ring on your compass will help you take bearings very accurately. Also the sighting lines in a compass binnacle are valuable for this purpose; but lacking such equipment the best thing to do is to head your boat directly toward the object and read the bearing from the lubber line of the compass.

A single bearing will never give you a fix, but cross-bearings will give you a fix quite accurately. Suppose a prominent lighthouse bears south by east. A glance at your deviation chart shows that the correct magnetic bearing is due South. Lay one edge of your parallel ruler through the center of the nearest magnetic rose on the chart so that it also passes through the opposite point, North. Walk the ruler across the chart until one edge passes through the lighthouse, and draw a line North from the lighthouse. Now suppose a prominent flagstaff bears Southeast by East. Suppose your deviation chart shows that the correct magnetic bearing is Southeast. With your parallel rules, lay off a line Northwest from the position of the flagstaff as shown on the chart until it intersects the other line. It is obvious that if the lighthouse is directly South of you, you must be somewhere on a line directly North of the lighthouse. And if the flagstaff is directly Southeast of you, you must be somewhere on a line directly Northwest of the flagstaff. The only point common to both lines is their intersection, and that is where you are. This is the method of determining a fix by cross-bearings.

Now if you can determine a third bearing on a dock or a windmill lay that off on the chart and if that crosses the intersection of the other two lines you will be sure that your fix is accurate. Two bearings are all that are necessary for a fix, but a third bearing is an excellent method of checking on the accuracy of the first two.

Another excellent method of obtaining a fix is by a single bearing and a range. Suppose you see a black can buoy and a lighthouse and the chart shows that the can buoy is directly Northwest of the lighthouse. Draw a line through the can buoy and the lighthouse. When the two come directly in line, you are somewhere along the line that you have drawn on the chart. If at that moment you can take a bearing on another prominent object and lay off the bearing on the chart, you are at the intersection of the two lines. A range of two objects is much more accurate than a bearing and it is surprising to find how many ranges can be pressed into service in coastwise navigating. At the mouth of the Connecticut river, for instance, there are two white lighthouses, one raised considerably above the other. When those two lighthouses are in range by day or when the two lights are in range, that is to say one light directly above the other, by night, you will know that you are in the channel and have merely to keep sailing in that direction until the first lighthouse comes abeam. At Brown's Creek in Sayville on Great South Bay, two street lights happen to be similarly in range, and since both of these facts are noted in the Pilot Book, the stranger may enter those difficult harbors on a black night with perfect safety.

Another method of determining a fix if you are provided with a log is by doubling the angle on the bow. Let us assume that you are approaching a lighthouse off which there are dangerous rocks and you are anxious to know your exact distance from the lighthouse. When the lighthouse bears let us say two points on the port bow, take a reading of the log. Continue on your course until the light bears four points on the port bow and read the log again. The distance that you have run between the first reading of the log and the second reading of the log is your distance from the lighthouse, and the bearing of the lighthouse gives you your direc-

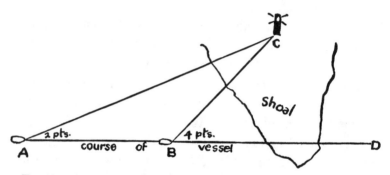

FIG. 70. Doubling the angle on the bow. It is obvious that if angle CBD is double the angle CAD, the distance BC is equal to the distance AB.

tion from it. If you have run one mile between the first and second readings, and the lighthouse bears South-west, you may draw a line Northeast from the light-house. Lay off the distance of one mile on that line, taking the distance with your dividers from the latitude scale and that point is exactly where you are. Now if the rocks extend a mile and a quarter out from the lighthouse, it will be obvious that you are not going to clear them, and you must alter your course accordingly.

A well-known method of obtaining a fix is by what

is known as the three-point fix. This is done on large ships by means of a sextant, but may be worked out on a small boat with a piece of tracing paper tacked down to a board, and four pins. Place one pin at a corner of the tracing paper near your eye. Select three points that are prominent. Sighting from the first pin, place the three other pins rapidly on the board in the directions of the three objects. Draw lines between the pins and move the tracing paper over your chart until these lines pass through the three objects on the chart. The point where the first pin was placed, which is the point common to all three lines, is your position. You must be careful to have all three points on a straight line or the middle point should be a little nearer to you than the other two. Otherwise all three points may fall in the circumference of a circle and if that is the case your fix is indeterminate, as it would plot anywhere on the circumference of the circle. This method unfortunately is not practicable in a small boat, except in very calm water.

No chapter on piloting would be complete without a word about the lead and line. A hand lead, or in its absence a heavy fishing sinker, attached to a long line will give you the depth of the water. In shoal water such soundings may readily be done with the settin' pole which should be marked clearly in feet. In deep water the lead line should be marked in feet to about twice the draft of your boat. In addition, it should be marked in fathoms so that you may be able to know your depth even when the depth is very great.

Seamen have a standardized way of marking a lead

line with bits of leather, bits of cord, red flannel and white cotton; but unless you are using a lead and line quite frequently, it is very hard to remember these markings. Small metal tags giving the exact reading are much less nautical but much more practical for the beginner.

A regulation lead has a hollow part which may be filled with tallow or other sticky substance, the most useful and generally employed being a plain ordinary piece of brown laundry soap. This is known as the arming of the lead. If you drop the lead armed with a piece of soap the soap will pick up little pieces of the bottom and it is easy to tell from the chart whether the character of the bottom agrees with the character of the bottom as shown on the chart. If you have a single bearing and your lead line shows a depth of 20 feet and the character of the bottom is gray sand, it is fairly easy to trace out along the bearing on the chart to the point where the depth reading shows 20 feet and if the character of the bottom is also gray sand, you have obtained a fairly accurate fix. It is the mark of a careful navigator to use his lead whenever he is in doubt.

The leadsman always whirls the lead, casts it ahead of the boat, and takes his reading when the lead strikes bottom and the boat is directly over it. If there are two hands available for this work, however, it is easier for one man to drop the lead from the bow, while the other handles the line from the stern. Thus the boat is sailing ahead while the lead is dropping and when the lead finds bottom the line is up and down.

All these rules for coastwise navigation have been

set down at length. The sailor of a small boat rarely employs them to the degree of accuracy that this chapter would seem to indicate is necessary. After all, rules for navigating are important in huge commercial vessels of hundreds of tons, and proportionately less important as boats are smaller. But navigating is always interesting and always good fun; and it is worth any sailor's time and effort to become a good and careful navigator.

CHAPTER XXIV

MARLINESPIKE SEAMANSHIP

THE author of any book on sailing is always confronted with the desire to show off when he reaches a chapter on knots. Knots are such pleasant things to play with and there are so many combinations of them, so many are pretty and ornamental, that there is always the danger of writing too much and especially too much that will not be useful. Knots of some sort or other are as old as rope, but the heyday of the knot was the day of the square-rigger when hundreds of different kinds of knots had to be tied for very specific uses. This day has passed. Many of the knots have been forgotten, and the complicated art of the rigger is almost lost. The sailor on the small boat needs to know very few knots, but in addition he should understand how to take care of his ropes. If he is interested in learning to tie a sheepshank, a carrick bend, a true lover's knot, a hangman's knot, a tomfool's knot, and the thousand and one other knots that were part of the old windjammer's lore, he is referred to Boy Scout manuals, navy manuals, the encyclopedia, and the numerous other publications on yachting. All that the beginner or the sailor in small boats needs to know is how to tie the three knots covered in Chapter V, how to tie a few variations of these knots, how to splice, and how to preserve his lines.

The following tools should be on board every boat to aid in the necessary knot work. First in order is a knife. The knife should be a clasp knife, not a sheath knife. Nothing is more dangerous than to run around the slippery deck of a small, pitching boat with a long sheath knife in a leather sheath. Yet every boy seems to have the ambition to carry such a weapon. It takes only one second more to open a clasp knife that is in good condition than to draw a sheath knife, and the clasp knife closed and put into a pocket is perfectly safe and sane. If you must wear a sheath knife, wear it as a sailor does—on a belt as near as possible to the middle of your back. Do not wear it in front. A knife worn in front may cut through the sheath if you should fall or even sit down suddenly, and it is right in the position where it may continue down, sever the femural artery, and cause your death within a few minutes. Worn on the back, it is comparatively safe, yet it is said that Indians who are always pictured with sheath knives, invariably carry their knives in the middle of their packs where no possible fall could cause an accident.

The knife should be sharp, but the edge need not necessarily be smooth. A rough, fairly jagged edge is most effective in cutting rope. A jagged-edged bread knife is a particularly good tool for wet and stubborn rope. In addition to the knife, you should have a serving mallet. The serving mallet consists of a piece of hard wood about 2½" long, hollowed on one side to receive a rope. A short handle projects from the other side. The serving mallet is most useful in serving or wrapping the end of a rope to prevent it from unlaying. Third, you should have a marlinespike or pricker. A marlinespike is a smooth tapered rod of hard wood usually about two feet long. It is especially useful with large, heavy line, but the pricker will be found to be more useful with smaller ropes. The pricker is the same shape as the marlinespike but is made of steel and is about five or six inches long. There is a useful tool on the market consisting of a strong knife blade and a steel pricker mounted in a steel handle to which is attached a ring so that the tool is not readily lost. The skipper should be provided also with a sail-maker's palm, a sort of reverse thimble of steel set into a short, fingerless glove of rawhide and leather and provided with a hole for the thumb. Sail needles, heavy cotton cord or light fish line and a ball of marline complete his equipment.

Let us for a minute review the principles underlying all sailor's knots. First, a knot must be tied so that it remains tied under any and all circumstances. It must never slip or let go. Second, a knot must be tied in such a manner that it can be cast off instantly without jamming. Third, the knot must be adapted to the purpose for which it is intended so that the strain put upon it tends to make it more secure rather than less secure.

In Chapter V we discussed the reef knot, a useful variation of the reef knot, the clove hitch, the clove hitch around its own standing part, and the bowline.

We also defined the three parts of a knot—the standing part, the bight, and the fall. It is advisable at this point to read over Chapter V before continuing to read this chapter.

You will note that in the discussion of the reef knot, it is mentioned that this knot is unsuitable for tying together two ropes of different diameters. The best knot for this purpose is generally known as the weaver's knot. A weaver has a trick method of tying it, and there is a reason for the trick method as well as for the knot, because if the weaver's knot is tied in backward the knotted yarns will catch when passed through the fabric. There is no necessity for the sailor's tying the weaver's knot in this complicated way. For the sailor's purpose, it may be tied as follows:

Hold the end of one line in your left hand, and the second line in your right. Fold over an end of the left-hand line, forming a "U"-shaped loop. Now take the rope that is in your right hand, pass it under and through the loop of the other line, pass it over one end of the loop, under both ends of the loop, and back under itself. Draw tight. (See Fig. 71.) You will note that this knot is rather similar to the reef knot. It differs from the reef knot in that the fall of the rope held in your right hand passes under its own standing part and not through the bight of the other line as in the case of the reef knot. One of these lines can be an inch in diameter and the other can be ¼″, and it will still hold. It is cast off by jerking loose either end as in the case of the reef knot. If the rope in your left hand is finished with an eye splice, the right-hand rope can be passed through and around the splice just as if the splice were a double rope. This is a very handy little stunt to remember. (See Fig. 72.)

In the description of the clove hitch, you will recall the warning that the clove hitch must be tied about a timber so that the pull is approximately at right angles to the timber. If the pull comes lengthwise to the timber the clove hitch will slip.

A variation of the clove hitch that will not slip under such circumstances is made as follows: First take a hitch in the regular manner, with the fall below the standing part. Now take a round turn (not a hitch) on the timber below the hitch. Now put a hitch on the timber above the first hitch just as you would do in making an ordinary clove hitch. You will find that you have made the two hitches with the round turn in between. This knot has various names, but perhaps the best name is "a hitch, a round turn, and a hitch." The round turn prevents the knot from slipping lengthwise of the timber. It is very useful if you are tying up to a dock where the top of a pile or bollard is below the level of your deck. (See Fig. 73.)

In tying a clove hitch, it is occasionally useful to be able to pick up a rope with one hand in such a manner that the hitch is already in the rope ready to be cast over a pile. Suppose you are approaching a dock and have run forward to make fast. Your boat is pitching and plunging into the waves, and you must steady yourself to avoid falling overboard—with "one hand for yourself and one for the ship," as the old windjammers used to say. In such circumstances the ability to pick up a clove hitch in this manner may be most

FIG. 71. The weaver's knot. Note that this knot is effective even with lines of different diameters.

FIG. 72. A bend and an eye splice on the same principle as the weaver's knot.

FIG. 73. A hitch, a round turn, and a hitch.

FIG. 74. Picking up a clove hitch. A. Line thrown out on deck, hand supine; B. Hand prone, fall crosses standing part; C. Hand supine, fall crosses standing part again; D. Hand prone, standing part picked up between the two crossings of the fall.

useful. Pick up the rope four or five feet from the end and throw it out on deck with both the standing part and the fall away from you, and your hand with the palm up (see Fig. 74). Turn your hand over smartly with the knuckles up so that the fall crosses the standing part. Now bring your hand back to its original position, palm up, so that the fall crosses the standing part again, making a U-shaped loop across the standing part. Still holding the bight in your hand, turn your hand over, knuckles up and little finger away from you, and pick up that part of the standing part which lies within the U-shaped loop made by the fall. Shake the line clear, and you will find in your hand a perfect clove hitch.

When a bowline is tied about its own standing part (see Fig. 75), it makes what is known as a running bowline, which is an excellent slip knot.

A bowline in a bight is a very useful knot. Suppose you want to hook a tackle onto a line, both ends of which are fast. It then becomes necessary to tie some sort of knot in the middle of the line to which you can attach the tackle. The knot most used for this purpose is the bowline in a bight. It is tied as follows: Take the middle of a piece of line. Pull it out in the shape of a loop, with the loop in your right hand and the two parts forming the loop in your left exactly as if it were just one piece of rope in which you were to tie an ordinary bowline. Strike the two pieces above your left hand with the loop in your right hand and form the bight as in the first part of the ordinary bowline. The next movement, however, is very different

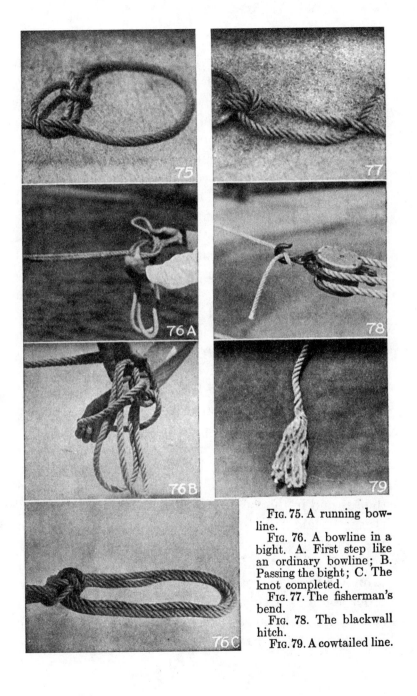

Fig. 75. A running bow-
line.

Fig. 76. A bowline in a
bight. A. First step like
an ordinary bowline; B.
Passing the bight; C. The
knot completed.

Fig. 77. The fisherman's
bend.

Fig. 78. The blackwall
hitch.

Fig. 79. A cowtailed line.

Open out the loop after it has passed through the bight; pass the entire knot through it so that the loop comes up over the standing part and pull it tight. (See Fig. 76.)

A knot with which you should be familiar is the fisherman's bend. The fisherman's bend and the bowline are both used extensively in making a line fast to the ring in an anchor. The fisherman's bend is tied as follows: With the fall of your line, take a round turn around the ring. Then another round turn. Then pass the fall behind and around the standing part and through the two round turns on the ring. The proper way to finish this knot is to unlay one strand of the line a few inches above the knot and poke the end of the fall through it. (See Fig. 77.)

Another knot that you should know is the blackwall hitch. The reason for describing this hitch in this chapter is not because it is so eminently useful but because if you understand it you will have a proper appreciation of the principle that underlies all knots. The blackwall hitch is used when a line is made fast to a hook such as a hook in the end of a block. The fall is first passed behind the shank of the hook and then is laid in the loop of the hook. The standing part is merely laid over the fall and the strain is put upon the standing part. Study this knot a moment. You will find a bight passing around the hook so that it cannot slip. The reason it cannot slip is because in order for it to slip the fall must move, and the fall cannot move because it is held in place by pressure from the standing part. The strain which is put on the standing part holds the entire knot. The blackwall hitch is useless without a strain on the standing part. (See Fig. 78.)

Closely related to Irish pennants are cowtails. They are the mark of a careless skipper. If you see Irish pennants aloft, you are quite sure to find the ends of the halliards and sheets cowtailed or unlaid and unraveled. If the ends of the line are not preserved, the line rapidly loses much of its available length and the result is exceedingly messy. There are in general three ways of terminating a line so that it will be neat and serviceable. First, it may be served. Second, it may be knotted. Third, it may be backspliced. In general, a line should be served unless you wish the end of the line to be larger than the line itself, so that it will not slip through a block. Serving is done with a serving mallet and light cotton cord. Lay the end of your cord along the rope with its end toward the standing part. Lay the serving mallet with its groove on the rope. Take a turn with the cord around the rope and around the head of the mallet on the standing part side of the handle. Then take two turns around the rope and around the mallet on the opposite side of the handle. Then take a turn around the handle. Keeping a slight pressure with your thumb on the part of the cord that is on the handle, pass the mallet around the rope and after each turn pass the ball of cord around also. You will find that the cord is whipped around the rope perfectly evenly. As you approach the end of your serving, cut the line and place the end of it along the rope headed back toward the serving.

Twist the mallet until at least four turns of the line are covering the end. Then pull the end up taut and cut it off. If you lack a serving mallet, the serving can be done as follows: Cut off a piece of cord of sufficient length for the serving and thread one end through a sail needle. Lay the opposite end upon the rope headed toward the standing part. Wrap the rope beginning with the end and working toward the standing part so that the wrapping covers the end of the wrapping line. When you have served the rope for at least a half an inch, pass the sail needle under four or five turns of the serving. Pull taut and cut off.

To end a rope with a knot is the next problem. This takes less time than serving and can be done in a few minutes at any time. If you intend to serve the end of a rope but lack the opportunity to do the serving, you can knot it temporarily, then later serve it above the knot and cut the knot off. The knot generally used for this purpose is the wall and crown. Historically, this knot is of interest as it was used originally in the ends of the cat-o'-nine-tails so liberally used for punishment on board ships. The wall and crown could be depended upon to draw blood at every stroke and no amount of whipping could untie the knot.

To tie the wall and crown, unlay the end of the line for a distance of about five inches. It is helpful to whip the line with light cord at this point, but the whipping is not really necessary. For convenience, we will number the strands 1, 2, and 3. Take any strand, 1, and pass it down by the standing part so as to form a bight. Hold it in this position with your thumb (see

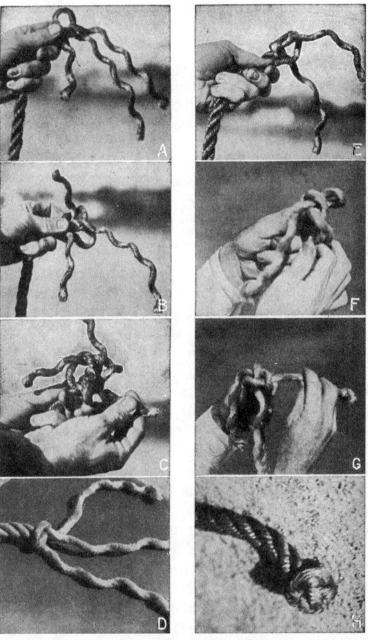

FIG. 80. The wall and crown knot. A. First strand in wall; B. Second strand in wall; C. Third strand in wall; D. Wall completed; E. First strand in crown; F. Second strand in crown; G. Third strand in crown; H. Wall and crown completed.

Figure 80). Now take the next strand 2, the one that is nearer to you than strand 1, pass it over the fall of strand 1, forming another bight with the fall of strand 1 through it. Now take strand 3, pass it over and around the fall of strand 2 and up through the bight of strand 1. Now pull up all three falls tight, working the bights around smoothly with your thumb. You will note that each strand passes upward through the bight of the next strand to it. This is the wall knot.

On top of the wall we place the crown. Bend strand 1 over so that its end comes between strands 2 and 3. Bend strand 2 over the fall of strand 1 so that it comes between strand 3 and the bight of strand 1. Then bend strand 3 over strand 2 and tuck it through the bight of strand 1. Examine this knot and you will find that each strand passes under the bight of the strand next to it. Draw up the three strands tight and cut them off close, using a sharp knife and a sawing motion, and be careful that the friction of the cutting does not pull the cut ends out of the bights.

The combination of these two knots is known as the wall and crown. If you study out this knot, you will see that the wall is really nothing but a crown that is tied around the standing part.

Another knot that is useful for ending a rope is the Matthew Walker. This is tied as follows. Unlay the line for a slightly greater distance than for the wall and crown. Hold the line so that one strand, 2, is nearer to you than the other two. Take the strand to the left of strand 2 and call it strand 1. Pass strand 1 around the standing part with the lay of the rope and tuck the end up through its own bight.

Now take strand 2 and pass it around in the same way and up through the bights of both 1 and 2. In doing this, you must be careful to pass the bight of 2 on the near side of the fall of 1, so that the fall of 1 is not included in the bight of 2. Now pass the strand 3 in the same manner on the near side of the fall of 2 so that the fall of 2 is not included in the bight of 3, and pass it up through the bights of 1, 2 and 3. Draw up all three falls evenly until you have a perfectly round, hard knot. Pull this knot in the direction of the end of the rope and cut off the strands as in the wall and crown. The Matthew Walker is not crowned.

The Matthew Walker is useful as a stopper knot to prevent a line, such as the main sheet or centerboard pennant from running through a block. The line is unlaid for the necessary distance, the Matthew Walker is tied as described, and then the strands are twisted and laid up again in the original form of the rope and the end is served.

This is a logical place to discuss the back splice, because the back splice is a very useful knot for preventing cowtails. But the back splice will be easier to describe and easier to understand if we first describe the principles of splicing.

In general, there are two kinds of splices—a long splice and a short splice. Nine-tenths of all splicing is of the short splice variety. The short splice is just as strong as the long splice, but the long splice has merit which the short splice lacks. The long splice can be passed through a block whereas the short splice cannot. To make a short splice, take two pieces of rope of equal diameter and unlay the ends for about five or six inches. Call these two ropes 1 and 2. Place the two ropes together so that the three strands of rope 1 are placed in the three spaces between the strands of rope 2, and the three strands of rope 2 are placed in the spaces between the strands of rope 1. Pull them up close together and tie a temporary whipping around the standing part of rope 2 and the strands of rope 1. The object now is to weave the strands of rope 2 into the standing part of rope 1. Number these three strands A, B, and C. Take strand A. Pass it over the nearest strand of rope 1 and under the next strand of rope 1 *against the lay of the rope.* Now take strand B of rope 2, pass it over the next strand of rope 1 and under the remaining strand in exactly the same manner. Do the same with strand C. If this is done correctly, strand B will pass over the strand under which strand A has just been passed, and strand C will pass over the strand under which strand B has just been passed, and strand C will pass over the strand under which strand A was passed in the first place. The three strands will now project from the same part of rope 1. The first tuck of the splice is now completed. We will now repeat the process by taking a second tuck, passing each strand over the nearest strand in the standing part of rope 1 and under the next strand to it. This completes the second tuck. We take a third tuck in the same manner, and ordinarily three tucks are enough to make a good short splice,

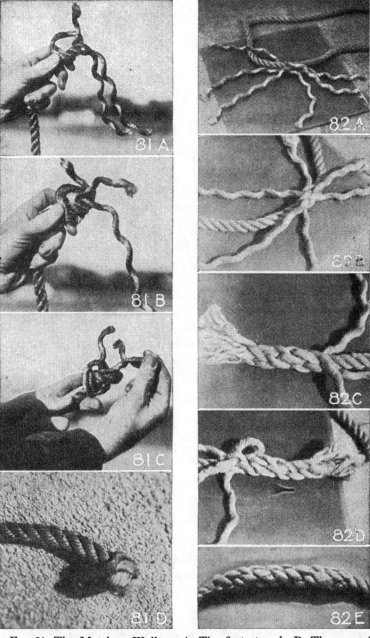

FIG. 81. The Matthew Walker. A. The first strand; B. The second strand tied in front of the first; C. The third strand tied in front of the second; D. The knot completed. FIG. 82. The short splice. A. Strands in each half of line opened and passed between strands of other half; B. The first tuck, one side; C. Three tucks completed, one side: D. First tuck, second side; E. The splice completed.

although if extra strength is desired you may take a fourth or a fifth.

Now remove the whipping which you placed temporarily around the standing part of rope 2 and the loose strands of rope 1. Number these strands of rope 1 X, Y and Z. Pass these three strands over the strand of rope 2 next to them and under the strand next to that, so that strand Y passes over the strand under which strand X has just been placed; strand Z over the strand under which Y has just been passed and under the strand over which X was passed in the first place. Take three tucks with strands X, Y, and Z, just as you did with strands A, B, and C. Now place the splice on the floor under your foot and roll it back and forth several times. This will make the splice small, round, and neat. The ends may now be cut off close to where they project. If you wish to do a really good job, point the strands and take one or two more tucks on each end. Lay back the outside fibers of each strand so that about half the strand is laid back and the remaining half forms the core of the strand. With the aid of a safety razor blade, shave down this core so that it tapers nicely. Put back the strands that you have laid back and take fresh tucks, bringing the splice down to a tapered end.

An eye splice is made in the same manner as an ordinary short splice. The end is unlaid for five or six inches and that end of the rope which is not yet unlaid is placed against the standing part to form a loop or eye of the desired size. Twist open the strands of the standing part at this point. As you hold the two parts of the rope together, you will notice that the three strands are arranged in a line—one to the left, one to the right, and one in the middle. Begin with the middle strand and pass it under a strand of the part of the rope which you have untwisted. Now take the strand to the left and pass it under the next strand in the standing part, to the left of the strand just used. Take the strand to the right and pass it under the remaining strand of the standing part to the right of

A.   B.
Fig. 83. The eye splice
A. The first tuck; B. The splice completed

the strand first used. If you have done this work carefully, the three strands of the end of the rope will have passed through the strands of the standing part at exactly the same point and all the strands will have been tucked under against the lay of the rope. Take two more tucks in the manner of making the short splice. The ends may be tapered if a good-looking job is required. The most difficult part of the eye splice is to get the first three strands passed correctly and without unnecessary twisting or unlaying of the rope.

Beginning with the center strand and working right and left is your best safeguard. Also it must be borne in mind that all strands are to be passed under against the lay of the rope and not with the lay of the rope, and that all should project from the standing part at the same point.

An eye splice may be made in the middle of a piece of rope as follows: twist the rope against itself as you would do in unlaying the strands but continue to do so

A.   B.

Fig. 84. The eye splice in the middle of a rope
A. The untwisted strands tucked once; B. The splice completed

until the three strands form long, double pigtails about 6″ long. Form your eye and take tucks with these pigtails just as if they were the ends of the lines.

A cut splice is made in the middle of a piece of line by taking a short piece of line of the same diameter and splicing both ends into the line in the manner of a short splice.

A back splice is tied as follows: First crown the rope as described in the wall and crown knot. Next tuck the three strands over the nearest strands in the stand-

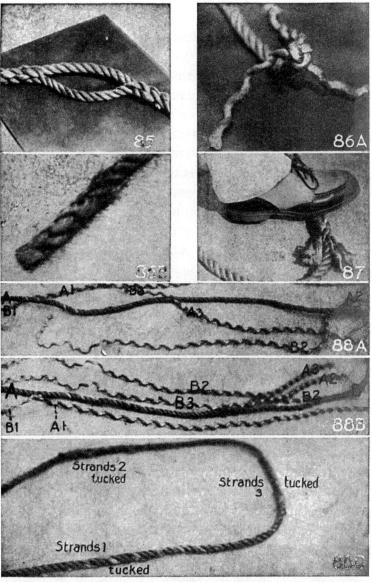

FIG. 85. The cut splice. FIG. 86. The back splice. A. Started with a crown knot; B. The splice completed. FIG. 87. Rolling a splice under the foot. FIG. 88. The long splice. A. Strands unlaid, strand A 1 unlaid all the way, strand B 1 laid up in its place; B. Strand B 2 unlaid to receive strand A 2; C. All strands tucked; the splice completed.

ing part and under the strands next to them just as in putting in the ordinary short splice. Three tucks should be sufficient but the ends may be pointed for a fourth or fifth tuck. All splices should be rolled under the foot during and after the tucking.

The long splice is used only to join two ropes or the broken ends of a single rope. Unlay both ends for a distance of two to three feet. For convenience we will call the ropes A and B, and the strands of rope A, A1, A2, and A3, and the strands of rope B, B1, B2, and B3. Place the strands together as in making a short splice. Now unlay A1 for a further distance of about one foot and lay B1 in the space A1 occupied. Next unlay B2 for the same distance, and lay A2 in the space B2 occupied. The splice now appears as in Figure 88-B. The three pairs of strands, 1, 2, and 3, are now knotted with an ordinary overhand knot, but care must be taken to make this knot with the lay of the rope.

Each strand is then tucked in the manner of the short splice except that it is passed over one strand and under two. Three tucks on each of the six strands are sufficient. Stretch the splice well and roll it under your foot, then cut the ends off close. If there is but little room in the blocks through which it is intended to reeve the splice, the strands must be halved before tucking.

CHAPTER XXV

STANDING AND RUNNING RIGGING

THE standing rigging of a boat is usually made of wire and, as the word implies, it "stands" throughout the season except for minor adjustments the way it is set up at the start of the season. The running rigging, on the other hand, is usually made of rope and, as its name implies, it runs through blocks and is constantly being hauled and adjusted. The understanding of the rigging of a boat plays an important part in its safe and efficient management.

The wire used in wire rigging is generally too light in racing boats and too heavy in all other boats. The frequency with which the tall masts of racing boats break and go over the side is largely an indictment of the wire rigging. Rigging can be too heavy in that a large wire offers considerably more wind resistance than a small wire, so that the skipper must always compromise between strength and windage. The development of the airplane has led to wires of very small diameter and very great tensile strength, and in general airplane wire is becoming most popular on small boats. Small wire in good condition is better than heavy wire in poor condition, but heavy wire lasts much longer than light wire in that the outer strands may be rusted and the inner strands still have sufficient strength to support the mast. However you look at it, wire rigging is cheaper than new spars, and it is the part of wisdom, safety and economy to renew your wire rigging every two or three years.

Where wire rigging passes around the mast or into a turnbuckle it is usually spliced. The beginner would do well not to attempt to splice wire. In most wire there are seven strands to keep track of, as against the three or four in rope. In addition, it is a bloody job. The wire when unlaid straightens out like a maniac. The sharp ends of it pierce the skin, splinters remain under the skin, and in general it is a tough job even for the old hand. If splicing is necessary and you cannot get an experienced rigger to do the splicing for you, it is possible to resort to clamps, especially designed for this purpose which hold the wire about as well as splicing it. If splicing is resorted to, the splice should be served with marline. Serving is covered in the chapter on Marlinespike Seamanship. After the splice has been served, it makes a neat and seamanlike job to sew a piece of rawhide over the served splice.

The wire is usually held to the boat by means of turnbuckles. A turnbuckle consist of two male screw members with threads running in opposite directions and a female screw member between them which draws up on the threads when turned in one direction and slacks off on the threads when turned in the opposite direction. Most turnbuckles are too small for the job in hand and they break far more frequently than the wire rigging they are supposed to support, thus proving that they are the weakest link in the chain. The male members of many turnbuckles end in hooks. These are undesirable, as hooks have a habit of straightening out under a strain. Also they catch in the clothing and tear sails, especially the spinnaker. If you have hooks on your turnbuckles get rid of them. And if you disregard this advice, be sure to mouse the hook by wrapping several turns of marline about the end of the hook and the shank, then tying the wrapping together by the ends of the marline passed back and forth around the middle of the wrapping and tying the ends in a reef knot. Another type of turnbuckle has its male members terminating in rings. Rings are better than hooks, but must be shackled to the chain plates and to the shrouds and shackles are a nuisance. The best form of turnbuckle is terminated with a double ending like a fork, through which a bolt is passed and secured by a cotter pin. Turnbuckles generally break right on the thread where a male member enters a female member. It is a good rule to have the cross section of the male members of the turnbuckle slightly larger than the cross section of the wire. The female member comes in several forms. The poorest form is the open type with two vertical struts connected to the two screw ends. This is the weakest form and offers no protection to the threads of the male member. A better form is that of a long, thin barrel with holes for a tool which can be thrust through the barrel to turn it. The best form has such a barrel with a hexagonal nut cast in the middle so that a husky wrench can be used to turn it. There should be some means of preventing the turnbuckle from turning of its own accord under strain. It should be secured either with cotter pins through both male and female members or else clamped down with locknuts on either end. If your turnbuckles are not provided with these checks, do not grease them under any circumstances. If they are provided with such checks, grease them liberally.

The chain plates are frequently a cause of trouble, first if they are too short; and second, if they are improperly secured to the boat. Chain plates should always be bolted; never screwed. They should be long enough to cover several planks. If possible, they should fasten not only through planks but also through ribs, and lacking that, should have additional bracing inside the planks. One sailing enthusiast of my acquaintance had a boat built with chain plates passing all the way down the side of his boat and interlocking in the keel.

Chain plates may be inside or outside the planking but are generally placed inside. They should be of heavy bronze. If they are of steel, inspect them thoroughly and make sure that they are covered at all times with a thick layer of red lead and several layers of paint.

On gaff-rigged boats, the shrouds have just one duty and that is to prevent the mast from breaking. On Marconi-rigged boats the shrouds have a double duty. Not only must they keep the mast in the boat but they must be so adjusted as to permit a slight curvature in the mast which will develop the necessary drive in the sail.

Masts may be permitted to bend to a certain small

degree without danger of breaking. In fact, on the old square-riggers the shrouds were never set up too tight and the old shellbacks always insisted on having a certain give to the lanyards that were rove through the deadeyes at the foot of the shrouds in order to have a degree of elasticity to the masts and rigging. Elasticity is no longer recognized as necessary, and on the whole rigidity is to be preferred.

But let us study for a minute the amount of tension in the various stays comprising your standing rigging.

If you have a headstay which does not carry sail, you must judge its tension when the boat is under sail and the windward backstay is trimmed. At such times the headstay should be snugly taut, but it is quite acceptable to be loose when the mainsail is lowered and the backstay slackened off. The jib stay should be taut, but you cannot judge the tension in the jib stay except when the boat is under way and particularly with the jib set. Remember that tightening up on your stays is going to affect the position of the mast. If one shroud is more taut than the other, the mast will lean toward that side of the boat. If the headstay and jib stay are too taut, they will pull the mast forward. If they are too slack, the backstay and weight of the mainsail will pull the mast aft. It is a generally accepted practice to have the mast of a gaff-rigged sloop rake slightly forward. I do not know the real reason for this. The most plausible reason is that if the mast slants slightly forward the gaff does not swing off too far from the boom. Lacking a gaff, the Marconi rig does not come under this rule. The question of trim of a Marconi mast is highly controversial. The majority of authorities maintain that it should stand perfectly plumb or should rake slightly aft. Other authorities maintain, however, that it should rake forward in the manner of the gaff-rigged mast. All these matters will be proved by experiment in the next few years, but I think it is safe to maintain now that if the Marconi mast is curved aft it should be given a slight rake forward. On no account should a Marconi mast be so set up that it *curves* forward. Distinguish between a curve and a rake. The rake of a mast is its position in the boat. The curve of the mast is a change of direction in the stick itself. Remember that you can tauten your headstay and jib stay by taking up on the turnbuckles of the shrouds and if the mast is already too far forward the proper place to trim the headstay and jib stay is by tautening the shrouds rather than these stays.

Shrouds should be set up so that they are tight enough to take the strain off the mast. But they should not be set up too tight. Under the strain of the sail the mast is bound to bend somewhat. When it bends, the windward shrouds should be taut as a fiddle-string, but the leeward shrouds should be slack. If the shrouds are set up too tight, the mast develops a dangerous curve like the figure S.

Shrouds frequently come in pairs, upper and lower. The lower shrouds usually run from the mast to the inboard ends of the spreaders. The upper shrouds run over the spreaders to the top of the mast. When you have two pairs of shrouds, upper and lower, you also have two chain plates—one forward of the other. The upper shrouds should be made fast to the forward chain plates; the lower shrouds to the after chain plates. Boats are frequently seen with shrouds made fast to the wrong chain plates. This puts an unusual strain on the mast, prevents the spreaders from working properly, and endangers the entire rig.

On a Marconi mast, the upper shrouds support the very tip of the mast. Although there is greater leverage to the part of the mast supported by the upper shrouds, the sail is narrowed down to such a point that it is usually safe to have these shrouds slightly slack so that the mast may bend slightly to leeward and give greater draft in the luff of the sail. I know one very expert skipper in the Star class who adjusts his upper shrouds for every variation in the wind—slacking them off in light airs and tautening them up when it blows. He counts the threads on his turnbuckles and takes up so many threads for every variation in the wind.

The spreaders are a very important part of your rigging. They should end in a fork or loop through which the wire may pass freely. The wire where it passes through the spreaders should be served with marline to prevent it from chafing and should be bound in in such a manner that it may work freely up and down through the spreaders but may never jump out of the hole or the fork.

Spreaders have two bad habits. The worst of these is sagging. If a spreader starts to sag, you must tighten it where it joins the mast. Perhaps the screws have pulled out or the hinge bolt by which it may be secured to the mast may be worn or bent. Never allow your spreaders to sag. The second bad habit of spreaders is to swing forward. This happens, of course, only when the spreaders are hinged, but it is possible to make a little wooden strut passing around the forward end of a mast and holding the spreaders back. There is no strain on this strut. It simply prevents the spreaders from sagging forward and keeps them at right angles to the shroud, to the mast, and to the fore and aft line of the boat.

Some boats are equipped with a jackstay, a small stay which runs from the top of the mast forward of the mast over a short spreader and down to the foot of the mast or to the deck. The principal function of the jackstay is to prevent the mast from bending under the forward thrust of the gaff. Some jackstays are fastened into the deck at the foot of the mast. Jackstays so rigged perform the additional function of holding the mast down into the step.

If the top of the mast above the jaws of the gaff bends or waves forward and aft in a seaway, it means that you need a jackstay or that your jackstay, if you have one, is not set up tight enough.

Backstays or preventers are on the borderline between running and standing rigging. They perform the function of standing rigging in that they help to stay the mast, but they are handled like running rigging in that the lower ends terminate in blocks to which a tackle is attached, so that the windward backstay may be trimmed or slacked off.

The location of your backstay blocks and cleats on

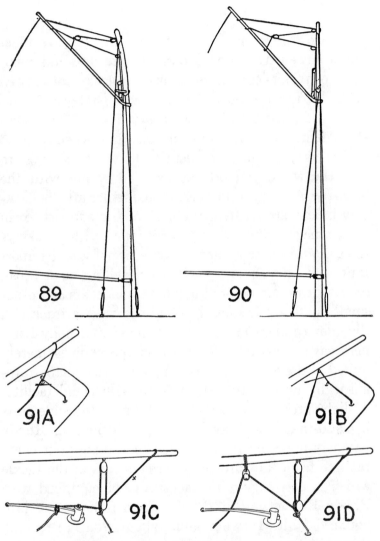

FIG. 89. Upper and lower shrouds leading to wrong chain plates. Note the bend in the top of the mast. FIG. 90. Upper and lower shrouds leading to correct chain plates. FIG. 91. A. Power of one; B. Power of two; C. Double and single block, power of three; D. Same rig with snatch block, power of five. Strain on boom distributed among three points.

the deck will repay close study. Here, too, we must compromise between maximum effectiveness and maximum convenience. If the backstay blocks are located fairly far forward on the deck it is possible to tack to windward with both the windward and leeward backstays trimmed taut. This means that when you go about, as you must frequently do when beating up into the wind, you do not have to bother with the backstays. On the other hand, the farther aft the backstay blocks are located, the greater the support given to the mast. When a boat is equipped with backstays they should never be neglected; especially is it important that they be trimmed when sailing on a broad reech or running before the wind. Star boats and other small boats are frequently equipped with a track and slide device known as "Rhody Runners." Rhody Runners save a lot of work because the slide is merely pulled to the after end of the track where it snaps automatically over a stud. It is freed with equal facility. A slight pressure with the thumb under the slide casts it off so that it will not interfere with the sail. Rhody Runners have the further merit of leaving your cockpit free from the yards and yards of line in the tackle which is necessary with backstays not equipped with Rhody Runners. But Rhody Runners have one pronounced fault. If, when going about, you fail to snap them into place before any strain comes on the mast from the new direction, you are absolutely licked. If it is blowing at all hard, your entire crew will not have power enough to pull the slide back to the point where it will snap over the stud. With the ordinary purchase, on the other hand, you can always tauten up a back-stay however late you may be in getting at it.

A permanent backstay is found on some of the more modern Marconi rigs with such tall narrow sail plans that the boom stops short of the counter. With such a rig it is possible to run a backstay from the truck of the mast to the center of the stern and set it up per-manently with a turnbuckle. Permanent backstays should be adjusted while under way and should be tautened or slackened in relation to the headstay. The headstay and permanent backstay should be con-sidered as a single unit, as a tension on each one affects the other. Permanent backstays were originated in Sweden, and at the time of writing, there is a tendency to call this stay a swedestay.

Let us consider now the running rigging.

Ropes are run through the blocks for two purposes. The first is to change the direction of the pull. The second is to give increased power to the man who is pulling on the rope. Where a rope is run through sev-eral blocks, it is known as a tackle—pronounced tayckle—or purchase. Generally speaking, a fixed pulley does not increase the power of the man pull-ing the rope, whereas every movable pulley multi-plies it. In the illustration (Figure 91) A shows a main sheet passing from the boom through a single block on the traveler and heading into the boat. This has a power of one. That is to say, the man who pulls on that rope has no more power than if it did not pass through the pulley. The block merely changes the direction of this pull. In B, we have a movable pulley on the boom—movable, that is to say, because it may be pulled down to the traveler or let out from the traveler according as the sheet is trimmed or slacked. There are two parts to this line passing over the single sheave on the boom. This has a power of two. In C we see a common rig. The line leads down from the end of the boom under one sheave on the traveler block, back over the sheave on the boom, and through the other sheave in the traveler. There are three parts to this line, and it has the power of three. If the part marked "X" were to run to the ring at the bottom of the movable block on the boom (see Figure 95), you would still have a power of three. In D we have the same rig, but the sheet in this case is passed back to the boom over a snatch block (see Figure 92), and we now have a power of five. In other words, if we had two men of equal strength pulling on rig A and on rig D, the man on rig D would exert five times the power as the man who trims on rig A.

You may determine the power by the number of parts of the line. In the figure you will see that the number of parts of a rope always corresponds to the power. Now let us take a common form of tackle (Figure 93).

It consists of two blocks—a single block at M and a double block at N. Let us assume that the hook on the block M is attached to a pile on the shore and the hook at block N is attached to a boat which you wish to haul up on shore. In such a case you would exert a power of four. But let us assume that you have made an error in rigging your tackle and you have made the hook at N fast to the pile and the hook at M fast to the boat. This time you would exert a power of only three. How is it possible to get two kinds of power from the same tackle? The answer is that if the fall of the line P is being pulled from the movable block of the tackle, you are exerting the power of P along with three other parts of the line. Whereas, if the fall P comes from the fixed block N, the sheave at N over which it passes merely changes its direction and not its power and it would be the same as if you were trimming on O in the opposite direction. With N attached to the boat and M attached to the pile, you have two pulleys in the movable end. With N attached to the pile and M attached to the boat, you have only one pulley at the movable end. This explanation of a purchase is necessary to understand why rope is rove through blocks. The power may be increased indefinitely by increasing the number of blocks. Unfortunately, however, what we gain in power we lose in speed, as we are obliged to haul so much more rope every time we add a pulley to our rigging.

If the end of a sheet, for instance, is fastened at the deck or to the traveler block, the power can be increased by having the end at the boom because it gives one more part of the purchase pulling on the boom which is the movable part.

The main sheet usually has one of its blocks secured to a traveler. The purpose of the traveler is to enable you to trim the sail down without at the same time trimming it in. If you did not have a traveler, you could trim the boom flatter but the gaff would sag off and the whole sail would be warped. With the traveler, you can trim the boom right straight down to a point on deck almost directly beneath it. Sometimes travelers are too long and it is impossible to trim the sail flat enough to go high into the wind. In such a case, the traveler can be shortened by placing a small block of wood under its ends. Frequently the block on the boom is attached not to the boom but to a wire bridle. The function of the bridle is twofold. First it permits the block to slide forward when the boom is broad off and you are sailing before the wind. This keeps the main sheet out of the water. Its second function is to distribute the strain of the sheet along the boom, thus keeping the boom from bending and possibly from breaking.

There are many forms of main sheet rigs but in general they may be divided into two classes—double-ended and single-ended. In the double-ended rig, both ends of the sheet lead to the deck. In the single-ended rig one end is made fast to the boom and the other end only leads to the deck. If you are sailing single-handed, there is no rig like the old-fashioned single-ended main sheet. You have only one end to bother with. It leads in right over the stern where it can be led through a fair-leader on top of your tillerhead and belayed around a pin in the tiller itself. This is the handiest of all rigs. But if you are sailing with a crew and you are depending on someone else to trim the main sheet for you, you will find that double-ended rig has a marked advantage in that it can be trimmed from either deck without the sheet tender interfering with

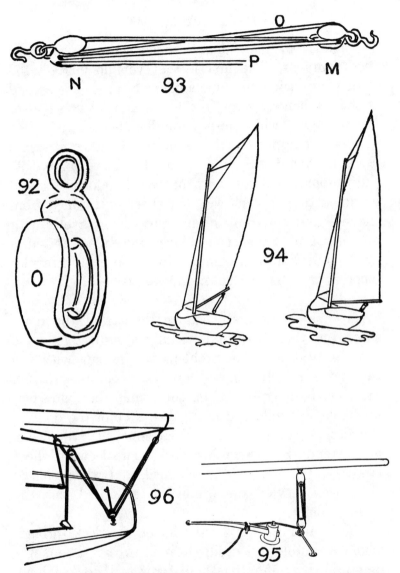

FIG. 92. A snatch block. FIG. 93. Most power from this tackle if N is the movable block. FIG. 94. The same sail sheeted with and without a traveller. Note how the gaff sags off when no traveller is used. FIG. 95. A common form of single ended main sheet. FIG. 96. A common form of double ended main sheet.

the helmsman. The double-ended rig has two slight disadvantages. The first is that you do not get the same power with the same amount of line. The second is that somebody may be careless and let one end of the sheet run while he is trimming the other.

A boat equipped with an outboard rudder presents certain difficulties in the rig of the sheet. Figure 97 shows some good rigs with outboard rudders. It will be noted that in each case the sheet is trimmed from the side and not from the traveler. The traveler with an outboard rudder passes over the tiller, and if a single-ended sheet is trimmed direct from the traveler block it must be cast off and made fast again on every tack.

Most skippers rarely change the rig of the main sheet, but the jib sheet is usually a subject for wide experimentation. The problem is different with the two types of jibs—loose-footed and clubfooted. On the loose-footed jib, the jib sheet must be made fast in the clew cringle and must always be of the double-ended type; that is to say, there must be two sheets, one extending down either deck. The leeward sheet is always the one that is trimmed, and when you go about you cast off the windward sheet and trim the leeward sheet.

The location of the fair-leader on the deck through which a double-ended jib sheet is rove is frequently determined by the "trial and error method." I have seen Star boats with no less than a dozen pairs of fair-leaders located at different points of the deck for different trims of the jib. The rule, however, seems to be fairly easy to express. The line of the jib sheet from the fair-leader to the clew cringle if extended to the luff should bisect the angle at the clew. The fair-leaders should be placed inboard at the closest point to the cockpit coaming at which the jib when trimmed flat will not backwind the mainsail.

On small boats, most double-ended sheets are single lines, not purchases. On larger boats it is sometimes necessary to have purchases in place of the single lines. On the New York Yacht Club Thirty-Foot Class, each of the two jib sheets is a double-ended line. One end is belayed to a cleat on the side deck near the helmsman. Thence it leads forward through fair-leaders on deck, through a block on the jib club, back through fair-leaders to another block through which a tackle is rove, the fall of which leads to the after end of the cabin. The single end is trimmed quickly when the boat is tacked; but when the jib is drawing, it is necessary to trim on the tackle to get power enough to flatten the jib.

But whether a purchase or a single line is used, the double-ended jib sheet should be used on all loose-footed jibs. With club-footed jibs, the problem is somewhat similar. The jib sheet may be single-ended or double-ended. If double-ended the fair-leaders are usually placed much farther forward than in the case of the loose-footed jib and may even be forward of the clew of the jib. The double-ended jib rig with a block on the club through which it is rove is a very simple and convenient rig and is recommended for the beginner. The location of the block, however, is important. Try moving the block forward and aft on the club until it is just right. You can tell when it is just right by the fact that the jib is trimmed down, not aft; and the fullness in the luff is not flattened out. If the block is too far forward, the jib will stand too flat; if the block is too far aft, the forward end of the club will swing off to leeward, the jib will be too full forward and will backwind the mainsail. There is also a critical point to be avoided at which the jib shakes and seems to pivot about the block. A little experimentation will soon determine the correct position for the block.

A rig which to my mind is superior to that of the double-ended sheet passing through a block on the club is a double-ended sheet made fast to the club at the point where the block would ordinarily be. This would mean that you have two sheets, both of which should be trimmed. The leeward sheet is used to trim it down and the windward sheet to trim it in. By playing with both these sheets, it is possible to make the jib set absolutely perfectly—far better, in fact, than with the sheet rove through a block. But it is an awful nuisance when you go about. Both sheets have to be cast off and retrimmed, and the trimming takes the fine hand of an artist.

Sometimes a single-ended jib sheet is used in connection with a traveler just as in the case of a main sheet. One word of caution must be sounded in connection with such a rig; when the jib sheet leaves the traveler block it should be headed forward, not aft. If it comes directly aft from the traveler block to a block or fair-leader located on deck in front of the mast, this block will prevent the traveler block from running out to the end of the traveler. The correct way to rig a jib sheet with traveler block is shown in Figure 98.

The trim of the jib sheet is dependent upon the location of the blocks, travelers, and fair-leaders. If the jib is improperly trimmed, it will interfere greatly with the efficiency of your boat, perhaps even more than the incorrect trim of your mainsail. Fullness at the throat and flatness at the leech must be attained. The leech should never be allowed to curve because that not only destroys the power of the jib but back-winds the mainsail and prevents the funnel effect on the leeward side of the mainsail. The function of the jib is not only to act as a sail and exert a propelling force to the boat; it also guides the wind so that it flows with greater velocity and smoothness past the leeward side of the mainsail, thus developing the suc-tion which gives most of the forward drive to that sail. Thus the jib is relatively much more powerful than the mainsail and its power comes not of itself but by imparting more power to the mainsail.

Consider now the halliards. The throat halliard blocks should be sufficiently high above the jaws of the gaff when the sail is hoisted to prevent the parts from being twisted or chafed against one another. The blocks of the throat halliard should be so arranged that the fall leads fairly down the port side of the mast. If the block on the mast is high enough, it will prevent to a large degree any danger of chafing on the jaws of the gaff. The peak halliard blocks should be set as high as possible on the mast and the top peak halliard block should be just below the topping lift block. The peak halliard should be rove so that the parts will not cross one another or chafe and so that it will lead fairly down the starboard side of the mast. It is a good idea to have the peak halliard blocks on the gaff arranged on wire bridles not only because the bridles distribute the strain but also they permit a better lead of the halliard when the sail is reefed.

Most Marconi mainsails are now equipped with a single wire halliard which passes over a sheave in the truck of the mast. Inasmuch as it is impossible to get much power on the end of a halliard of just one part, the halliard usually terminates in a purchase or tackle. This purchase consists of three or more parts of rope. The reason for the wire ending in a rope purchase is that the wire will not stretch and when the purchase is trimmed there is only a short length of rope—so short that the stretching is immaterial. Many boats equipped with Marconi sails have a long gooseneck at the boom and a purchase with which the boom can be hauled down after the sail is hoisted (Figure 99). This flattens the luff and is easier on the rigging than sway-ing up too hard on the halliard. It has been said by many experts that if the *Shamrock V* were equipped with such a long gooseneck and purchase, she would not have parted her halliard in the third race with the *Enterprise*. On small gaff-rigged boats in which the boom has jaws instead of a gooseneck, it is frequently a good idea to put a ringbolt in the deck directly under

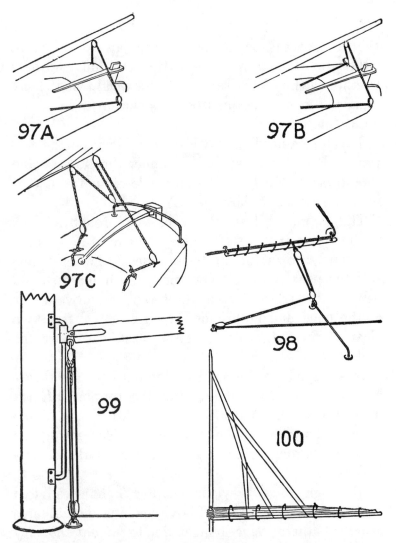

FIG. 97. Some good rigs with outboard rudders. FIG. 98. Correct lead of single ended jib sheet with traveller. FIG. 99. Long gooseneck and down-haul purchase. FIG. 100. Lazyjacks.

the jaws of the boom and tie the jaws down to it. Otherwise it is possible to flatten the luff line only by the weight of the sail. And the weight of the sail in a small boat is frequently not sufficient to have any noticeable effect.

The jib halliard should lead to a block on the forward side of the mast directly under the jib stay and should be led fairly to the port side of the mast outside the throat halliard.

The topping lift should be passed through a block at the very top of the after side of the mast and should lead fairly down the starboard side of the mast outside the peak halliard. The spinnaker halliard should be rove through a block at the top of the forward side of the mast and both ends should be made fast to a cleat on the forward side of the mast just above the deck.

It is a good idea to head the jib halliard, the throat halliard, the peak halliard and the topping lift aft by passing them under sheaves on either side of the mast and making them fast to the deck inside the cockpit coaming or to cleats fastened on the centerboard trunk.

Although in a previous chapter I have advised against coiling the sheets, I advise coiling the halliards because halliards have so much line to run out and they are so easily messed up on a boat that they should be coiled carefully in the bottom of the boat with the top coil leading directly to the cleat. Do not hang the halliard coils on nails or hooks. Do not stuff the coils under the standing part of the halliard. This is the surest possible way to foul them. Of course, if there are tubs or drawers in which the halliards could lie exactly as they fall, they are better uncoiled.

A topping lift may be rigged in three ways. A line running from the end of the boom over a block on the mast down to a pulley on deck and aft to the cockpit is the standard rigging. Another rig consists of a line made fast to the top of the mast leading down over a sheave in the end of the boom and heading into a cleat on the boom. This rig is trimmed from the boom. A variation of this rig has the line come down from the top of the mast, terminating in a single block. Another line fast to the end of the boom runs through this block, back through a block in the end of the boom, and forward to a cleat on the boom. This variation, too, is trimmed from the end of the boom. The third rig, and the one which I prefer, is a combination of both these rigs. Such a rig may be trimmed from the cockpit where the end of the line comes down from the mast or may be trimmed from the end of the boom. In a large boat it is a great convenience to be able to trim from the end of the boom because it is possible to get your shoulder under the boom and lift it clear of the crutch, at the same time trimming in on the topping lift. But if you do not also have the ability to trim the topping lift from the cockpit when the boom is broad off and when you are likely to need the topping lift most, you will regret the absence of this feature. On larger boats two topping lifts are used so that the one to windward may be trimmed and the other slacked off.

The lazyjacks call for very little attention. They are rarely found on boats of the size to which this volume is dedicated. Lazyjacks are always trimmed from the foremost part. Their sole function is to gather in the sail when it is lowered. But it is well to remember that lazyjacks hanging in loops below the boom may foul on skylights, deck cleats, or the back hair of your guests, and they should always be trimmed sufficiently to get them out of the way. A standard form of lazy-jack is as follows: Two lines come down from the mast on either side of the sail, terminating in cringles. Two other lines pass forward from near the end of the boom, head through the cringles and down toward the fore part of the boom, terminating in two more cringles. Two other lines start forward of this last line, run parallel to it, pass through its cringles, then lead forward, and are tied together through a ring underneath the forepart of the boom (see Figure 100).

No chapter on rigging would be complete without a word on downhauls. A downhaul is a very convenient line, especially if your sail has a habit of sticking aloft. The old sloops with long bowsprits were all equipped with downhauls so that when the skipper let the halliard run he could seize the downhaul, trim it in smartly, and have his jib housed in a few seconds. Sometimes we see the fall of the throat halliard made fast to the jaws of the gaff so that as the gaff is hauled up, the end of the halliard goes with it, and this line may be pulled to get the sail down after the halliard is cast off. This is a sloppy trick. It is impossible to make your halliards lie decently coiled, with one end of them slatting about up aloft. If you need a down-haul, be a sport and reeve a separate line for the pur-post. A downhaul is very useful on a Marconi main-sail.

When a boat is laid up for the night, you should never trim your halliards, topping lift, or lazyjacks flat. This always looks neat and shipshape but it is one of the earmarks of a landlubber. Rope shrinks when it is wet. I have known a shrinking halliard to break a boom on a large boat. Always allow three or four feet shrinkage and with that much slack allowed, make your lines fast.

I have managed to keep my boats looking trim by a little device which I have never seen anywhere else but which is worth the slight effort which it costs. I attach heavy fisherman's net sinkers to the slack in my halliards so that these weights keep the halliards trim yet allow full slack for shrinkage.

When running rigging starts to chafe, it is not always necessary to buy new rigging. The lines can be reversed; that is to say, turned end for end so that the wear and the chafing come at different parts of the line. It is always well to reverse your running rigging after half a summer.

New lines should not be rove until all the kinks have been gotten out of them. Stretch the line out straight in a grassy field and let the dew come on it. If that does not take the kinks out of it, tow the line over-board for an hour or two but do not reeve it until the line is perfectly pliable and free from kinks.

CHAPTER XXVI

LIGHT SAILS

THE jib and mainsail on a small boat are sometimes referred to as the working sails. The spinnaker, the ballooner, and Genoese jib are generally spoken of as the light sails. The description is a good one because they are made of very light, thin canvas; but the distinction between working sails and light sails is not fair, for light sails are not restricted to racing but can and should be used to work the boat in ordinary sailing.

The spinnaker is a large, baggy, triangular light sail which is set on the side of the boat opposite the mainsail when you are running before the wind. The spinnaker is set flying. That is to say, it is secured to the boat at only three points—the three clews of the sail. The head is hoisted by a halliard. The tack is secured to the outer end of a spinnaker boom, and the clew is sheeted to the deck somewhere forward of the mast. The spinnaker is a difficult sail to handle, especially in a quartering wind. When you are dead before the wind, it is rather easier, so let us consider first the technique of setting the spinnaker while sailing before the wind.

The spinnaker is first made perfectly clear without any twists in it and is bundled up with the three clews all together. One hand goes forward, casts off the spinnaker halliard from its cleat at the foot of the mast, snaps a snap hook on the halliard into the shackle at the head of the spinnaker, and passes the fall of the halliard aft to a second hand or to the helmsman. The spinnaker boom is placed on the weather deck with the outboard end headed forward. The tack of the spinnaker is snapped to a ring or shackle at the outboard end of the boom. The sheet which is fast to the clew is belayed to a cleat forward or in some instances a snap hook in the clew is snapped into a ringbolt in the forward deck. The man forward now passes the guy which is fast to the outer end of the spinnaker boom around outside the shrouds and back to the helmsman or to another man who stays aft for this purpose. Note that in all these operations only one man has gone forward. It should never be necessary to send more than one man forward and in a race this is most inadvisable, as it destroys the trim of the boat and permits your opponents to overtake you.

We now have the spinnaker boom on deck, the three clews fast to their particular positions, and the halliard and guy in the hands of the helmsman or of another man aft. Temporarily making fast the very end of the guy, the helmsman starts hoisting on the halliard and at the same time the hand forward pushes the spinnaker boom out over the bow of the boat, lifts up the inboard end, and rests the jaws against the mast. The spinnaker goes up in a big, fluttering mass. It is easy to hoist and easy to handle because it is just blowing out before the wind and is not pulling. When the halliard is hoisted all the way, the helmsman makes it fast on any convenient cleat, then grasps the guy and starts to trim the boom aft until it is at right angles to the boat. He must beware of a sudden hard strain on the guy, as the spinnaker fills when the boom is trimmed aft; and unless the helmsman is strong and

Photo M. Rosenfeld

FIG. 101. Spinnaker set and drawing

alert, the whole sail is likely to get away from him. The hand forward helps by pulling aft on the boom, at the same time steadying it against the mast. As soon as the boom is at right angles to the boat, the spinnaker is drawing and when the guy is fast it may be said that it is completely set.

Let us look for a moment at the rigging necessary to make a spinnaker set well. Consider first the halliard. It must be rove through a block at the forward side of the top of the mast. Since the spinnaker is a very light sail, no purchase is necessary. Just a single line rove through the block will do. One end of the halliard should be spliced into a swivel hook. The swivel is most necessary, as the spinnaker is often hoisted with a twist in it, and the only way in which the twist can be gotten out is by permitting the hook to revolve. There are excellent ball-bearing swivel hooks on the market that are recommended for this purpose. If a swivel hook cannot be readily obtained, a swivel shackle in the headboard of the spinnaker will serve the purpose. With a swivel hook, however, it is advisable to serve the halliard in three or four places at intervals of about one foot. This is necessary to prevent the halliard from unlaying when the swivel revolves.

Strength is a necessary factor in a spinnaker boom, but lightness is more to be desired. A boom that is too heavy is very difficult to handle. On the larger yachts, the outboard ends of spinnaker booms are carried by lifts similar to topping lifts, but this should never be necessary in a small boat. The jaws of the spinnaker boom should be lined with rawhide to make them stay on the mast at the point where the boom is placed. There are various patent devices for securing the inboard end of the spinnaker boom to the mast, but unfortunately, I have had no experience with them. A single line is all that is necessary for a guy. For although the pull is considerable, it can usually be handled by one man, and speed is so essential in the setting of the spinnaker that the extra power developed by a purchase is more than offset by the length of time it takes to trim with it.

I have described the setting of the spinnaker as though there were just one guy heading aft. On larger boats it is necessary to have two—one headed forward to the very bow of the boat. I have never seen a forward guy used in a very small boat, but if you have difficulty in managing your spinnaker with only a single guy, you can improve its operation by a forward guy as well.

A forward guy is valuable, especially in a quartering wind when the boom is headed forward of athwartship. On a small boat it is a good idea to snap the forward guy to the outboard end of the boom, lead it in to a point near the jaws, and make it fast. Then, if the spinnaker misbehaves, the guy is all ready to use. It may be led forward through the chocks in the bow and trimmed or started as the after guy is started or trimmed.

Remember the after guy must always be passed outside the shrouds before the halliard is hoisted. Spinnakers on larger yachts are nearly always set in stops. This is not necessary in a small boat, but it is sometimes very useful. In a leeward start in a race, for instance, if the spinnaker is hoisted in stops beforehand it is only the work of a few seconds to break it out as you cross the starting line. It is well to understand how to set your spinnaker in stops and a pleasant and exciting pastime.

The spinnaker is first laid out on deck very carefully with the luff and leech laid alongside one another. The middle of the sail is then rolled up very small and tight so that we get a long, thin roll from head to foot with the luff and leech side by side on the outside of the roll and the clew and tack together at the bottom. In this position the sail is tied by ordinary cotton thread. Do not use anything heavier than cotton thread for stops. Never use string or fish line. A single turn of the thread tied at intervals of about two and one-half feet is sufficient except near the foot of the sail, where two or three turns are advisable. The sail thus stopped is sent up the mast and the foot made fast until it is ready for use. The best place to keep the spinnaker on a small boat is just forward of the mast where it is clear of both the jib and the mainsail. The technique of breaking out a stopped spinnaker differs somewhat on large and small boats. In large boats whose spinnaker booms are provided with lifts, the tack is made fast to the outboard end of the boom, the boom is put in position and guyed out at right angles to the boat. Then, when it is all ready to set, the clew is hauled inboard by the sheet, thus breaking the stops. It is only necessary to break one or two stops with the sheet; the wind will break the rest.

On a small boat whose boom is not provided with lifts, it is better to make the clew fast on deck and the tack fast to the outboard end of the boom. Thrusting the boom forward will start to break the stops and when the jaws are placed against the mast and the guy is trimmed aft, the rest of the stops will go.

When you take in a spinnaker you reverse the process of setting it. First you send a man forward to take charge of the boom, then you slack off the guy, letting the boom go forward and spilling all the wind out of the sail. The hand forward unships the jaws from the mast and passes the boom aft. He must take care to look aft while doing this or he is quite likely to brain his shipmates with the end of the boom. The flapping sail is apt to make the boom jump around a bit, and care must be exercised in handling it. Particularly the man forward must be careful not to let the boom get into the water, as all sorts of disasters may result. If this happens, someone may be hit by the boom, the hand forward may be knocked overboard, the boom is quite likely to break, the spinnaker is quite likely to be split from head to foot, and if you are racing, the sail may take charge and cause you to foul the mark or another boat.

As soon as the boom is inboard, both the clew and the tack are cast off, the hand forward gathers as much of the spinnaker as he can reach into his arms, and then—and not until then—the halliard is let go. The hand forward gathers the spinnaker into a big bundle as it comes down, unsnaps the hook, and makes it fast immediately to the cleat. Both spinnaker and boom are now carefully housed in the cockpit, and the guy, which is probably trailing overboard, is hauled in and coiled, and the fall of the halliard is made fast.

If you have an auxiliary motor and a propeller, care must be taken to see that the guy which probably trails overboard during this performance does not foul the propeller.

Such is the technique of handling a spinnaker before the wind. The essence of it is that the sail that is being hoisted must go forward and must not be permitted to fill until the boom is guyed out at right angles. In lowering the sail, the same is true. Nothing can be done until the boom which is out at right angles is allowed to go forward and all the wind is spilled out of the sail. Everything forward is a good rule to remember in setting or taking in a spinnaker.

If you are racing, however, you will find that you seldom have a course directly before the wind. The run, so called, especially on a triangular course, is nearly always a broad reach. The wind is blowing over the quarter and not directly astern and in this position the handling and setting of the spinnaker is a little more difficult. The boom cannot be guyed out at right angles to the boat because if it is, the sail will be taken aback, the wind will blow on the forward side of it, and it will stop the progress of the boat. So that on a quartering wind the boom is considerably forward of the beam. This means that it will fill more quickly as the boom is guyed aft and will spill the wind less quickly when the boom is allowed to go forward. It is more difficult to guy the boom because the guy and the boom will be running in nearly the same direction instead of at a wide angle. The exact angle at which the boom should be trimmed is a matter for great care and judgment. If at the same time you get a wind that is not blowing steadily from one direction, you have to keep fishing for it with the guy, slacking and trimming alternately. At the same time the sheet must be adjusted to keep the spinnaker at its proper fullness. If the wind is fairly far forward, the sheet will have

Fig. 102. Mainsail spilling wind into spinnaker; spinnaker spilling wind into jib

to be passed around the headstay and trimmed to leeward of the jib. Of course, it is impossible to use a spinnaker at all unless the wind is abaft the beam.

If possible, it is advisable to trim your sails in such a manner that each sail will spill into another sail.

In the illustration (Figure 102), we see the mainsail spilling its wind into the spinnaker and the spinnaker spilling its wind into the jib so that all three sails are pulling and two of the sails are profiting from the spent wind of another sail. Incidentally, note the trim of the topping lift in this illustration. This picture was taken when this boat was about one hundred yards behind two other boats it was racing. About one minute before the photograph was taken, the topping lift was trimmed as shown, the boat immediately started to overhaul the two other boats, and passed them before the next mark, a distance of less than a mile. She had been dropping behind the two other boats up to the time the topping lift was hoisted, thus giving greater draft to the mainsail and helping to spill the mainsail's wind into the spinnaker.

In the absence of a balloon jib, a spinnaker can be used for the purpose. In the boat in the illustration, I often made it a practice to lash the spinnaker boom on the forward deck with the jaws against the mast and used it as a bowsprit to spread the spinnaker as a ballooner. Whenever the wind was not forward of the beam, the spinnaker would pull like a mule.

It should be noted that the two edges of the spinnaker are sometimes cut exactly alike, but one edge is roped and the other is not. The roped edge is the luff and should always run from the head to the outboard end of the boom.

The spinnaker has been described as a racing sail, and it is rarely used except for racing. This is a false concept. The spinnaker is a very valuable working

sail and properly used will greatly increase the pleasure
which you derive from your boat. I have often set a
spinnaker while running before a heavy wind just to
stop the boat from yawing and wallowing. I have used
it as a balloon jib to stop the pressure of a heavy
weather helm. I have used it as the sole sail on my

Photo M. Rosenfeld

FIG. 103. A ballooner

boat because it was easier to set it and to run under the
spinnaker than to tie two reefs in the mainsail. I have
used it in the light airs of an evening to run out from
the yacht-club dock to my mooring rather than take
the gaskets off the mainsail and hoist it, only to put it
to bed again a few minutes later. Yes, the spinnaker

is a grand working sail and multiplies the possibilities of your boat many times indeed.

The balloon jib, ballooner, or reaching jib, is a light sail somewhat similar to a spinnaker. It is cut a little differently from the spinnaker, however, and snaps on the headstay or the jib stay. The balloon jib is so

Photo M. Rosenfeld

FIG. 104. A Genoese jib

large that its sheet must always be passed outside the shrouds and trimmed from a point well aft. A useful thing to remember is that a balloon jib or a spinnaker trimmed as a ballooner may sometimes have its effectiveness increased if the sheet is passed over a snatch block on the boom before being made fast to the deck.

By use of this snatch block it is possible to trim the
ballooner to the proper degree of flatness and at the
same time trim it out from the boat so that it does not
backwind the mainsail.

The Genoese jib is a large jib that overlaps the mainsail for about one-third of its width. It is carried when
sailing to windward and is nearly as effective on a
broad reach as a ballooner. The Genoese jib is chiefly
valuable as a racing sail because it is a great nuisance
to tack with. In going about, the leeward sheet must
be cast off and a hand must go forward to carry the
jib around the windward shrouds, the mast, and the
leeward shrouds. This makes it a very uncomfortable
sail to handle, for any other purpose than racing. The
reasons for the remarkable efficiency of the Genoese
jib are not yet known. Some authorities maintain that
the reason boats win with the Genoese jib is that they
carry a much greater sail area than with the ordinary
jib and yet they are not penalized for this sail area
because the racing measurement rules take into
account the fore-triangle—in other words, the space
occupied by the jib in front of the mast—and the over-
lapping part of the jib does not count under the sail
area measurement rules. Other authorities maintain
that the Genoese jib is effective because it increases
the draft funnel on the leeward side of the mainsail
and thereby increases the power of that sail.

CHAPTER XXVII

RULES OF THE ROAD—RIGHT-OF-WAY

"Here lies the body of Michael O'Day,
Who died maintaining the right-of-way;
He was right—dead right—as he sailed along
But he's just as dead as if he'd been wrong."

I WISH I knew the author of this much-quoted epitaph, for to him much credit is due. It is far better at all times to avoid a collision or even the danger of a collision than to insist upon the right-of-way. So many people are sailing boats and so many thousands more are operating motor boats who have no idea of the rules of the road, that it is always safe to assume that the other sailor is a landlubber.

We will understand the rules of right-of-way very much better if we remember that they were formed at a time when most boats were square riggers. A square-rigged ship is very easy to handle when she is before the wind. A twist of the helm, slacking off some lines and trimming on others, and a square-rigged ship may alter her course to starboard or port with the greatest facility. On the wind, however, it is quite another story. It is a tough job to tack a square-rigged vessel. Some of the sails must be taken aback;

all hands are at their stations, and it is a long, slow, tedious process involving much labor with the outcome frequently in doubt. Therefore it is but natural that a boat before the wind should yield right-of-way to a boat that is on the wind, and infinitely harder to handle.

To-day the same distinction exists. A boat is close-hauled if she is sailing as close to the wind as she can manage efficiently. If her sheets are started and she is sailing any other course than close-hauled she is said to be free. The first rule to remember is that a boat close-hauled has right-of-way over a boat that is free.

But let us suppose that two boats meet, both of them close-hauled. They may meet for one of two reasons: either they are sailing on opposite tacks or they are sailing on the same tack and converging slowly together because one boat is able to point higher than the other.

If they sail on opposite tacks, the boat on the starboard tack has right-of-way. A boat is on the starboard tack when the wind is over the starboard side and her main boom is over the port side. If the two boats are converging on the same tack, the one that is to leeward and sailing closer into the wind has right-of-way.

If both boats are free—neither one close-hauled—and the sails are on opposite sides of the boat, the boat with its main boom over the port side and the wind presumably over the starboard side has right-of-way over the boat whose main boom is over the starboard side. If both boats are free and converging on the

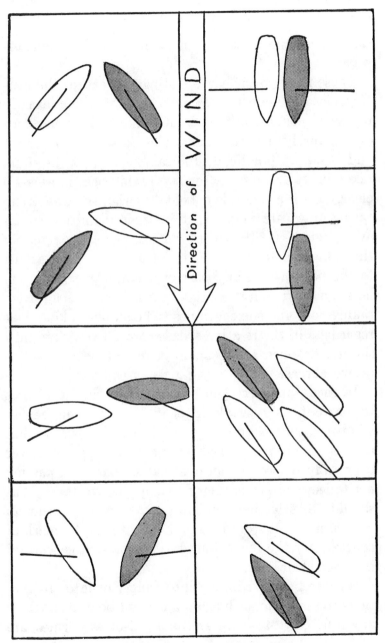

Fig. 105. The shaded boat in each instance has the right-of-way.

same tack, the boat that is to leeward has right-of-way.

These rules cover every contingency except the contingency arising when two boats are sailing exactly the same course and one is overtaking the other. An overtaking boat is one that comes up from clear astern and is sailing practically the same course as the overtaken boat. In all cases the overtaking boat must keep clear, and the overtaken boat has right-of-way. The racing rules are very exact in their definition of an overtaking boat. If two boats are sailing approximately the same course and one comes up from clear astern to the point where any part of her hull or spars overlaps the overtaken boat, this boat is known as an overtaking boat and she continues to be an overtaking boat regardless of the relative speeds of the two boats until she has dropped astern again or drawn clear ahead or drawn abreast out of any danger of collision.

In races, an overtaken boat may luff as she pleases to prevent an overtaking boat from passing her to windward, but a limit is placed on this power to luff after a certain point has been reached. She may never bear away to prevent an overtaking boat from passing her to leeward. In ordinary sailing, the overtaken boat should not alter her course in any way to prevent an overtaking boat from passing her, but it is the mark of courtesy for the overtaking boat to pass to leeward of the overtaken boat.

When a boat is running into danger or into obstructions to sea room such as an anchored boat, a shoal, or anything of that nature, the right-of-way rules are suspended. Such a boat not having the right-of-way may demand that another boat having the right-of-way yield to it.

Sailboats have right-of-way over power and steamboats. But when a steamboat starts tooting at you it is as well to know what the toots mean. A single blast of the whistle means "I am directing my course to my starboard." Two blasts mean "I am directing my course to my port." Three blasts mean, "My engines are reversed and my boat is going astern."

If one boat signals with a single blast or two blasts and another answers with four or more blasts in rapid succession, it means that that course of the first whistler is not satisfactory to the second whistler. A boat whistling three times and then once signifies that it is towing, and whereas theoretically a sailboat has right-of-way over a tug with a string of barges, it is well to give such an argosy all the room it requires.

Certain boats are sometimes not amenable to the rules of the right-of-way. A naval boat, for instance, on official business, may demand and take the right-of-way. Usually you will find that the boats of the navy are most punctilious in observing the rules. The worst offenders are the local steamboat captains who may happen to be carrying the U. S. mail. In a recent race, a boat carrying the mails ran right through the fleet at the finish line, ramming some boats and interfering with all of them, simply because the presence of a bag containing a few picture postcards gave the skipper an enlarged ego.

It must be remembered that Coast Guard boats

and naval boats are not obliged even to run with lights if it interferes with their mission.

If you engage in racing, do not be guided by the rules of the road as outlined here. Racing rules are vastly more complicated, but this is all you need to know for ordinary sailing.

CHAPTER XXVIII

HANDLING THE DINGHY

THERE is a ritual and a correct procedure in handling the dinghy that marks the salty skipper. In the first place, very few amateur yachtsmen know how to row. They may not splash with their oars or pull the boat

FIG. 106. The flip of the oars that sends you ahead
Note position of the wrists

in circles; but they can always be spotted by the height to which they lift their oar blades and by the fact that their strokes lack power.

The oar should never be dipped below the top of the blade. In leaving the water the oar should be flipped with a smart flexion of the wrist so that it comes out of the water at an angle of 45° and not at an angle of 90°. This little flip drives the boat ahead

281

almost as much as the entire stroke. When the oars
are shipped they should be laid in the boat with the
blades forward, not aft. This is accomplished by pressing the handles down smartly, flipping the oars out of
the rowlocks in a vertical position, twisting the wrists
so that the blades fall in the direction of the bow of
the boat and at the same time moving the hands aft.
The rowlock in the side of the dinghy that is next to
your sailboat when you come alongside should never
be left in the thole.

When you pull up alongside your boat, always approach it with the bow of the dinghy in the same direction as the bow of the sailboat. Never row directly at
your sailboat. Row astern of her and round up to her.
Of course this rule does not apply in a heavy sea when
your boat is to leeward. There you round with your
bow to the wind ahead of your boat and drift down
to her. If your sailboat is tide-borne so that she is not
heading directly into the wind always approach her
from the leeward side. The correct place to land on a
sailboat is abaft amidships, not forward of amidships.

A dinghy towed behind a sailboat should be given
enough scope of the painter to allow it to travel on the
forward side of the second following wave. That is the
position in which it tows the easiest. If you are making considerable leeway the dinghy should be towed
from the leeward quarter as it will be less interfered
with from the wake of the sailboat.

Handling a boat with one oar is an art by itself.
Most people manage to paddle a boat fairly well, but
to pole it or to scull it requires "know-how." To pole

a boat, stand near the stern and push over the side
directly aft with a long, steady push. Draw your oar
back through the water, using it as a rudder to correct
any little change in direction that may have been im-
parted by your push. Never pole a boat from the bow.
You should pole from the leeward side of a boat; never
from the windward.

Fig. 107. Sculling. *Left,* Note position of oar blade and hand
and disturbed water. *Center,* The black lines show the successive positions of the oar blade. The shaded area shows the path
of the oar through the water. *Right,* Sculling from a rowlock
set off center on the transom so as not to interfere with rudder
or outboard motor.

The art of sculling is a trick which some people
never learn. A boat is not sculled, as many people
imagine, by merely moving the oar from side to side
in the scullhole. Such movement merely tends to drive
the boat slightly backwards. The oar is placed in the
water with the flat side athwart the boat. With the
oar in this position, hold it in your right hand and

face the stern. Now turn your knuckles slightly down and move the handle of the oar to your right. Turn your knuckles up and move the handle of the oar to the left. Turn the knuckles down again, handle to the right. Knuckles up, handle to the left. And continue. At all times keep pressing down with the handle of the oar so that the blade of the oar is being forced against the water. Relax this tension slightly as you turn your hand at the end of each stroke. The path described by the oar is shown in Figure 107.

CHAPTER XXIX

CARE OF THE HULL

I HAVE recently purchased a sailboat that is twenty-six years old. Her gaff rig looks a little old-fashioned in comparison with a lot of the Marconi rigs now in vogue. But except for that, no one could tell the difference between this *Old Timer* (for such I have christened her) and a brand-new boat. A boat that is properly cared for almost never wears out and one should look for a life of thirty-five to fifty years in a small sailboat properly built and properly kept up.

But let a beginner take out a brand-new boat and in the course of a month she looks like a wreck. It is more than a question of economy, more than a matter of trying to protect an investment; it is an essential part of seamanship to keep a boat at her best at all times. A sailing boat that goes to sea and makes long passages must be cared for as a matter of life and death. It is wonderful to think how self-supporting and independent is the ship cut off from the land. She has her carpenter who is always called "Chips" and who makes instantly any repair that may become necessary. She has her sailmaker who always goes by the name of "Stitches" who spends every day and all day in making repairs to the sails. In the old days every seaman was an expert rigger and even to-day there is no sailing vessel but can boast a number of good riggers among her crew. A ship's stores include planks and nails, canvas and needles; the boatswain has his special stores of rope and wire, blocks and cleats and shackles and turnbuckles, paint and varnish, red lead and white lead, and everything necessary to keep the boat at all times in tiptop condition.

When supplies can be had at the nearest hardware store, when the services of a shipyard or a carpenter or a painter can be readily procured and when most of the little jobs about a boat can be done without much expenditure of time and effort, it is inexcusable to let the boat go to pieces for lack of care.

And yet, carelessness seems to be growing apace. It may be due to our country's orgy of sudden wealth and to the spirit of wastefulness that accompanies it. It may be due to mass production of automobiles and the ever-present tendency to turn in a used car for a new one; but this attitude should not carry over to one's boat. It is of the very essence of the sea that a boat should be kept up.

Beware of scars on the hull. They come from a number of causes and first may be listed slamming hard into a dock. Always try to stop your boat before she gets to the dock; never attempt to make a landing until you are sure you can handle your boat safely considering all the circumstances. After you have made the dock get out your fenders even if there is no boat alongside of you; put out the fenders anyway because a boat may tie up beside you the minute your back is turned.

Occasionally boats are damaged by hitting floating objects. This is not so serious in a sailboat as in a power boat because a sailboat travels at lower speed and because it has no propeller to be bent or broken. Nevertheless a keen lookout should be kept at all times for floating wreckage and especially is this true at night or in a fog.

The dinghy is guilty of causing many scars. The bow of your dinghy should be protected by a big, soft pudding; and a clean, new cotton rope should be strung as a fender along the gunwale. Care should be taken at all times in bringing the dinghy alongside. When the dinghy is pulled up from her position astern, always pull her up by the side of the boat—never directly into the stern. Do not let your passengers volunteer to pull the dinghy alongside; do it yourself and do it properly.

The anchor is another offender. When you haul it in be sure that you wash off the mud before taking it aboard and that you do not strike the overhang of your bow with its sharp fluke. Anchors ready for service are often carried on the bows with the stock in place and one fluke resting over the side. If you run up to a dock with the anchor in this position and should strike a piling of the dock against the anchor it may drive the fluke right through the planking. If your anchor is carried on deck it should be lashed down so that it will not roam around.

Wounds and scars of any nature should be repaired as promptly as possible. A new section of plank should be put in if the wound is a bad one; otherwise the paint should be scraped off, and the scar filled in with plastic wood a little higher than the surrounding surface. The plastic wood should then be planed or sandpapered off until the surface is perfectly smooth and the whole repair should be painted.

The worst enemy of a boat is dry rot. Dry rot is a germ disease. It is a fungus growth which spreads rapidly and eats and destroys the wood. There are two medicines for warding off dry rot. There is only one medicine after it has set in. The two preventive medicines are ventilation and paint; do not keep your boat closed up; let the air and the sunlight get to it. Even an open boat has nooks and corners where the light and air never penetrate. Lockers are built under the stern and these lockers are closed with ornamental doors. Leave these doors open just as much as possible and especially leave them open when the boat is laid up for the winter. When your winter cover is put on, be sure that there is an adequate opening forward and aft so that a draft of fresh air may go through it.

Always keep your wood covered with paint or varnish. If the paint or varnish wears off, so that the wood is bare, there is always danger of dry rot setting in.

There is only one medicine that will cure dry rot after it once starts: tear the affected wood out, get out every particle of it. One little spot that is rotted will soon destroy the entire boat, for the disease spreads like wildfire. Painting over dry rot does not help it but rather hastens the spread of the disease underneath the paint.

Worms are another major cause of trouble. Worms

are worse in some localities than in others. The teredo or marine borer is the worst of the lot. He abounds in tropical waters but he is found in great numbers in many ports pretty far north. He prefers salt water to brackish water.

It is important to keep your bilge clean. Pump it out frequently, whether it really needs it or not. Never let the dead sandwiches from the last picnic float about in the bilge. This is sometimes easier to say than to do. I remember pumping chicken soup in small quantities for an entire month after my stove upset.

Keep fresh poisonous paint on the bottom. The most popular anti-fouling paints contain copper, bronze, or mercury. It is a good plan to paint the bottom at least twice during the season. Copper paint should be applied just before launching and some paint manufacturers recommend that the boat should be launched while the paint is still wet. I have found to my sorrow that this does not always work out.

After the worms get a start, you can try poisoning them by putting destructive fluids in their holes. Kerosene is a favorite remedy that is probably only partly efficacious. Watch your boat carefully after any such treatment. If the worms continue to spread, have the boat hauled out and the worm-eaten parts ripped off and renewed. Otherwise they will go through your boat and destroy it utterly.

The places where worms usually get a start are behind the rudder post and in the centerboard trunk. There are two reasons for this: these places are particularly hard to reach with a paint brush and the worms probably can bore there with less disturbance from the water. A swab on the end of a stick can be used to paint below the water line in the center-board trunk. Every time you haul out, be sure to try to work some paint between the rudderpost and dead-wood.

Many authorities recommend coppering the bottom of a boat as a protection against worms. Others equally authoritative claim that copper is more dangerous than the lack of it, for if the worms once get under the copper it is the end of your boat.

Most marine growths other than worms are not par-ticularly destructive but they slow down the boat amazingly and certainly do it no good. Marine growths should be scrubbed off daily as far under the boat as you can reach and the boat should be beached at fre-quent intervals and the bottom thoroughly scrubbed with a coarse scrubbing brush.

In some localities gases arise from the water and form a black scum under the overhang. In localities frequented by motor boats there is always a certain amount of oil floating on the water which deposits a nasty brown scum at and just above the water line. These scums can be scrubbed or chamoised off if the boat is not allowed to turn too dark.

Your topsides should be gone over regularly with a sponge and chamois and washed with fresh water if that is convenient. The bright work or varnished sur-faces should be sanded down and varnished about every three weeks early in the day with an offshore wind blowing. If you do not care to keep your blocks,

cleats, turnbuckles and traveler brightly shined with
brass polish, paint them or coat them so that they will
not turn green. There are preparations on the market
to smear over polished brass that preserve the polish
so that daily polishing is not necessary.

CHAPTER XXX

CARE OF SAILS

EXCEPT in a new boat, good sails represent from 25% to 50% of your investment. If for no other reason, they deserve the best possible care. But there are other reasons for caring for sails quite apart from monetary consideration. Good-looking sails enhance the beauty of a boat more than any other part of her. Powerful, efficient sails improve the boat's performance so greatly that they add immensely to the pleasures of sailing. So true is this that most skippers who have ever sailed a boat in the topnotch of perfection rarely derive much pleasure thereafter from sailing a badly equipped or badly dressed boat.

Keep your sails clean. There is rarely an excuse for getting them dirty. Do not walk on them when they are lowered and do not permit anyone else to walk on them. Do not let them fall into a dirty bilge or onto that part of the deck where you have just been pumping or where you have laid a dirty anchor. Never let them touch the pump or the mop or a slimy, green cable. Never handle them with hands that have been wrestling with a stubborn motor or hauling a muddy chain.

A sail has four roaches or curves—one along the head, one along the luff, one along the foot, and the last one along the leech. The first three of these roaches are pulled into straight lines when the sail is bent and hoisted, and therefore they impart a curvature to the sail that develops its power when the wind blows on it. Canvas is very elastic, and is easily stretched. But there is a limit to its elasticity and if the stretching goes beyond the elastic limit the sail stays stretched and the roaches are destroyed. Sails are stretched out of shape first by pulling on them too hard; second by permitting them to get wet and to shrink while thus stretched; third, by improper drying; fourth, by too much strain as a combined result of stretching and wind. Sails lose their driving force by becoming too baggy or by becoming too flat. Sometimes a sail that is too baggy becomes an excellent power plant in light airs. Sails that have become too flat for ordinary use are still useful and powerful in strong blows.

In the chapter on bending and hoisting sail much emphasis has been placed on the necessity for drawing out the outhaul only hand-tight and never putting too much strain upon it. It takes courage to do this, especially when the dockside critics will all tell you that your sail should be stretched out to the ends of the spars. The spars should always be longer than the sails so that you will have a little room to stretch them; but to pull the sails out until they are drum-tight murders the sails and spoils the performance of your boat.

If your sails get wet while you are sailing, be sure

to slack off the outhaul at the clew. It is equally necessary to slack off the outhaul at the peak if the sail
becomes wet from rain, dew, or fog. Spray rarely
reaches the head so that in ordinary sailing the clew
outhaul is the only line that needs attention. The outhauls that are fast to the reef cringles must be cared
for in the same way. Never tie your boat up for the
night or permit the sails to dry with a reef tied in. It
is the work of only a few minutes to shake out all your
reefs. If you have more than one suit of sails, do not
use your best suit on a day when you have to reef.
When you shake out reefs, do not stop with merely
untying the reefing points; shake them out completely
and literally. Pull them clear of their furl and give
them a good hearty shaking throughout their length.

In a small boat, the sails should be unbent and taken
ashore every night; especially if you have a track and
slides on mast and boom there is no excuse for leaving
your sails bent. If you insist upon doing so, however,
be sure that they are properly furled and covered with
the sail covers. It is common practice to roll the jib
on the jib club. There is no harm in this if the jib is
dry and if you slack off the lacing on the club before
rolling the jib around it. But at least take the jib
ashore and do not tuck it under the deck to slop around
in the bilge water.

Sails should be dry before they are furled and there
are right and wrong ways of drying sails. The best
way to dry sails is to sail on them. Do your sailing
in sheltered water where you will not kick up any
spray. Have your outhaul fairly slack and do not hoist

too high on your halliards. The second-best method of drying sails is to take them ashore and spread them over clothes lines hung in a warm, dry loft or attic. If you lack these facilities, spread them over clothes lines outdoors. In using clothes lines be sure that the sails are hung loosely over several lines. Do not fasten them up by the corners, as the whole weight of the sail will pull on those corners and distort the shape.

If sails must be dried at anchor observe the following procedure: first shake out all reefs; second, have the outhauls loose; third, hoist the sail about two-thirds of the way. Then, by passing a line over mast hoops or slides tie up the slack part of the sail near the foot. A sail that has been stretched out of shape will often recover if hoisted in this way and allowed to shiver and shake in a light breeze for several hours.

A sail should be furled as follows: first take the leech and pull it out toward the end of the boom, getting the bunchiness away from the mast. Hoist the gaff about ten inches and keep it parallel with the boom. Now beginning near the head of the sail, pull the sail aft, shake it, and fold it in to the hammock formed by the head itself. Grasp the sail a foot or two lower and repeat the process, each time pulling the sail aft, shaking it and turning it into the hammock formed by the head. Continue thus until you reach the foot, walking a step or two aft as you go along to see that the leech is well pulled out. When you reach the foot, you will find that the sail is neatly furled with the head forming a smooth covering on one side and the foot a smooth covering on the other. Tie down a gasket a little forward of the peak, then slack off the halliards, cast off the gasket and tie it again. Gaskets are usually made of canvas. Lacking canvas, you may use rope. And lacking rope you may use the ends of your halliards, topping lift, and main sheet, but this is always a confession of slovenliness and a mark of an ill-equipped boat.

Gaskets are tied as follows: the middle of the gasket is laid over the gaff and the ends allowed to fall below the boom on either side. Both ends are passed below the boom in opposite directions. They are then brought to the top side of the gaff and tied hard with a firm reef knot. After tying in the gasket forward of the peak, tie other gaskets at three to four feet intervals all along the sail. The after part of the sail beyond the end of the peak is usually rolled up after the part under the gaff is tied down. A good furling job should be a source of pride to any skipper.

Second only to stretching, the worst enemy of a sail is mildew. Sometimes it seems impossible to keep a sail from mildewing. But if the cause of mildew is known, its prevention can be achieved by proper care. Sails become mildewed when they are furled and covered while wet and allowed to dry in the hot sun when rolled up tightly in a cover. If you must put wet sails to bed, always furl them very loosely, making a bundle about three times the size of the normal furl and never under any circumstances put the sail covers on wet sails. If your boat should be rained on during the night, get out early the next morning and hoist them and dry them. A few hours of midsummer sun is all that is necessary to give mildew a start.

Mildew spreads fairly rapidly. When your sails are new make particular efforts to prevent even a small spot of mildew from getting a foothold.

Battens often do considerable damage to sails. The principal damage from this cause is from breaking a batten and having the sharp, jagged end tear a hole through the sail. Try to avoid breaking battens. It is easy enough to do if you make it a rule never under any circumstances to step on your sails. Once more, let me repeat, that battens should always be an inch or two shorter than their pockets. If the batten is too long and is pushed hard down into the pocket, it will not only cause the sail to set badly but will stretch the leech and cause a hard line to develop in the sail. Battens should be tied into the grommets at the outboard end of the pockets. The tying line may be knotted permanently into one of the grommets but in tying in the batten, the line should pass through both grommets and through a hole in the batten as well.

The right way to fold the sail is as follows:

Spread the sail out on a clean floor. Place one man at the luff and one at the leech. Each man then takes hold of the sail approximately at the first row of reefing points and lifts it up toward the head. The sail is again seized at the same points and at the points immediately beneath them, and the three layers are again carried forward an equal distance. This is continued until the sail forms a long, flat bundle as wide as the distance from the foot to the first reef. This bundle is then rolled (not folded) from the leech toward the luff and the sail is stowed in a clean, dry canvas bag. A sail so rolled is very easy to bend on the spars. The luff line appears at the edge of the bundle with all the grommets in the proper order, so that they may be bent to the hoops or the slides may be put on the

Fɪɢ. 108. Folding a sail—part **one**

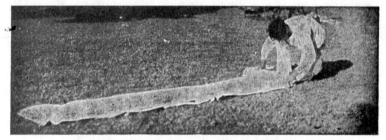

Fɪɢ. 109. Folding a sail—part two

Marconi track without undoing the bundle. When the luff is properly bent the entire sail may be unrolled along the boom. It will there appear as a flat, carefully folded package with the head along the gaff and the foot along the boom both ready for lacing, and the whole sail may be bent before the bundle is further disturbed or falls into the bilge water or is carelessly trampled on. In folding a sail for the winter, a slightly different procedure is necessary:

You begin in the same manner as outlined above but each successive fold is made just an inch or two shorter so that if anything should rub up against the sail during its winter storage the sail will not be soiled in streaks. Moth balls are liberally sprinkled in every layer as a safeguard not only against insects but also against rats and mice which seem to delight in nesting in a bundle of sails and soiling and destroying them.

If the foot of the sail is equipped with slides, it should be folded in the ordinary manner; but the folded sail should be rolled in the reverse order, beginning with the luff and rolling it so that the leech is on the outside of the bundle. Then, when the sail is bent, the slides may be placed on the track of the boom as the bundle is unrolled.

The skipper should take care to see that his leech line is always properly adjusted. The leech line is the thin cotton line sewed loosely into the leech of the sail. It generally leaves the hem of the leech through a brass grommet about four inches above the foot. This line is intended as a puckering string to be used in case the leech should become too loose. This is not a very common fault in sails as most leeches are too tight; but if the leech shakes or has a tendency to fold over, it may be corrected by a very slight tension on the leech line. In adjusting the leech line it must be borne in mind that the sail derives its power not so much by the wind blowing on it as by blowing off it. The wind must be allowed to flip off the leech without being hindered in any way. A leech that forms a pocket to hold the wind or to change its direction is a serious handicap in any boat. Too tight a leech line results in a nigger-heeled sail. The adjustment of the leech line should result in a leech that is flat in its lateral curvature but curved outward or roached in its fore and aft curvature.

CHAPTER XXXI

WINTER STORAGE AND CARE

CONSIDERABLE thought should be given to the selection of a boatyard where your boat will be stored for the winter. The most expensive yard is by no means necessarily the best. A yard should be selected only after talking to yacht owners who have stored in various yards and who are willing to relate their experiences. A yard that does not keep its promises or that is not efficiently managed or lacks the facilities, the workmen, or the finances for turning out good work should not be encouraged to stay in business. If you find a good yard, take the attitude that it should be encouraged. Be willing to pay a fair price for labor and materials and do not try to get something for nothing. Many of the most accommodating yards are carelessly run. If you borrow a pint of turpentine or a handful of copper nails, be sure that you remember it and account for it; for little losses of that sort make staggering totals to a yard that tries to please the yachtsman and does not load its bills with all sorts of extras. The yard is entitled to a certain amount of work on your boat; usually the painting of the topsides and bottom are insisted upon. This is a fair provision, but never store in a yard that insists upon doing all of the work on your boat or that will prevent you from doing work yourself. Most yachtsmen take a keen joy in putting their own boats in condition and this is impossible in the wrong kind of yard.

See to it personally that your boat is hauled out on the day agreed upon. If it is neglected it may stay afloat under adverse conditions until late in the fall or early in the winter. After the boat is hauled out, make sure that the plugs are knocked out of it. If the plugs

FIG. 110. Improper cradling—danger of sagging

cannot be found, drill a half-inch hole through the garboards near the keel. This is necessary to drain out the rain and the snow that will accumulate during the winter. You should see to it that your boat is properly cradled. It should be supported firmly at several points along the bottom and braced so that it will not topple over in a high wind. There is a further reason for proper cradling and that is that you are likely to work on or under your boat in the following spring and proper cradling is necessary for your personal safety. Only recently I heard of a boat that rolled over while the owner was working beneath it. It crushed his chest and killed him instantly.

Apart from security, the cradling should be studied with a view to support. A boat that is supported only on the ends is apt to sag in the middle. A boat supported in the middle but not at the ends is apt to hog and get higher in the middle and lower on the ends. Boats improperly stored have been known to increase their water-line length nine or ten inches through hogging and to lose four or five inches through sagging.

Fig. 111. Improper cradling—danger of hogging

See that the middle and the ends of your boat are properly supported by heavy beams resting on solid ground and that these beams are really bearing against the boat by having wedges driven between the boat and the beam.

You should see that your boat is properly covered. A boat stored in a shed does not need a cover. A boat stored in the open does. The object of the winter cover is to spare the boat from alternate periods of wetness and dryness and particularly from snow and ice forming on it in the winter. An old sail loosely thrown over the boat is not an adequate cover. If a ridgepole is built down the middle of the boat and slats run off to the side and the old sail then nailed onto the slats so as to form a tent, it will then be satisfactory. The sides of the cover should come well down over the boat and should be tacked securely to it so as to prevent the loose ends from flapping in the wind and wearing away the paint.

An excellent winter cover can be made for very little money out of tar paper. The flat-headed nails for applying the tar paper come with each roll. It has been my experience that tar-paper tops are easy to build if the strips are laid across the boat rather than lengthwise.

Ventilation is most necessary and can be provided for by leaving an opening forward and aft. If your boat has a cabin, the companionway and portholes should be left open, and all closets and lockers on any boat —open or cabin—should be left with the doors open. Floor boards should be taken up and all inside ballast should be removed. The mast should be unstepped and placed in a shed. The wire rigging should be examined for defects and greased or varnished. Just before putting on the winter cover, the bright work should be given a good thick coat of varnish. The varnish will not look like anything in the spring but at least it will prevent the wood from being bare and turning black.

Every loose part of your boat, including the ballast and spars, the running and standing rigging, the pump, the boat hook, the anchors and cable, should have a tag bearing the name of the boat, the name of the owner and his address. It is important to make out an inventory in duplicate giving one copy to the yard and keeping one copy for yourself. The yard is responsible for your boat and all her equipment. And if someone steals your equipment through error or intention the yard is responsible.

The spars should be stored so that they will neither sag nor hog. If your mast has warped or been bent it is possible to straighten it out again by storing it in such a way that it will rest on its ends with a weight tied at the worst point of the bend; but it will be well to inspect the mast occasionally during the winter to see that this treatment does not over-correct.

The sails should be taken to your home or stored somewhere apart from the yard where you will be sure that they will be dry and free from rats, mice, and other vermin. The rigging should be "made up" in coils and hung from hooks.

It is very important to have fire insurance on your boat during winter storage. A boatyard is a very dangerous fire risk. There is wood and sawdust everywhere. Everything in the yard is inflammable and every workman and every visitor to the yard smokes perpetually. Furthermore there is gasoline in many of the boats and a fire once started is apt to sweep through an entire yard.

When you haul out in the fall, you should tell the yard the date on which you expect delivery of your boat in the spring. Then stick to this delivery date. Do not change your mind. If the yard is properly run, your boat will be placed where she can be put overboard at the date specified; for other boats that will go overboard earlier will be placed between her and the water, and boats that will go overboard later will be hauled farther out on land. It is well to give instructions to the yard for repairs and reconditioning both orally and in writing at the time you haul out. If the work includes alterations or repairs they should be done by the yard during the winter; but painting and varnishing should not be done until a short time before the boat goes overboard in the spring. It is well to repeat these instructions by letter again in the middle of the winter and to repeat them once more as soon as the weather is good. Under no circumstances wait until the week before you expect your boat before telling the yard what to do. Bear in mind that the spring is the outfitting season; that the yards are always rushed at that time and that painting and varnishing always take at least three times as long as they should take because of the prevalence of rain.

Visit your boat occasionally in the winter. See that nothing has happened to her. See that the cover has not been ripped off in a storm and that the drain holes have not been plugged by something loose in the bilge. When the warm days of late April and early May arrive, the winter cover should be taken off and the boat opened up as far as possible to the sunlight.

CHAPTER XXXII

FITTING OUT

SPRINGTIME! What does that mean to the sailor? Not the sinking of the plowshare in the moist, brown earth nor the return of the birds, the first green buds upon the trees or the gay new apparel in the shop windows.

No, spring expresses itself to the sailor in the tapping of the caulking mallet, the pungent smell of copper paint, the good will and the hard work and the cheery good fellowship in the shipyard; the warm sun overhead and the cold, forbidding, empty blue water just beyond. Spring is a joyous time in a shipyard. The boats emerging grimily from their winter covers seem to stretch and yawn and cast an eye seaward. There is joy in the scraping and painting and puttying; in the overhauling of gear and equipment. And when at last the old hooker slides down the ways and bobs gayly in her new coat of paint, it is a moment of sheer, unalloyed joy.

The spring overhaul begins with a thorough inspection. Every inch of the boat must be examined for worms and dry rot, particularly the bottom, the chines, the garboards, the centerboard trunk, the deadwood and the rudderpost. Seams should be inspected to see if they have opened up during the winter. If the caulking is dry and hard or has fallen out, recaulking is probably necessary. But don't reach this conclusion without first getting advice from experts and don't recaulk unless you really have to. Recaulking is a long, tedious, expensive job and unless the work is done carefully it may do more harm than good. If you must caulk, be sure that you don't overcaulk. If your boat is made of cedar or other light material it will swell a great deal when it is launched. A boat too tightly caulked may have her planking sprung from the ribs by the swelling. The caulking should be done gently but firmly and all the caulking should be below the level of the seam. Do all your caulking from the outside, never from the inside. The materials used for caulking are caulking cotton, cotton wicking, and oakum. Oakum is generally used in large ships only or in very bad leaks in small boats. It consists of fiber similar to the fiber of rope that is soaked in pitch or tar. Caulking cotton is generally used in small, heavily built boats but cotton wicking is the best material for a small, lightly built boat. Cotton wicking comes in balls and is laid up with five or six strands. If the seams you are to caulk are small, peel off some of these strands; one or two may be enough for you to use. The cotton is placed at the end of the seam and driven home by a caulking iron and a mallet. Then the wicking is twisted into a tight, hard roll, laid along the seam and driven in with the iron and mallet or with a caulking wheel. A caulking wheel consists of a little iron wheel placed in a handle. This wheel is run along the edge of the cotton which is placed over the seam. If you have much caulking to do, by all means get a wheel. It will materially shorten the work.

After the caulking has been driven in, the seams are covered with white lead applied with a putty knife, scraped off smooth and left slightly hollow. If you prefer, you may use a seam composition— a plastic substance which comes for that purpose, or you may even cover the seams with marine glue. Marine glue is advisable in the case of rowboats which are frequently hauled out and left out of water, as it is elastic, and will stretch when the wood dries out. There are two kinds of marine glue—solid and liquid. The solid marine glue is supposed to be used for seams, while the liquid marine glue is to be applied under canvas decks. The solid marine glue must be heated and it is a devilish thing to handle. I have tried the liquid marine glue for this purpose and found it very satisfactory and much easier to use. If you should run out of white lead (and one always runs out of whatever he needs the most) take the paint skins out of the bottom of an old paint can and apply the moist side to the seams. Paint skins make an excellent substitute.

Examine particularly the butt ends of your planks. Boats frequently leak at the butts if nowhere else. If your boat is old and in bad condition some refastening may be necessary. Be sure that you refasten with the same material as has already been used in the boat. If the boat has been fastened with copper use copper rivets or brass nails or screws. Don't mix iron and brass in your fastenings.

This is the time of year to get the bottom smooth. Use sandpaper liberally; knock off all the barnacles and blisters. Sand down any rough spot that may appear. There are many kinds of bottom paint and they seem to work with varying degrees of success in different localities. Get the best local advice you can. The poison materials in bottom paint are copper, bronze, and mercury. I have found bronze more satisfactory though more expensive than copper. Mercury is the poisonous substance used in white bottom paint. A dark-colored boat with a white bottom is very beautiful when she is heeled over. The light color is said to be a deterrent to marine growth and on the whole I have found white mercury bottom paint very satisfactory in all respects except one: its tendency to blister. Bronze paint is good for anti-fouling, but it forms a rough bottom that is not particularly suitable for racing. Copper paint comes in three colors: green, red, and brown. The green seems to give the fastest bottom, but the brown is by far the best so far as anti-fouling properties go. The red is next best, and the green is a very poor third. Don't experiment with trick paints and marvelous new discoveries. I have often noticed that the people who start the season with some wonderful new discovery are back the next season with the old copper and white lead.

Of course if you plan to race your boat you will pay more attention to having a fast bottom than one that is free from fouling, and you will use a bottom paint that is hard and glossy. Liberal use of the sandpaper is necessary before applying your bottom paint, and

even afterwards the body must be rubbed and rubbed
—first with coarse sandpaper and then with fine
sandpaper until you get it as smooth as a piano.
At least two coats of bottom paint are always necessary.

The top sides should be carefully prepared for painting. Wash off all the old dirt before the first coat goes
on. Fill the rough spots with some plastic material designed for that purpose. Never change the color of a
boat without first burning off the paint that is underneath it. A white boat, for instance, that is painted
black, looks fine when it leaves the yard; but every
bump and scratch makes a white mark and the boat is
soon a sorry-looking sight. I do not know whether
there is any reason for it, but I have often noticed that
boats that have been painted a different color without
a previous burn-off always seem to blister. Most boats
are easier to look at when painted white than when
painted any other color. It seems, however, a little
easier to keep a black boat black than a white boat
white. One of the complaints against boats painted
black is that the black absorbs the heat of the sun and
it is very hard to keep them tight above the water line.

If you attempt to burn off a boat yourself, handle
the torch carefully. The paint should merely be softened, not burned, and care should be taken not to
scorch the wood in the least. Particularly you should
be careful not to let the torch reach any of the bright
work.

When it comes to painting your top sides white, you
must make a choice between two kinds of paint. Some

people prefer one kind, and some the other. Here are their reasons; choose for yourself:

The man who wants glossy paint says, "I want a paint that is hard and that resists wear. It stays cleaner than soft, flat paint. I can scrub it and get the dirt off, but the paint stays on."

The other fellow replies: "I want a soft, flat finish, chalky paint. When I scrub my boat I take off not only dirt but paint as well. I can always get down to a layer of fresh paint by removing the top part. I may put on a little more paint than you do at the start of the season, but my boat is always easily cleaned, and at the end of the season she has on her just enough paint to take her comfortably through the winter. My boat never gets paint sick from having too many coats of paint."

Two to three coats of top-side paint are always required. Two thin coats are always better than one thick coat. If your bright work is in very good condition, it can be restored with sanding and varnishing. If it is not in good condition it is necessary to get down to bright wood. First, paint remover must be applied and the varnish scraped. Paint remover is of many different qualities. The best for use on a boat contains a considerable amount of a waxy substance that holds the paint-removing agent where you place it long enough for it to eat away the paint. The paint remover must be allowed to stand for from five to ten minutes before you start to scrape. You can tell when it has stood long enough by the little wrinkles and blisters which it raises. If it stands too long, it will harden the paint or varnish and make it more difficult to remove. Do not attempt to work too big a surface all at one time.

There are numerous types of scrapers on the market, but the best is the cheapest—an ordinary, flat piece of steel known as a cabinet scraper. Such a scraper is sharpened by means of a file. The edge of it is filed by pressing the file over it in one direction only so that the edge of the scraper is turned to form a little bead or hook. It is this turned edge that gets the paint and varnish off without biting too deeply into the wood. It is a good plan to have at least two scrapers and one file, so that if the scraper you are using becomes dull you can pick up the other one and continue work before the paint remover has a chance to harden. One word of caution in regard to the use of paint remover: do not let it get on your skin. It is said that it has the power to penetrate the pores and get inside the body where it causes pernicious anemia.

When the varnish has been scraped down to bare wood any black spots may be bleached by a strong solution of oxalic acid. Heat some water in a pot and dissolve the acid in it until it will take no more. Apply it with a paint brush, in the sun if possible. The results are astounding. I have bleached oak, white pine, and mahogany with equal facility, using oxalic acid in this way. The bleached wood should be carefully sanded to remove the acid before varnishing. In doing this work, however, you must be careful not to breathe the dust as that is pure, concentrated oxalic acid, and more dangerous even than when it is dissolved in water. If you bleach wood and do not have a chance to varnish it on the same day, be sure to cover it with a piece of canvas, as the dew will turn it black again.

You should always apply at least three coats of varnish over bare wood, and each coat should be sanded down before the next coat is applied. There are many different kinds of varnish and there are at least three kinds all known as spar varnish and recommended for use on boats. These three kinds are made from three different gums. There is the old varnish which we knew years ago made of kauri gum. There is a more modern varnish made from resin, and a still more modern kind made from a synthetic gum with a Bakelite base. I have used but one brand of varnish with a Bakelite base but have found it so superior to any other varnish that I have ever used that there is no comparison. It dries quickly, with a brilliantly bright finish and stays bright. The second best is the old-fashioned varnish made from kauri gum but it is difficult to use and takes a long time to dry. I think if I were restricted to varnishes made from resin I would never again have any bright work on a boat. Your success in varnishing depends largely upon the weather. You should not varnish if there is any moisture or dampness in the air, or if the temperature is below seventy degrees. You should varnish as early in the day as possible; never in the late afternoon. And you should be sure always to varnish in a land breeze. On Long Island or in Westchester you should varnish only when the wind is blowing from the northwest.

The appearance of your boat will be vastly enhanced

if you carefully touch up the little things—the porthole rims if you have a cabin, your boat hook and settin' pole and even the handle of your mop. The top of the centerboard where it sticks up above the trunk when lifted should not be neglected, and the floor of your cockpit deserves the friendly touch of the paint brush. Even the ballast might well be painted. Red lead on iron ballast should be applied as a first coat.

Avoid too many colors. They will make your boat garish and cheap.

The spars call for sanding and varnishing, and demand particular attention where the boom and gaff may have worn bare spots on the mast. Overhaul your wire rigging carefully. Bend new running rigging if you have any doubt as to the strength of the old. And do not haul yourself aloft on a boatswain's saddle unless you know you can trust the halliard, the block, and its fastening to the mast.

Don't shout with scorn if I advise you to be sure to drive your plugs home and to see to it personally that this is done before the boat is launched. This is so obvious a caution that it would seem to be entirely unnecessary; yet year after year I have seen boats launched in shipyards with the plugs forgotten. Whittle a long plug a foot or two in length with a long, careful taper. Drive it in, then saw it off close to the boat. Don't drive too short a plug, because you may drive it flush with the boat and still not fill the hole completely. The plug should be made of soft wood, not hard.

Before you put the boat overboard, soap the seams with ordinary brown laundry soap, turn the hose into her and fill her with water so that she may soak from the inside. It will save a powerful lot of pumping and cleaning if you do this. After you have launched your boat, let her swell for several days before you attempt to carry sail. Remember that a boat that is not swollen is but a flimsy aggregation of ribs and planks and she is apt to weave and warp if she is strained in this condition, and you will be obliged to use the pump all summer.

And now that we are launched, may you have a summer of fair winds and fast passages; with just enough adventure to make sailing for you, as it is for every sailor—the king of all sports.

THE HAUL-OUT

AN APPENDIX

This book was launched a year and a half ago and was reprinted after eight months. It has had two full seasons "in the water" and has been "handled" by many famous skippers.

Now it is time for a haul-out. As far as the author can learn, the book has behaved pretty well and has fulfilled the purpose for which it was built. But there are a few seams that need re-caulking, some barnacles that will need to be scraped off, some dowels to be sandpapered. And, on the whole, she should sail (or sell) better with new bottom paint in the form of a "Second Edition."

A book, like a boat, is built to certain pretty definite restrictions on cost. But when it has had a fair measure of success, the publisher is justified in spending more money to increase its usefulness. It is hard for an author to see his book as a whole when it is on the building ways. It looks very different in the water—in type and bound in blue buckram. A book for the beginner achieves more by being orderly than by being complete. Its helpfulness is determined as much by what is judiciously left out as by what is put in. But

317

when the book is launched, one sees many things that should be added.

The kindly criticisms of numerous skillful yachtsmen have disclosed several minor shortcomings. The letters from readers which the author has received have revealed still more. So we will review the book, chapter by chapter, adding, explaining, clarifying.

Speaking of letters from readers—the author welcomes them and answers them. They should be addressed in care of the publisher.

WHAT IT'S ALL ABOUT

There is a fraternity of the sea, not understood by landsmen. You may golf or ride or drink with a man and never see below the surface. But sail with him and you know him. Go through danger and hardship and adventure together and the knot of friendship is firmly tied. Yachtsmen visit one another in the ports they touch. The yacht clubs compete in extending hospitality. Yachtsmen help one another whenever possible. There is more genuine good fellowship among yachtsmen than among almost any other group of humans. Perhaps it is the salt water in the blood.

THE SELECTION OF A BOAT

The beginner should be guided in his selection by someone who knows boats. It is very easy to be deceived by appearances. A rotten, worm-eaten boat, ready to fall apart, may be painted and fixed up to look most alluring. On the other hand, a boat sadly in need of paint, may be sound and seaworthy, and be thoroughly worthy of the necessary expenditure of money to put her in first-class condition.

Examine the frames to see if they are broken. Stick a knife blade into the planking to see whether it has rotted. The knife should be placed crosswise of the grain of the wood, as the knife can easily penetrate sound planking if its edge is placed with the grain. Look for dry rot in the garboards (planking next to the keel). Examine the seams. See if the caulking has been pulled out. Look for dry rot in all places that are badly ventilated. Examine the boat for signs of strain. See if she has hogged up in the middle or has sagged, and if the line of her sheer is a true, graceful curve. Look for signs of worms in the keel, and especially in the centerboard and trunk. Examine the rigging and the sails. The age of the sails may be determined pretty accurately by the appearance of the roping. If the rope looks new and is bright in color and sound inside, the sails are pretty good for several seasons for all purposes except racing, even though they may look dirty and mildewed. The purchase of a small boat does not usually warrant a survey by a naval architect, but in buying a large boat, a survey is to be recommended.

THE MOORING

In many localities, moorings are put down with pipes or piles driven into the bottom. Devices of this kind do not offer maximum protection. Whereas the mooring should be of sufficient size to prevent dragging, it is far better to have a mooring drag than let go altogether. A mushroom anchor, or similar device, may drag for a long way in a storm without the loss of the boat, whereas a post, pipe, or similar device, will cause the loss of the boat if it is torn from its initial position.

In a recent hurricane, I nearly lost my boat through the chafing of a brand-new rope pennant that was carefully protected by chafing gear, with four wrappings of new canvass carefully sewed on with waxed sail twine.

My next pennant will be a cable of flexible, stainless steel, covered with rubber hose. I cannot recommend such a device from my own experience, but it is highly recommended by many eminent yachtsmen who have resorted to it since the comparatively recent introduction of flexible stainless steel.

ACQUIRING A VOCABULARY

This chapter had a curious omission. I neglected to list some of the verbs most common in sailing parlance.

To trim a line means to pull it in.

To trim it flat means to pull it in as far as possible.

To start a line means to let it out. It is usually spoken, however, of a line that is fast and is let out a short distance and then made fast again.

When one lets out a lot of line, it is usually spoken of as paying out.

When you pay out a lot of your anchor cable, you give it scope.

When you pull a line through blocks, so as to get

the blocks further apart, you are said to overhaul it. Thus you overhaul your back-stays or jigs.

You do not cast anchor; you let go your anchor. On the other hand, when you raise it, you break it out.

When an anchor is brought close to the boat before breaking out, you heave short. When the anchor is directly below the boat, it is up and down.

You hoist a sail, but hoist *on* a halliard.

When you pull down your sail, you lower it but do not use the words take *down*. You describe it as take *in* or take *off*. To tighten a halliard or wire rigging you use the term "set up." Thus, you set up your shrouds.

LOOKING HER OVER

It is important, especially in a cabin boat, to stow your duffle so that it will be secure when a boat heels. This is something which yachtsmen constantly forget.

On a recent cruise my paid hand placed a half gallon of varnish directly over a loosely furled spinnaker and also placed a bottle of muriatic acid on top of the ice box. They were safe while the boat was on an even keel, but as soon as she heeled to the breeze outside, the varnish spilled over the spinnaker and ruined it and the acid broke over the ice box, spoiling all the food and preventing further use of the ice box for several days.

Try to picture your boat heeled down to the deck or further and stow your duffle accordingly.

It is well to study the trim of the boat. On a small boat the weight of a spare sail will materially affect the trim. Even the anchor should not be placed in the bow if it will bring the bow below her proper lines.

THREE USEFUL KNOTS

The knot described as a square knot, which isn't a reef knot, has had a curious history. I learned it from a reader of this book who spent his youth on a brig plying between Long Island and South America. Originally, the knot was called a Thief Knot or a Cabin Boy Knot. It was used by the cook to tie up the sugar or other delicacies. If the cabin boy stole any of the sugar, he was careful to tie the knot exactly as he had found it, and naturally mistaking the thief knot for a reef knot, he would steal his sugar and tie it up with a reef knot, thus disclosing his peculations to the cook.

Sometimes it pays to tie a clove hitch backwards. To do this you take the first hitch with the fall above the standing part. Then take a turn below the standing part and pass the fall between the standing part and the lower turn. This is not recommended to the beginner until the normal way of tying the clove hitch becomes perfectly automatic. Frequently if the pull on the hitch is along the length of the timber, the clove hitch, tied backwards, will stay while an ordinary clove hitch will slip.

I have often heard it said that tug-boatmen and some old sailors can throw a bowline in a line by taking the fall, heaving it around the standing part, so that it makes the first bight, whirling it about the standing part above the bight, and having the end drop in place.

I have tried it for ten years without success. Perhaps it can be done. It makes an interesting exercise.

BENDING AND HOISTING SAIL

In bending the sail to the hoops, the forward side of the hoop should be turned upwards. If they are kept horizontal while being laced they are much more apt to stick on the mast.

The instructions in this chapter on backing out the bottom screw on the track were intended as an emergency guidance in case you have no other means of keeping the slides on the track. Some boats are provided with buttons to prevent slides from dropping off the bottom of the track. With a Marconi rig, I strongly recommend the use of slide magazines on the mast and boom. These magazines consist of a section of track which snaps onto the mast and onto the boom. When the sail is lowered all the slides on the luff slip over the spare section on the mast. Then the outhaul is cast off and the slides on the boom are pulled forward onto the boom section. By squeezing together two clips, the entire sail is lifted off the mast and a similar procedure lifts it off the boom and the slides are automatically retained on these sections.

To bend sail, you simply clip the slides into place, bend on your halliard and outhaul, haul out on the boom and hoist on the halliard. It saves the tedious business of threading the slides onto the track.

One word of caution. Do not use track and slides on the gaff. They work well on the boom of any sail, Marconi or gaff headed. They do not work on a gaff. The reason for this is obvious. The weight of the sail pulls down on the gaff, but the gaff is carried at an acute angle to the direction of the pull. Unless the head of the sail is firmly secured to the gaff at each grommet, the full weight of the sail falls on the peak and the sail may be quickly pulled out of shape. The more expensive sails are now made with wire lines in the luff. If your sail has a wire luff line the caution about hoisting too tight on the throat or main halliard may be disregarded. The wire luff line will prevent your stretching the sail out of shape.

Some of my readers have been a little confused by the section devoted to obtaining the proper roach in the leech. I think this will be clear if you bear in mind that wind must be permitted to blow, not only on the sail, but off it. If the leech of the sail curves to windward it will pocket the wind and prevent its swift flow off the leech. Even a slight curve to windward at the leech will change the direction of the flow of wind and this seriously retards progress.

REEFING

The strain on the mast in a gaff-headed rig takes a different direction when the sail is reefed. With full sail, the mast bends to leeward in an even symmetrical curve. With a reefed sail, however, it is apt to bend to windward—the middle of the mast curving away to leeward. If a mast with full sail breaks in the middle, the top half will go over to leeward. With a reefed sail, the top half will be pulled to windward by the shrouds and the mast will break first on the leeward side.

This difference in strain is not really of importance unless the shrouds are set up too tight. The reader is cautioned to watch his sail while reefed. If he sees a dangerous curve to leeward in the middle of the mast, it might be wise to slack off the shrouds slightly.

THEORY OF SAILING

It might be well to add that the theory expounded in this chapter explains what makes a boat go to windward. As a boat sails more freely until it gets almost dead before the wind, the power of the wind on the leeward side is decreased and the power of the wind on the windward side is increased. It is well for the beginner to remember that the principal drive is achieved, not by the wind blowing on the sail, but by the wind blowing off it.

Anything that breaks up or disturbs or pockets the wind, or sets up eddies in the wind, decreases its power and interferes with the efficiency of the boat.

BEFORE THE WIND

The maneuver of "tacking down wind" has been explained as a precautionary measure against the accidental jibe. This is not its only function. The boat sails faster with a quartering breeze than she does directly before the wind, and frequently you can save a good deal of time by tacking down wind. In the first race between *Enterprise* and *Shamrock,* the *Enterprise* won by this maneuver.

The helmsman's hail when jibing is "coming over." He does not say "hard alee" because, obviously, his helm is not alee. The jibing equivalent of "ready about" is usually "prepare to jibe."

The precaution against making the sheet fast applies only to a small boat. On a large boat the sheet must be made fast as the strain is too great to hold it in your hand.

A very old skipper who sailed for many years on the Hudson River has objected to my description of the North River jibe as a dangerous maneuver. It seems that in the old days the skipper of the big North River sloops were obliged to use that method of jibing in sailing before the wind down the many turns in the river. They reduced it to a fine art and were able to go into a flying jibe all standing in such a way that the sail would spend its force against the air backed up behind it; but the old boatmen left the helm, to be sure they were not caught in the path of the sheet. The boats had no back stays and nothing to carry away. I stick by my guns. The North River jibe is not a safe maneuver.

SAILING TO WINDWARD

Some of my readers have been confused and alarmed by the description of the critical angle of heel. I do not know how else to describe it. There is a point in all boats where it is easier for the boat to go over than to return to an even keel. The phrase "Critical angle of heel" is not mine. It is a common term in naval architecture. If this angle is low, it is rarely reached. On any well-designed boat, the deck and the cockpit will be well under water before the critical angle of heel is reached, but I had a boat once in which the critical angle of heel was very high. When there was only a little water on deck, the boat wanted to go right over. I never upset in her, but she had the reputation for being capsized more often than any other boat on that bay, and I had more narrow escapes in that boat than in all other boats that I ever sailed combined.

With a keel boat and ample ballast, and self-draining cockpit, capsizing is practically impossible; for the stabilizing effect of the keel increases as the boat heels over and, at the same time, the effect of the wind decreases.

REACHING

The advisability of sailing a compass course on a reach should be stressed. Small boats unfortunately do not carry compasses to the degree that safety and good sailing make desirable. The value of sailing a compass course is particularly noticeable when a boat is sailing on a reach in a cross current. In the short distances which small boats sail, it is rarely necessary to make the computations outlined in the chapter on Coastwise Navigation. As a rule, the small-boat sailor, when reaching across current, lays his course somewhat up-current from his objective. If, then, he sails for a landmark it will be necessary continually to change his course because the current is setting him down and when, after numerous adjustments, he has run down his distance, he will find himself up-current from his objective.

If, on the other hand, he sets his course with due

allowance for current and notices his compass heading, all that is necessary is to keep the boat on that heading. The current will set the boat progressively as she approaches her objective and, if his calculations and helmsmanship have been good, she will hit the objective on the nose.

MAKING OR CLEARING A DOCK OR MOORING

The section on the proper way to fend with a boathook caused one reader to tell me a gruesome story of a similar danger which should be cited as a warning. A man in a large catboat sailed up to a dock with more way on than he calculated. He stood between the mast and the dock. His chest was crushed like an eggshell and he dropped overboard dead.

Large boats, tugs, steamers, and the like always use a light heaving line to get out a cable to a dock or another boat. The light heaving line is attached to another cable. The heaving line is thrown and caught and by its means the bigger cable is pulled across the water. Small boats rarely use line large enough to be handled in this way, but even a moderate-size line is rather difficult for a girl or boy to heave. The use of a light line for this purpose may prove helpful.

Mention should be made of the stunt of approaching a dock or mooring not quite up wind with sheets started well off. If the sheets are absolutely free, the boat will lose way in almost the same manner as if the boat were driven right up wind. If, in such circumstances, you fetch short, it is easy to trim sheets for another quick kick ahead. It is necessary, however, to caution the reader that this method of approaching a dock or mooring requires much more sea room than if the boat looks right into the eye of the wind.

On approaching a dock or mooring, the jib should be absolutely free. If there is plenty of sea room and the skipper is sure that he can reach his mark, it is always advisable to lower away the jib at once. If, however, there is danger of missing the mark, the jib sheets should be absolutely free, but the jib should not be lowered, as it may be very necessary to use the jib to bear away so as to be able to sail up again.

The necessity for keeping the jib hoisted is much greater with a gaff-headed rig than with a Marconi mainsail. Boats with Marconi mainsails balance fairly well without a jib, whereas a jib is most necessary with a gaff-headed rig. In general, the bigger the jib, the more necessary it is to have it hoisted for such maneuvers.

HELMSMANSHIP

Some readers have been confused by the fact that their helms are heavier when it is blowing hard and also when the wind is abaft the beam. This phenomenon is perfectly normal and does not mean that the boat is badly balanced. The helm is always heaviest with a quartering wind. Also, inasmuch as in a perfectly hung boat the center of effort is slightly aft of the center of resistance, it must be evident that the tendency of the boat to point into the wind is increased with increased wind pressure on the sails. This, in turn, increases the weight of the helm.

Several readers have asked how to determine in advance exactly where the center of effort and the center of resistance should be situated. I have been forced to answer that I do not know. That is a job for the naval architect. Most naval architects pretend to understand this matter and treat it as a phase of an exact science, but their frequent failure to achieve it indicates that they are obliged to approach the matter by the cut-and-fit method. It took the famous *Istalena* two years to get properly hung. The *Whirlwind* was never able to compete properly against the other Cup defenders. There was nothing basically wrong with the *Whirlwind*, but her mast and sails were evidently in the wrong place.

The New York '40's proved so heavy on the helm that a wheel had to be substituted for a tiller. The New York '30's, probably the most successful one-design class ever built, were launched with an eighteen-inch bowsprit and a helm so heavy that a longer bowsprit and a larger jib had to be substituted. The increase of the bowsprit to three feet made them balance perfectly. Star boats and other small craft are equipped with movable steps and movable partners so that the entire mast may be moved forward and aft in the boat. Boats that have been most successful one year have proved to be rank failures the next by driving the wedges around the mast in the wrong order, placing wide wedges where narrow wedges had been and vice versa. It does not take much to throw a boat out of trim and it is all a matter of proper relationship between the center of effort and the center of resistance.

BALLAST AND TRIM

In building a new boat it is a sound plan not to place all of the ballast in the keel. Sufficient ballast for trim should be deducted from the outside ballast and stowed inside.

On a long trip in light airs, it is sometimes wise to shift the ballast to leeward to get the boat down to her sailing lines. If you are learning to sail in a rowboat equipped with a sail, it is always wise to carry ballast in the bow to counteract your weight in the stern of the boat.

SEVENTEEN WAYS TO GET INTO TROUBLE

It is very easy for the beginner to say that he will never fall overboard, but since this book was published I have had so many members of my crew drop overboard into the waters of the Sound that I think it would be wise to list a few of the ways in which people customarily fall overboard. These men were by no means inexperienced. One man who dropped overboard on a blustery night had been five times across the Atlantic under sail.

The first way is stepping on a deck that isn't there. The jib is down. It spreads out over the deck and the man steps on the jib at a point where there is no deck underneath. It is a proper punishment for stepping on a jib, a practice which should never be tolerated.

The next most frequent cause is stepping on a jib sheet or other line lying on the deck. The line rolls under the foot at the same moment that the boat gives a lurch. I dropped one man overboard by means of a spinnaker. The spinnaker pulled him out to the end of the boom before it dunked him.

Losing one's balance is a very frequent cause of falling overboard. Few beginners know how to run forward and, at the same time, keep their weight low. I have often seen men fall overboard while poling. The weight of the body is on the pole. You throw your weight into it, pushing hard on the pole. Then the boat suddenly moves out from under, and you stay with the pole instead of the boat.

The next method of falling overboard is by holding onto a line that either parts or is not fast. This is dramatic and sudden. Slippery soles are a very frequent cause. The worst soles that a yachtsman can wear are made of crepe rubber. They slip suddenly and treacherously and give no hold on the deck. Besides, they track up the deck amazingly. Corrugated soles, designed for golf or other sports, are almost equally bad. The best sole for a yachtsman is perfectly flat, without holes, cleats, corrugations or other similar devices. It should be made of felt, impregnated with rubber. Another satisfactory sole is made of cord impregnated with rubber. These wear badly and are the worst possible nuisance if you walk in sand; but if they are worn only on the boat and changed before you go ashore, they are reasonably satisfactory.

Inability to get down sail is not always due to sticking hoops or slides or to fouled halliards. I got into a frightful mess in a thunderstorm one night last summer before the eyes of an assembled fleet when one of my crew, a newcomer to sailing, made fast the peak halliard when the sail was half lowered. It was black as the inside of a cow. The halliard appeared perfectly clear, and I worked and sweated for half an hour suspecting that the blocks were fouled aloft while all the time the fall was neatly belayed to the cleat.

SEVENTEEN WAYS TO GET OUT OF TROUBLE

If the boat runs aground and you are forced to leave her, be sure to protect the sails. Furl them carefully, raise them as high as possible with a toppinglift and secure them so that they will not get into water when the boat is hove down with the tide.

I feel that a few more words are necessary about behavior in a fog. It is very easy to lose your head in a fog, particularly if steamer traffic is bearing down on you. It is almost as easy to get a bearing on the whistle of a steamer as it is to get a bearing on a navigation light. When you hear a steamer blowing its whistle, change your course to bring the sound of it abeam. As it draws nearer, keep it abeam until it begins to recede. In that way you will be certain to avoid collision.

Recently a friend of mine who had sailed across the Atlantic in a small boat told me that before starting on his passage he had plugs made of soft wood to fit every plumbing opening in the hull. They were carefully painted, accurately tagged, and securely hung in a prominent place on board so that if any of the plumbing gave way, it was an easy matter to plug the hole with a plug which was certain to fit. The small-boat sailor might do well to have similar equipment for drain plugs even if he has no plumbing.

The recent loss of a mast enables me to give some advice I was not able to give when this book was written. One of my crew was going forward to tighten the leach line just before the stick went out. If I had not called him back, he would certainly have been knocked down and possibly killed when everything let go. In heavy blows, do not pass to leeward of the mast. Also, keep your passengers and crew out from beneath the boom. If you lose a mast, the boom falls with sufficient force to smash your house, rail, and deck, and such a blow is apt to be serious. If the mast goes of its own accord, or by virtue of the loss of a shroud, the mast falls in one or more pieces over the lee side and is not apt to do damage in falling. If, however, it breaks because of failure of the head stay or jib stay, the mast is apt to fall into the boat and that is serious. It is not likely to fall to windward so that your chances of escaping being hurt are exceptionally good, so long as you stay on the windward side. This precaution need not be observed unless you suspect weakness in the mast or unless it is blowing hard. Ordinary shoal draft boats with reasonably sound sticks will capsize before the mast will break.

I have always feared that the pieces of a broken mast might threaten to poke a hole in the planking.

While the danger is greater at sea than in sheltered waters, I now think it is less than I imagined. The sail tamps down the motion of the floating spars considerably.

CAPSIZING

A capsized boat should give a signal, if possible. The foghorn should be kept where the helmsman can find it after the boat has upset. For night sailing every boat should be equipped with a number of flares, screwed tightly into a tin can. The flares and continuous blowing on the foghorn will almost certainly attract attention and help.

WHAT TO DO IN A THUNDERSTORM

One of the prominent twelve-meter boats sailing on Long Island Sound carries a radio set and uses it constantly to determine the course to windward on days when thunder squalls seem to threaten. Listening to the static to determine the course in a race is simply another application of the suggestion contained in this chapter.

One month after I replaced the broken mast mentioned above, my new mast was struck by lightning while the boat was at her mooring. It is interesting to note the action of the lightning. It knocked to the deck the ball and the metal staff at the truck of the mast, splintered the head of the mast down to the shrouds but did absolutely no other perceptible damage. It must have traveled down the shrouds or the jib stay and jumped directly to the water without following the chain plates or the hull. The insurance inspector who surveyed the damage said that he had seen many cases in which lightning behaved in just that way, doing no damage except to the very head of the mast.

SAILING IN A TIDEWAY

Since the publication of this book a new publication has been issued by the U. S. Coast and Geodetic Survey. It is entitled "Special Publication 174, Tides and Currents in Long Island and Block Island Sounds."

This book is the first of a series which, when complete, will probably cover the entire coast line. It is a very real aid in making calculations for tidal currents. It contains a series of small charts covering Long Island and Block Island Sounds. The first of these charts shows the maximum current at the strength of flood at The Race, which is the body of water between Plum Island and the two Gull Islands on the one side, and Fishers Island on the other side of the eastern entrance to Long Island Sound. Each successive chart shows the tidal currents one hour later than the preceding chart. These charts are all exactly alike, except for current arrows. These arrows are placed at all significant points on each chart. They show direction and strength of current accurately.

The way to use these charts is as follows: When undertaking a long sail on the Sound, look up the time of the maximum flood at The Race for the day on which you are sailing, in the annual Current Tables. Write that time down on the chart marked "Strength of Flood at The Race." Be sure to note that the time is Eastern Standard Time, and not Daylight Saving Time. Mark every successive chart one hour later. Then, at any time on your trip, you can look at your watch, turn to the chart marked with the time nearest to that noted, find your position on the chart, and read from it the strength and direction of the current. By forecasting where you will be in one, two, or more hours, it is easy to see what the current conditions will be and to plot your course to take the most advantage of the current.

The tidal currents around England are similarly noted in Pearson's *Nautical Almanac*.

The matter of lee-bowing the tide deserves elaboration. It should be borne in mind that in sailing to windward, it is better to have the tide on your lee bow than directly astern. The reason for this is obvious. If the tide is astern it merely sets you ahead faster on the course you are sailing If the side is on your lee bow, it sets you to windward. To travel a mile to windward it is necessary to go much more than a mile on two tacks at 45° from the wind. This consideration is important in determining a course to windward. In a long race last summer I defeated many faster boats by taking a long tack across the Sound, so that when the tide turned I would be able to lee-bow the current on another long tack. My competitors short-tacked along the shore and, although they were admittedly faster boats, they did not do so well.

LAYING TO

I distinguish between "laying to" to stop a boat from sailing and "heaving to" in a storm to prevent disaster. The business of heaving to does not properly come within the scope of a book for a beginner, but the principle underlying both maneuvers is the same. I remember once seeing a scallop fisherman lay his boat to and leave her in his dinghy. He did not return for half an hour and in all that time the boat lay without perceptible motion exactly as if she had been anchored. It is worth the effort to learn this trick. One cannot really be said to know his boat until he can lay her to in any circumstances.

WAVES

In a recent hurricane, when my boat was laboring at her mooring, and it was impossible to get out to her, I tried to plan some scheme for having an oil bag that would be blown overboard automatically in the event of a bad blow. I have not yet worked it out, but it should be easy to do, and would afford valuable protection to a boat left at a mooring in an exposed anchorage.

COASTWISE NAVIGATION

The use of new charts is strongly to be recommended. Geography does not change very much, except where currents wash over shoals and through narrow openings, but aids to navigation are constantly being changed and unless they are noted on the chart, the chart is not of very great value.

Charts of recent publication, corrected weekly for changes in navigational aids, are most necessary. Every change in navigation is published in a weekly bulletin "Notices to Mariners," which is sent free, upon application to the Coast and Geodetic Survey.

Another aid to navigation which I neglected to mention in this chapter is the Light List. This list, published annually, gives a full and complete description of all marks, buoys, lights, and other aids, and their day and night characteristics, with their exact location. With a recent light list, it is possible to navigate with old charts, but new charts are worth the investment.

MARLINESPIKE SEAMANSHIP

The ordinary serving of a line can be improved by threading the end of the service twine through a sail needle and passing several turns around the service between the strands of the line. This helps to hold the serving onto the end of the line and makes a neat and workmanlike job.

Wire splicing is too complicated for description in a book of this scope. Since wire rope is usually made up of seven strands, it is easy to conceive the complications. This much, however, may be said in passing. In making a splice in wire, the tucks are taken with the lay of the strands, not against them, and each tuck is taken under its own strand, not under the adjacent strand.

STANDING AND RUNNING RIGGING

The most efficient angle for the spreaders is that at which they bisect the angle of the shrouds. This means that the spreaders should be cockbilled upwards, so that the angle of the spreader and the part of the shroud above it is equal to the angle of the spreader and the part of the shroud beneath it.

A shroud arrangement, frequently found on Marconi rigged boats, is the so-called "Diamond rig," in which the upper shrouds are returned to the mast to form a diamond-shaped structure. With such a rig, the upper end of the lower shrouds takes its origin at the point of attachment of the spreader of the upper shrouds. Thus, the part of the mast between the upper and lower ends of the upper shrouds forms a unit by itself, and this is supported at midpoint by the lower shrouds.

Two terms frequently used for lines described in this chapter are the following: Back stays are often called runners. The terms are interchangeable where there is a single set of these lines. Where there are two sets, however, one further aft than the other, the forward set is called the runners and the after set the back stays. The tackle described on the jib sheet is often called a jig.

The rigs described for the main sheet should be studied carefully. It is advisable to rig the sheet for racing in such a way that it can be handled by a hand other than the helmsman, and lead clear of the helm. This is a great nuisance while sailing single-handed, and separate rigs are advisable for the two uses of the boat.

LIGHT SAILS

To jibe with a spinnaker set, the following procedure is observed: The forward guy is cast off from the deck, led inside the jib stay, and head stay, and outside the shrouds and back-stays on the same side as the main-sail. The after guy is then let go. The boom moves for-ward, is unshipped from the mast and passed inboard on the lee side of the boat under the main boom. One hand stays forward to gather in the spinnaker, but the halliard remains hoisted. The mainsail is then jibed, the spinnaker pole pushed forward on the opposite side of the jib stay and head stay, and is guyed aft by the line which originally was the forward guy. The forward guy thus becomes the after guy, and the after guy may be used as a forward guy. The spinnaker is then sheeted properly for the new bearing of the wind.

Genoa jibs are now equipped with tricing lines. A light line is sewed about in the middle of the jib and leads forward on both sides of the sail through small blocks in the luff, thence down the luff to blocks located at the tack, and then led inboard.

When a boat tacks, the tricing lines are trimmed to pull the leech and the clew of the jib forward. After the boat has filled away on the other tack, the tricing lines are let go and the leeward jib sheet is trimmed. The tricing lines thus make it unnecessary to send a man forward to guide the clew of the Genoese jib around the forward side of the mast.

RULES OF THE ROAD—RIGHT OF WAY

It is often confusing to determine at just what point one rule leaves off and another applies. In general, it is determined by what may be called a "zone of colli-sion." If either of the two boats may turn a complete circle, with the helm hard down, without striking the other boat, these boats are outside one another's zone of collision. If they are so close together that one of the boats cannot turn a complete circle, with the helm hard down, they are within the zone of collision.

Thus the rights of the boats are determined by their manner of entering into the zone of collision. A boat is an overtaking boat, for instance, or a converging boat, when she enters that zone, and it does not matter where she was half an hour before or where she came from.

HANDLING THE DINGHY

Yachting etiquette distinguishes between the port and starboard side of a vessel for the purpose of boarding and leaving. The owner, his family and guests use the starboard side. The crew uses the port side. Thus the starboard side becomes the front door, while the port side is the servants' entrance.

While this rule is observed in large yachts, it is not important in the etiquette of small boats.

CARE OF THE HULL

The following method of painting the inside of the centerboard trunk is worthy of mention. With the boat hauled out of the water, plug the space between the bottom of the board and the bottom of the trunk, with thin strips of wood and caulk in between with a caulking material, preferably oakum. Then pour copper paint down into the trunk until it is filled. Drill a hole through the caulking and drain off the paint for further use. Then pull out the strips of caulking. A good idea is to prepare one of the strips with a hole and plug beforehand. It is easier to drain after the painting is complete.

Painting the inside of the centerboard trunk should precede the painting of the bottom so that the paint recovered from the trunk will not go to waste.

To keep varnish looking its best, it should be rubbed down every morning with a chamois before the dew has an opportunity to dry on it. If this is impossible, it may be washed with fresh water and then chamoised down; but utilizing the dew is the better practice.

CARE OF SAILS

A torn sail is usually mended with what is known as a "herringbone stitch." The materials for sewing a sail are a sail needle, sailmaker's palm, sail twine and wax. The sail needle is short, strong, and triangular in section. The sailmaker's palm is an abbreviated mitten, with a space for the thumb. It is made of rawhide and has an inverted thimble in the palm of the hand so that the needle may be held between the fingers and the thumb and its after end placed in the inverted thimble.

After the needle is threaded, the simplest practice is to pierce the twine with the needle and pull it down over the end, thus forming a knot to keep the twine from slipping out of the needle. This is a nuisance in any sewing, but is particularly aggravating in sewing canvas. The twine is heavily waxed to lend strength, prevent kinking, and secure an even tension.

The herringbone stitch is made as follows: Stretch

out a tear so that the two sides are smooth and even. Poke the needle through from the back, half an inch away from one side of the tear. Cross over the tear in front and poke through to the back. Pass the needle up through the break on the side of the first stitch, opposite the side on which the second stitch will be taken. Pass it over the twine and down through the tear again. Then pass up through the canvas close to the first stitch and repeat, crossing the tear, going down through the canvas, up through the tear, between the first and second stitches, down through the tear on the opposite side of the stitch, up through the canvas again, etc. If the canvas is old and weak, take long and short stitches alternately. Try to draw up the twine so that the tension is even on all stitches.

WINTER STORAGE AND CARE

The bottom of the boat should be cleaned thoroughly when the boat is hauled out in the fall. Barnacles and other marine growth should be carefully scraped off. It is well to paint the bottom in the fall and for this purpose many yachtsmen prefer an ordinary lead and oil paint, not an anti-fouling paint. To build up a racing bottom, the work should be done in the fall so that the bottom will be very hard and dry and glossy before the final coat is put on in the spring.

FITTING OUT

Recent experiments which I have made with anti-fouling paint prompt me to mention a new theory which I have evolved which may or may not bear the test of time. I have tried this stunt for two summers. The first summer it worked remarkably well. The second summer it was not successful. I painted the bottom with a hard, green racing bottom paint, allowing it to set and carefully sanding it and making it as smooth as possible. Over this I put bronze paint. The first year I tried it, the bronze came off, leaving the green underneath, but it took an entire summer to do so. My boat was launched late in May, and by the middle of September there was no bronze left, but the bottom was clean.

The second summer I tried the same stunt. The bronze stayed on; but, in spite of a mid-season haul-out, the bottom was foul. Perhaps the difference was in the paint used, and perhaps my failure this second year was due to the fact that the green bottom paint was too hard and set. The theory of the plan is as follows: Use an undercoater and a top coat of two different paints so that the top coat will not adhere to the undercoater. Then, when the top coat washes off, all the marine growth that adheres to it will be washed off with it.

A CATALOG OF SELECTED
DOVER BOOKS
IN ALL FIELDS OF INTEREST

A CATALOG OF SELECTED DOVER
BOOKS IN ALL FIELDS OF INTEREST

CONCERNING THE SPIRITUAL IN ART, Wassily Kandinsky. Pioneering work by father of abstract art. Thoughts on color theory, nature of art. Analysis of earlier masters. 12 illustrations. 80pp. of text. 5⅜ x 8½.　　　　23411-8 Pa. $4.95

ANIMALS: 1,419 Copyright-Free Illustrations of Mammals, Birds, Fish, Insects, etc., Jim Harter (ed.). Clear wood engravings present, in extremely lifelike poses, over 1,000 species of animals. One of the most extensive pictorial sourcebooks of its kind. Captions. Index. 284pp. 9 x 12.　　　　23766-4 Pa. $14.95

CELTIC ART: The Methods of Construction, George Bain. Simple geometric techniques for making Celtic interlacements, spirals, Kells-type initials, animals, humans, etc. Over 500 illustrations. 160pp. 9 x 12. (USO)　　　　22923-8 Pa. $9.95

AN ATLAS OF ANATOMY FOR ARTISTS, Fritz Schider. Most thorough reference work on art anatomy in the world. Hundreds of illustrations, including selections from works by Vesalius, Leonardo, Goya, Ingres, Michelangelo, others. 593 illustrations. 192pp. 7⅛ x 10¼.　　　　20241-0 Pa. $9.95

CELTIC HAND STROKE-BY-STROKE (Irish Half-Uncial from "The Book of Kells"): An Arthur Baker Calligraphy Manual, Arthur Baker. Complete guide to creating each letter of the alphabet in distinctive Celtic manner. Covers hand position, strokes, pens, inks, paper, more. Illustrated. 48pp. 8¼ x 11.　　　　24336-2 Pa. $3.95

EASY ORIGAMI, John Montroll. Charming collection of 32 projects (hat, cup, pelican, piano, swan, many more) specially designed for the novice origami hobbyist. Clearly illustrated easy-to-follow instructions insure that even beginning papercrafters will achieve successful results. 48pp. 8¼ x 11.　　　　27298-2 Pa. $3.50

THE COMPLETE BOOK OF BIRDHOUSE CONSTRUCTION FOR WOODWORKERS, Scott D. Campbell. Detailed instructions, illustrations, tables. Also data on bird habitat and instinct patterns. Bibliography. 3 tables. 63 illustrations in 15 figures. 48pp. 5¼ x 8½.　　　　24407-5 Pa. $2.50

BLOOMINGDALE'S ILLUSTRATED 1886 CATALOG: Fashions, Dry Goods and Housewares, Bloomingdale Brothers. Famed merchants' extremely rare catalog depicting about 1,700 products: clothing, housewares, firearms, dry goods, jewelry, more. Invaluable for dating, identifying vintage items. Also, copyright-free graphics for artists, designers. Co-published with Henry Ford Museum & Greenfield Village. 160pp. 8¼ x 11.　　　　25780-0 Pa. $10.95

HISTORIC COSTUME IN PICTURES, Braun & Schneider. Over 1,450 costumed figures in clearly detailed engravings–from dawn of civilization to end of 19th century. Captions. Many folk costumes. 256pp. 8⅜ x 11¾.　　　　23150-X Pa. $12.95

STICKLEY CRAFTSMAN FURNITURE CATALOGS, Gustav Stickley and L. & J. G. Stickley. Beautiful, functional furniture in two authentic catalogs from 1910. 594 illustrations, including 277 photos, show settles, rockers, armchairs, reclining chairs, bookcases, desks, tables. 183pp. 6½ x 9¼. 23838-5 Pa. $11.95

AMERICAN LOCOMOTIVES IN HISTORIC PHOTOGRAPHS: 1858 to 1949, Ron Ziel (ed.). A rare collection of 126 meticulously detailed official photographs, called "builder portraits," of American locomotives that majestically chronicle the rise of steam locomotive power in America. Introduction. Detailed captions. xi + 129pp. 9 x 12. 27393-8 Pa. $13.95

AMERICA'S LIGHTHOUSES: An Illustrated History, Francis Ross Holland, Jr. Delightfully written, profusely illustrated fact-filled survey of over 200 American lighthouses since 1716. History, anecdotes, technological advances, more. 240pp. 8 x 10¾. 25576-X Pa. $12.95

TOWARDS A NEW ARCHITECTURE, Le Corbusier. Pioneering manifesto by founder of "International School." Technical and aesthetic theories, views of industry, economics, relation of form to function, "mass-production split" and much more. Profusely illustrated. 320pp. 6⅛ x 9¼. (USO) 25023-7 Pa. $9.95

HOW THE OTHER HALF LIVES, Jacob Riis. Famous journalistic record, exposing poverty and degradation of New York slums around 1900, by major social reformer. 100 striking and influential photographs. 233pp. 10 x 7⅞. 22012-5 Pa. $11.95

FRUIT KEY AND TWIG KEY TO TREES AND SHRUBS, William M. Harlow. One of the handiest and most widely used identification aids. Fruit key covers 120 deciduous and evergreen species; twig key 160 deciduous species. Easily used. Over 300 photographs. 126pp. 5⅜ x 8½. 20511-8 Pa. $3.95

COMMON BIRD SONGS, Dr. Donald J. Borror. Songs of 60 most common U.S. birds: robins, sparrows, cardinals, bluejays, finches, more–arranged in order of increasing complexity. Up to 9 variations of songs of each species. Cassette and manual 99911-4 $8.95

ORCHIDS AS HOUSE PLANTS, Rebecca Tyson Northen. Grow cattleyas and many other kinds of orchids–in a window, in a case, or under artificial light. 63 illustrations. 148pp. 5⅜ x 8½. 23261-1 Pa. $5.95

MONSTER MAZES, Dave Phillips. Masterful mazes at four levels of difficulty. Avoid deadly perils and evil creatures to find magical treasures. Solutions for all 32 exciting illustrated puzzles. 48pp. 8¼ x 11. 26005-4 Pa. $2.95

MOZART'S DON GIOVANNI (DOVER OPERA LIBRETTO SERIES), Wolfgang Amadeus Mozart. Introduced and translated by Ellen H. Bleiler. Standard Italian libretto, with complete English translation. Convenient and thoroughly portable–an ideal companion for reading along with a recording or the performance itself. Introduction. List of characters. Plot summary. 121pp. 5¼ x 8½. 24944-1 Pa. $3.95

TECHNICAL MANUAL AND DICTIONARY OF CLASSICAL BALLET, Gail Grant. Defines, explains, comments on steps, movements, poses and concepts. 15-page pictorial section. Basic book for student, viewer. 127pp. 5⅜ x 8½. 21843-0 Pa. $4.95

THE CLARINET AND CLARINET PLAYING, David Pino. Lively, comprehensive work features suggestions about technique, musicianship, and musical interpretation, as well as guidelines for teaching, making your own reeds, and preparing for public performance. Includes an intriguing look at clarinet history. "A godsend," The Clarinet, Journal of the International Clarinet Society. Appendixes. 7 illus. 320pp. 5⅜ x 8½.   40270-3 Pa. $9.95

HOLLYWOOD GLAMOR PORTRAITS, John Kobal (ed.). 145 photos from 1926-49. Harlow, Gable, Bogart, Bacall; 94 stars in all. Full background on photographers, technical aspects. 160pp. 8⅜ x 11¼.   23352-9 Pa. $12.95

THE ANNOTATED CASEY AT THE BAT: A Collection of Ballads about the Mighty Casey/Third, Revised Edition, Martin Gardner (ed.). Amusing sequels and parodies of one of America's best-loved poems: Casey's Revenge, Why Casey Whiffed, Casey's Sister at the Bat, others. 256pp. 5⅜ x 8½.   28598-7 Pa. $8.95

THE RAVEN AND OTHER FAVORITE POEMS, Edgar Allan Poe. Over 40 of the author's most memorable poems: "The Bells," "Ulalume," "Israfel," "To Helen," "The Conqueror Worm," "Eldorado," "Annabel Lee," many more. Alphabetic lists of titles and first lines. 64pp. 5³⁄₁₆ x 8¼.   26685-0 Pa. $1.00

PERSONAL MEMOIRS OF U. S. GRANT, Ulysses Simpson Grant. Intelligent, deeply moving firsthand account of Civil War campaigns, considered by many the finest military memoirs ever written. Includes letters, historic photographs, maps and more. 528pp. 6⅛ x 9¼.   28587-1 Pa. $12.95

ANCIENT EGYPTIAN MATERIALS AND INDUSTRIES, A. Lucas and J. Harris. Fascinating, comprehensive, thoroughly documented text describes this ancient civilization's vast resources and the processes that incorporated them in daily life, including the use of animal products, building materials, cosmetics, perfumes and incense, fibers, glazed ware, glass and its manufacture, materials used in the mummification process, and much more. 544pp. 6¹⁄₈ x 9¹⁄₄. (USO)
                                                                                  40446-3 Pa. $16.95

RUSSIAN STORIES/PYCCKNE PACCKA3bl: A Dual-Language Book, edited by Gleb Struve. Twelve tales by such masters as Chekhov, Tolstoy, Dostoevsky, Pushkin, others. Excellent word-for-word English translations on facing pages, plus teaching and study aids, Russian/English vocabulary, biographical/critical introductions, more. 416pp. 5⅜ x 8½.   26244-8 Pa. $9.95

PHILADELPHIA THEN AND NOW: 60 Sites Photographed in the Past and Present, Kenneth Finkel and Susan Oyama. Rare photographs of City Hall, Logan Square, Independence Hall, Betsy Ross House, other landmarks juxtaposed with contemporary views. Captures changing face of historic city. Introduction. Captions. 128pp. 8¼ x 11.   25790-8 Pa. $9.95

AIA ARCHITECTURAL GUIDE TO NASSAU AND SUFFOLK COUNTIES, LONG ISLAND, The American Institute of Architects, Long Island Chapter, and the Society for the Preservation of Long Island Antiquities. Comprehensive, well-researched and generously illustrated volume brings to life over three centuries of Long Island's great architectural heritage. More than 240 photographs with authoritative, extensively detailed captions. 176pp. 8¼ x 11.   26946-9 Pa. $14.95

NORTH AMERICAN INDIAN LIFE: Customs and Traditions of 23 Tribes, Elsie Clews Parsons (ed.). 27 fictionalized essays by noted anthropologists examine religion, customs, government, additional facets of life among the Winnebago, Crow, Zuni, Eskimo, other tribes. 480pp. 6⅛ x 9¼.   27377-6 Pa. $10.95

CATALOG OF DOVER BOOKS

FRANK LLOYD WRIGHT'S DANA HOUSE, Donald Hoffmann. Pictorial essay of residential masterpiece with over 160 interior and exterior photos, plans, elevations, sketches and studies. 128pp. 9¼ x 10¾. 29120-0 Pa. $12.95

THE MALE AND FEMALE FIGURE IN MOTION: 60 Classic Photographic Sequences, Eadweard Muybridge. 60 true-action photographs of men and women walking, running, climbing, bending, turning, etc., reproduced from rare 19th-century masterpiece. vi + 121pp. 9 x 12. 24745-7 Pa. $10.95

1001 QUESTIONS ANSWERED ABOUT THE SEASHORE, N. J. Berrill and Jacquelyn Berrill. Queries answered about dolphins, sea snails, sponges, starfish, fishes, shore birds, many others. Covers appearance, breeding, growth, feeding, much more. 305pp. 5¼ x 8¼. 23366-9 Pa. $9.95

ATTRACTING BIRDS TO YOUR YARD, William J. Weber. Easy-to-follow guide offers advice on how to attract the greatest diversity of birds: birdhouses, feeders, water and waterers, much more. 96pp. 5³⁄₁₆ x 8¼. 28927-3 Pa. $2.50

MEDICINAL AND OTHER USES OF NORTH AMERICAN PLANTS: A Historical Survey with Special Reference to the Eastern Indian Tribes, Charlotte Erichsen-Brown. Chronological historical citations document 500 years of usage of plants, trees, shrubs native to eastern Canada, northeastern U.S. Also complete identifying information. 343 illustrations. 544pp. 6½ x 9¼. 25951-X Pa. $12.95

STORYBOOK MAZES, Dave Phillips. 23 stories and mazes on two-page spreads: Wizard of Oz, Treasure Island, Robin Hood, etc. Solutions. 64pp. 8¼ x 11. 23628-5 Pa. $2.95

AMERICAN NEGRO SONGS: 230 Folk Songs and Spirituals, Religious and Secular, John W. Work. This authoritative study traces the African influences of songs sung and played by black Americans at work, in church, and as entertainment. The author discusses the lyric significance of such songs as "Swing Low, Sweet Chariot," "John Henry," and others and offers the words and music for 230 songs. Bibliography. Index of Song Titles. 272pp. 6½ x 9¼. 40271-1 Pa. $9.95

MOVIE-STAR PORTRAITS OF THE FORTIES, John Kobal (ed.). 163 glamor, studio photos of 106 stars of the 1940s: Rita Hayworth, Ava Gardner, Marlon Brando, Clark Gable, many more. 176pp. 8⅜ x 11¼. 23546-7 Pa. $14.95

BENCHLEY LOST AND FOUND, Robert Benchley. Finest humor from early 30s, about pet peeves, child psychologists, post office and others. Mostly unavailable elsewhere. 73 illustrations by Peter Arno and others. 183pp. 5⅜ x 8½. 22410-4 Pa. $6.95

YEKL and THE IMPORTED BRIDEGROOM AND OTHER STORIES OF YIDDISH NEW YORK, Abraham Cahan. Film Hester Street based on Yekl (1896). Novel, other stories among first about Jewish immigrants on N.Y.'s East Side. 240pp. 5⅜ x 8½. 22427-9 Pa. $6.95

SELECTED POEMS, Walt Whitman. Generous sampling from *Leaves of Grass*. Twenty-four poems include "I Hear America Singing," "Song of the Open Road," "I Sing the Body Electric," "When Lilacs Last in the Dooryard Bloom'd," "O Captain! My Captain!"—all reprinted from an authoritative edition. Lists of titles and first lines. 128pp. 5³⁄₁₆ x 8¼. 26878-0 Pa. $1.00

THE BEST TALES OF HOFFMANN, E. T. A. Hoffmann. 10 of Hoffmann's most important stories: "Nutcracker and the King of Mice," "The Golden Flowerpot," etc. 458pp. 5⅜ x 8½. 21793-0 Pa. $9.95

FROM FETISH TO GOD IN ANCIENT EGYPT, E. A. Wallis Budge. Rich detailed survey of Egyptian conception of "God" and gods, magic, cult of animals, Osiris, more. Also, superb English translations of hymns and legends. 240 illustrations. 545pp. 5⅜ x 8½. 25803-3 Pa. $13.95

FRENCH STORIES/CONTES FRANÇAIS: A Dual-Language Book, Wallace Fowlie. Ten stories by French masters, Voltaire to Camus: "Micromegas" by Voltaire; "The Atheist's Mass" by Balzac; "Minuet" by de Maupassant; "The Guest" by Camus, six more. Excellent English translations on facing pages. Also French-English vocabulary list, exercises, more. 352pp. 5⅜ x 8½. 26443-2 Pa. $9.95

CHICAGO AT THE TURN OF THE CENTURY IN PHOTOGRAPHS: 122 Historic Views from the Collections of the Chicago Historical Society, Larry A. Viskochil. Rare large-format prints offer detailed views of City Hall, State Street, the Loop, Hull House, Union Station, many other landmarks, circa 1904-1913. Introduction. Captions. Maps. 144pp. 9⅜ x 12¼. 24656-6 Pa. $12.95

OLD BROOKLYN IN EARLY PHOTOGRAPHS, 1865-1929, William Lee Younger. Luna Park, Gravesend race track, construction of Grand Army Plaza, moving of Hotel Brighton, etc. 157 previously unpublished photographs. 165pp. 8⅞ x 11¾. 23587-4 Pa. $13.95

THE MYTHS OF THE NORTH AMERICAN INDIANS, Lewis Spence. Rich anthology of the myths and legends of the Algonquins, Iroquois, Pawnees and Sioux, prefaced by an extensive historical and ethnological commentary. 36 illustrations. 480pp. 5⅜ x 8½. 25967-6 Pa. $10.95

AN ENCYCLOPEDIA OF BATTLES: Accounts of Over 1,560 Battles from 1479 B.C. to the Present, David Eggenberger. Essential details of every major battle in recorded history from the first battle of Megiddo in 1479 B.C. to Grenada in 1984. List of Battle Maps. New Appendix covering the years 1967-1984. Index. 99 illustrations. 544pp. 6½ x 9¼. 24913-1 Pa. $16.95

SAILING ALONE AROUND THE WORLD, Captain Joshua Slocum. First man to sail around the world, alone, in small boat. One of great feats of seamanship told in delightful manner. 67 illustrations. 294pp. 5⅜ x 8½. 20326-3 Pa. $6.95

ANARCHISM AND OTHER ESSAYS, Emma Goldman. Powerful, penetrating, prophetic essays on direct action, role of minorities, prison reform, puritan hypocrisy, violence, etc. 271pp. 5⅜ x 8½. 22484-8 Pa. $7.95

MYTHS OF THE HINDUS AND BUDDHISTS, Ananda K. Coomaraswamy and Sister Nivedita. Great stories of the epics; deeds of Krishna, Shiva, taken from puranas, Vedas, folk tales; etc. 32 illustrations. 400pp. 5⅜ x 8½. 21759-0 Pa. $12.95

THE TRAUMA OF BIRTH, Otto Rank. Rank's controversial thesis that anxiety neurosis is caused by profound psychological trauma which occurs at birth. 256pp. 5⅜ x 8½. 27974-X Pa. $7.95

A THEOLOGICO-POLITICAL TREATISE, Benedict Spinoza. Also contains unfinished Political Treatise. Great classic on religious liberty, theory of government on common consent. R. Elwes translation. Total of 421pp. 5⅜ x 8½. 20249-6 Pa. $9.95

MY BONDAGE AND MY FREEDOM, Frederick Douglass. Born a slave, Douglass became outspoken force in antislavery movement. The best of Douglass' autobiographies. Graphic description of slave life. 464pp. 5⅜ x 8½. 22457-0 Pa. $8.95

FOLLOWING THE EQUATOR: A Journey Around the World, Mark Twain. Fascinating humorous account of 1897 voyage to Hawaii, Australia, India, New Zealand, etc. Ironic, bemused reports on peoples, customs, climate, flora and fauna, politics, much more. 197 illustrations. 720pp. 5⅜ x 8½. 26113-1 Pa. $15.95

THE PEOPLE CALLED SHAKERS, Edward D. Andrews. Definitive study of Shakers: origins, beliefs, practices, dances, social organization, furniture and crafts, etc. 33 illustrations. 351pp. 5⅜ x 8½. 21081-2 Pa. $8.95

THE MYTHS OF GREECE AND ROME, H. A. Guerber. A classic of mythology, generously illustrated, long prized for its simple, graphic, accurate retelling of the principal myths of Greece and Rome, and for its commentary on their origins and significance. With 64 illustrations by Michelangelo, Raphael, Titian, Rubens, Canova, Bernini and others. 480pp. 5⅜ x 8½. 27584-1 Pa. $9.95

PSYCHOLOGY OF MUSIC, Carl E. Seashore. Classic work discusses music as a medium from psychological viewpoint. Clear treatment of physical acoustics, auditory apparatus, sound perception, development of musical skills, nature of musical feeling, host of other topics. 88 figures. 408pp. 5⅜ x 8½. 21851-1 Pa. $11.95

THE PHILOSOPHY OF HISTORY, Georg W. Hegel. Great classic of Western thought develops concept that history is not chance but rational process, the evolution of freedom. 457pp. 5⅜ x 8½. 20112-0 Pa. $9.95

THE BOOK OF TEA, Kakuzo Okakura. Minor classic of the Orient: entertaining, charming explanation, interpretation of traditional Japanese culture in terms of tea ceremony. 94pp. 5⅜ x 8½. 20070-1 Pa. $3.95

LIFE IN ANCIENT EGYPT, Adolf Erman. Fullest, most thorough, detailed older account with much not in more recent books, domestic life, religion, magic, medicine, commerce, much more. Many illustrations reproduce tomb paintings, carvings, hieroglyphs, etc. 597pp. 5⅜ x 8½. 22632-8 Pa. $12.95

SUNDIALS, Their Theory and Construction, Albert Waugh. Far and away the best, most thorough coverage of ideas, mathematics concerned, types, construction, adjusting anywhere. Simple, nontechnical treatment allows even children to build several of these dials. Over 100 illustrations. 230pp. 5⅜ x 8½. 22947-5 Pa. $8.95

THEORETICAL HYDRODYNAMICS, L. M. Milne-Thomson. Classic exposition of the mathematical theory of fluid motion, applicable to both hydrodynamics and aerodynamics. Over 600 exercises. 768pp. 6⅛ x 9¼. 68970-0 Pa. $20.95

SONGS OF EXPERIENCE: Facsimile Reproduction with 26 Plates in Full Color, William Blake. 26 full-color plates from a rare 1826 edition. Includes "The Tyger," "London," "Holy Thursday," and other poems. Printed text of poems. 48pp. 5¼ x 7. 24636-1 Pa. $4.95

OLD-TIME VIGNETTES IN FULL COLOR, Carol Belanger Grafton (ed.). Over 390 charming, often sentimental illustrations, selected from archives of Victorian graphics—pretty women posing, children playing, food, flowers, kittens and puppies, smiling cherubs, birds and butterflies, much more. All copyright-free. 48pp. 9¼ x 12¼. 27269-9 Pa. $7.95

PERSPECTIVE FOR ARTISTS, Rex Vicat Cole. Depth, perspective of sky and sea, shadows, much more, not usually covered. 391 diagrams, 81 reproductions of drawings and paintings. 279pp. 5⅜ x 8½. 22487-2 Pa. $7.95

DRAWING THE LIVING FIGURE, Joseph Sheppard. Innovative approach to artistic anatomy focuses on specifics of surface anatomy, rather than muscles and bones. Over 170 drawings of live models in front, back and side views, and in widely varying poses. Accompanying diagrams. 177 illustrations. Introduction. Index. 144pp. 8⅜ x11¼. 26723-7 Pa. $8.95

GOTHIC AND OLD ENGLISH ALPHABETS: 100 Complete Fonts, Dan X. Solo. Add power, elegance to posters, signs, other graphics with 100 stunning copyright-free alphabets: Blackstone, Dolbey, Germania, 97 more–including many lower-case, numerals, punctuation marks. 104pp. 8⅛ x 11. 24695-7 Pa. $8.95

HOW TO DO BEADWORK, Mary White. Fundamental book on craft from simple projects to five-bead chains and woven works. 106 illustrations. 142pp. 5⅜ x 8. 20697-1 Pa. $5.95

THE BOOK OF WOOD CARVING, Charles Marshall Sayers. Finest book for beginners discusses fundamentals and offers 34 designs. "Absolutely first rate . . . well thought out and well executed."–E. J. Tangerman. 118pp. 7¾ x 10⅝. 23654-4 Pa. $7.95

ILLUSTRATED CATALOG OF CIVIL WAR MILITARY GOODS: Union Army Weapons, Insignia, Uniform Accessories, and Other Equipment, Schuyler, Hartley, and Graham. Rare, profusely illustrated 1846 catalog includes Union Army uniform and dress regulations, arms and ammunition, coats, insignia, flags, swords, rifles, etc. 226 illustrations. 160pp. 9 x 12. 24939-5 Pa. $10.95

WOMEN'S FASHIONS OF THE EARLY 1900s: An Unabridged Republication of "New York Fashions, 1909," National Cloak & Suit Co. Rare catalog of mail-order fashions documents women's and children's clothing styles shortly after the turn of the century. Captions offer full descriptions, prices. Invaluable resource for fashion, costume historians. Approximately 725 illustrations. 128pp. 8⅜ x 11¼. 27276-1 Pa. $11.95

THE 1912 AND 1915 GUSTAV STICKLEY FURNITURE CATALOGS, Gustav Stickley. With over 200 detailed illustrations and descriptions, these two catalogs are essential reading and reference materials and identification guides for Stickley furniture. Captions cite materials, dimensions and prices. 112pp. 6½ x 9¼. 26676-1 Pa. $9.95

EARLY AMERICAN LOCOMOTIVES, John H. White, Jr. Finest locomotive engravings from early 19th century: historical (1804–74), main-line (after 1870), special, foreign, etc. 147 plates. 142pp. 11⅜ x 8¼. 22772-3 Pa. $10.95

THE TALL SHIPS OF TODAY IN PHOTOGRAPHS, Frank O. Braynard. Lavishly illustrated tribute to nearly 100 majestic contemporary sailing vessels: Amerigo Vespucci, Clearwater, Constitution, Eagle, Mayflower, Sea Cloud, Victory, many more. Authoritative captions provide statistics, background on each ship. 190 black-and-white photographs and illustrations. Introduction. 128pp. 8⅞ x 11¾. 27163-3 Pa. $14.95

LITTLE BOOK OF EARLY AMERICAN CRAFTS AND TRADES, Peter Stockham (ed.). 1807 children's book explains crafts and trades: baker, hatter, cooper, potter, and many others. 23 copperplate illustrations. 140pp. 4⅝ x 6.
23336-7 Pa. $4.95

VICTORIAN FASHIONS AND COSTUMES FROM HARPER'S BAZAR, 1867–1898, Stella Blum (ed.). Day costumes, evening wear, sports clothes, shoes, hats, other accessories in over 1,000 detailed engravings. 320pp. 9⅜ x 12¼.
22990-4 Pa. $15.95

GUSTAV STICKLEY, THE CRAFTSMAN, Mary Ann Smith. Superb study surveys broad scope of Stickley's achievement, especially in architecture. Design philosophy, rise and fall of the Craftsman empire, descriptions and floor plans for many Craftsman houses, more. 86 black-and-white halftones. 31 line illustrations. Introduction 208pp. 6½ x 9¼.
27210-9 Pa. $9.95

THE LONG ISLAND RAIL ROAD IN EARLY PHOTOGRAPHS, Ron Ziel. Over 220 rare photos, informative text document origin (1844) and development of rail service on Long Island. Vintage views of early trains, locomotives, stations, passengers, crews, much more. Captions. 8⅞ x 11¾.
26301-0 Pa. $13.95

VOYAGE OF THE LIBERDADE, Joshua Slocum. Great 19th-century mariner's thrilling, first-hand account of the wreck of his ship off South America, the 35-foot boat he built from the wreckage, and its remarkable voyage home. 128pp. 5⅜ x 8½.
40022-0 Pa. $4.95

TEN BOOKS ON ARCHITECTURE, Vitruvius. The most important book ever written on architecture. Early Roman aesthetics, technology, classical orders, site selection, all other aspects. Morgan translation. 331pp. 5⅜ x 8½.   20645-9 Pa. $8.95

THE HUMAN FIGURE IN MOTION, Eadweard Muybridge. More than 4,500 stopped-action photos, in action series, showing undraped men, women, children jumping, lying down, throwing, sitting, wrestling, carrying, etc. 390pp. 7⅞ x 10⅝.
20204-6 Clothbd. $27.95

TREES OF THE EASTERN AND CENTRAL UNITED STATES AND CANADA, William M. Harlow. Best one-volume guide to 140 trees. Full descriptions, woodlore, range, etc. Over 600 illustrations. Handy size. 288pp. 4½ x 6⅜.
20395-6 Pa. $6.95

SONGS OF WESTERN BIRDS, Dr. Donald J. Borror. Complete song and call repertoire of 60 western species, including flycatchers, juncoes, cactus wrens, many more—includes fully illustrated booklet.   Cassette and manual 99913-0 $8.95

GROWING AND USING HERBS AND SPICES, Milo Miloradovich. Versatile handbook provides all the information needed for cultivation and use of all the herbs and spices available in North America. 4 illustrations. Index. Glossary. 236pp. 5⅜ x 8½.
25058-X Pa. $7.95

BIG BOOK OF MAZES AND LABYRINTHS, Walter Shepherd. 50 mazes and labyrinths in all—classical, solid, ripple, and more—in one great volume. Perfect inexpensive puzzler for clever youngsters. Full solutions. 112pp. 8⅛ x 11.
22951-3 Pa. $5.95

PIANO TUNING, J. Cree Fischer. Clearest, best book for beginner, amateur. Simple repairs, raising dropped notes, tuning by easy method of flattened fifths. No previous skills needed. 4 illustrations. 201pp. 5⅜ x 8½. 23267-0 Pa. $6.95

HINTS TO SINGERS, Lillian Nordica. Selecting the right teacher, developing confidence, overcoming stage fright, and many other important skills receive thoughtful discussion in this indispensible guide, written by a world-famous diva of four decades' experience. 96pp. 5⅜ x 8½. 40094-8 Pa. $4.95

THE COMPLETE NONSENSE OF EDWARD LEAR, Edward Lear. All nonsense limericks, zany alphabets, Owl and Pussycat, songs, nonsense botany, etc., illustrated by Lear. Total of 320pp. 5⅜ x 8½. (USO) 20167-8 Pa. $7.95

VICTORIAN PARLOUR POETRY: An Annotated Anthology, Michael R. Turner. 117 gems by Longfellow, Tennyson, Browning, many lesser-known poets. "The Village Blacksmith," "Curfew Must Not Ring Tonight," "Only a Baby Small," dozens more, often difficult to find elsewhere. Index of poets, titles, first lines. xxiii + 325pp. 5⅝ x 8¼. 27044-0 Pa. $8.95

DUBLINERS, James Joyce. Fifteen stories offer vivid, tightly focused observations of the lives of Dublin's poorer classes. At least one, "The Dead," is considered a masterpiece. Reprinted complete and unabridged from standard edition. 160pp. 5$\frac{3}{16}$ x 8¼. 26870-5 Pa. $1.00

GREAT WEIRD TALES: 14 Stories by Lovecraft, Blackwood, Machen and Others, S. T. Joshi (ed.). 14 spellbinding tales, including "The Sin Eater," by Fiona McLeod, "The Eye Above the Mantel," by Frank Belknap Long, as well as renowned works by R. H. Barlow, Lord Dunsany, Arthur Machen, W. C. Morrow and eight other masters of the genre. 256pp. 5⅜ x 8½. (USO) 40436-6 Pa. $8.95

THE BOOK OF THE SACRED MAGIC OF ABRAMELIN THE MAGE, translated by S. MacGregor Mathers. Medieval manuscript of ceremonial magic. Basic document in Aleister Crowley, Golden Dawn groups. 268pp. 5⅜ x 8½. 23211-5 Pa. $9.95

NEW RUSSIAN-ENGLISH AND ENGLISH-RUSSIAN DICTIONARY, M. A. O'Brien. This is a remarkably handy Russian dictionary, containing a surprising amount of information, including over 70,000 entries. 366pp. 4½ x 6⅛. 20208-9 Pa. $10.95

HISTORIC HOMES OF THE AMERICAN PRESIDENTS, Second, Revised Edition, Irvin Haas. A traveler's guide to American Presidential homes, most open to the public, depicting and describing homes occupied by every American President from George Washington to George Bush. With visiting hours, admission charges, travel routes. 175 photographs. Index. 160pp. 8¼ x 11. 26751-2 Pa. $11.95

NEW YORK IN THE FORTIES, Andreas Feininger. 162 brilliant photographs by the well-known photographer, formerly with *Life* magazine. Commuters, shoppers, Times Square at night, much else from city at its peak. Captions by John von Hartz. 181pp. 9¼ x 10¾. 23585-8 Pa. $13.95

INDIAN SIGN LANGUAGE, William Tomkins. Over 525 signs developed by Sioux and other tribes. Written instructions and diagrams. Also 290 pictographs. 111pp. 6⅛ x 9¼. 22029-X Pa. $3.95

ANATOMY: A Complete Guide for Artists, Joseph Sheppard. A master of figure drawing shows artists how to render human anatomy convincingly. Over 460 illustrations. 224pp. 8⅜ x 11¼. 27279-6 Pa. $11.95

MEDIEVAL CALLIGRAPHY: Its History and Technique, Marc Drogin. Spirited history, comprehensive instruction manual covers 13 styles (ca. 4th century thru 15th). Excellent photographs; directions for duplicating medieval techniques with modern tools. 224pp. 8⅜ x 11¼. 26142-5 Pa. $12.95

DRIED FLOWERS: How to Prepare Them, Sarah Whitlock and Martha Rankin. Complete instructions on how to use silica gel, meal and borax, perlite aggregate, sand and borax, glycerine and water to create attractive permanent flower arrangements. 12 illustrations. 32pp. 5⅜ x 8½. 21802-3 Pa. $1.00

EASY-TO-MAKE BIRD FEEDERS FOR WOODWORKERS, Scott D. Campbell. Detailed, simple-to-use guide for designing, constructing, caring for and using feeders. Text, illustrations for 12 classic and contemporary designs. 96pp. 5⅜ x 8½. 25847-5 Pa. $3.95

SCOTTISH WONDER TALES FROM MYTH AND LEGEND, Donald A. Mackenzie. 16 lively tales tell of giants rumbling down mountainsides, of a magic wand that turns stone pillars into warriors, of gods and goddesses, evil hags, powerful forces and more. 240pp. 5⅜ x 8½. 29677-6 Pa. $6.95

THE HISTORY OF UNDERCLOTHES, C. Willett Cunnington and Phyllis Cunnington. Fascinating, well-documented survey covering six centuries of English undergarments, enhanced with over 100 illustrations: 12th-century laced-up bodice, footed long drawers (1795), 19th-century bustles, 19th-century corsets for men, Victorian "bust improvers," much more. 272pp. 5⅜ x 8¼. 27124-2 Pa. $9.95

ARTS AND CRAFTS FURNITURE: The Complete Brooks Catalog of 1912, Brooks Manufacturing Co. Photos and detailed descriptions of more than 150 now very collectible furniture designs from the Arts and Crafts movement depict davenports, settees, buffets, desks, tables, chairs, bedsteads, dressers and more, all built of solid, quarter-sawed oak. Invaluable for students and enthusiasts of antiques, Americana and the decorative arts. 80pp. 6½ x 9¼. 27471-3 Pa. $8.95

WILBUR AND ORVILLE: A Biography of the Wright Brothers, Fred Howard. Definitive, crisply written study tells the full story of the brothers' lives and work. A vividly written biography, unparalleled in scope and color, that also captures the spirit of an extraordinary era. 560pp. 6⅛ x 9¼. 40297-5 Pa. $17.95

THE ARTS OF THE SAILOR: Knotting, Splicing and Ropework, Hervey Garrett Smith. Indispensable shipboard reference covers tools, basic knots and useful hitches; handsewing and canvas work, more. Over 100 illustrations. Delightful reading for sea lovers. 256pp. 5⅜ x 8½. 26440-8 Pa. $8.95

FRANK LLOYD WRIGHT'S FALLINGWATER: The House and Its History, Second, Revised Edition, Donald Hoffmann. A total revision—both in text and illustrations—of the standard document on Fallingwater, the boldest, most personal architectural statement of Wright's mature years, updated with valuable new material from the recently opened Frank Lloyd Wright Archives. "Fascinating"–*The New York Times*. 116 illustrations. 128pp. 9¼ x 10¾. 27430-6 Pa. $12.95

CATALOG OF DOVER BOOKS

PHOTOGRAPHIC SKETCHBOOK OF THE CIVIL WAR, Alexander Gardner. 100 photos taken on field during the Civil War. Famous shots of Manassas Harper's Ferry, Lincoln, Richmond, slave pens, etc. 244pp. 10⅝ x 8¼. 22731-6 Pa. $10.95

FIVE ACRES AND INDEPENDENCE, Maurice G. Kains. Great back-to-the-land classic explains basics of self-sufficient farming. The one book to get. 95 illustrations. 397pp. 5⅜ x 8½. 20974-1 Pa. $7.95

SONGS OF EASTERN BIRDS, Dr. Donald J. Borror. Songs and calls of 60 species most common to eastern U.S.: warblers, woodpeckers, flycatchers, thrushes, larks, many more in high-quality recording. Cassette and manual 99912-2 $9.95

A MODERN HERBAL, Margaret Grieve. Much the fullest, most exact, most useful compilation of herbal material. Gigantic alphabetical encyclopedia, from aconite to zedoary, gives botanical information, medical properties, folklore, economic uses, much else. Indispensable to serious reader. 161 illustrations. 888pp. 6½ x 9¼. 2-vol. set. (USO) Vol. I: 22798-7 Pa. $9.95
Vol. II: 22799-5 Pa. $9.95

HIDDEN TREASURE MAZE BOOK, Dave Phillips. Solve 34 challenging mazes accompanied by heroic tales of adventure. Evil dragons, people-eating plants, blood-thirsty giants, many more dangerous adversaries lurk at every twist and turn. 34 mazes, stories, solutions. 48pp. 8¼ x 11. 24566-7 Pa. $2.95

LETTERS OF W. A. MOZART, Wolfgang A. Mozart. Remarkable letters show bawdy wit, humor, imagination, musical insights, contemporary musical world; includes some letters from Leopold Mozart. 276pp. 5⅜ x 8½. 22859-2 Pa. $7.95

BASIC PRINCIPLES OF CLASSICAL BALLET, Agrippina Vaganova. Great Russian theoretician, teacher explains methods for teaching classical ballet. 118 illustrations. 175pp. 5⅜ x 8½. 22036-2 Pa. $5.95

THE JUMPING FROG, Mark Twain. Revenge edition. The original story of The Celebrated Jumping Frog of Calaveras County, a hapless French translation, and Twain's hilarious "retranslation" from the French. 12 illustrations. 66pp. 5⅜ x 8½. 22686-7 Pa. $3.95

BEST REMEMBERED POEMS, Martin Gardner (ed.). The 126 poems in this superb collection of 19th- and 20th-century British and American verse range from Shelley's "To a Skylark" to the impassioned "Renascence" of Edna St. Vincent Millay and to Edward Lear's whimsical "The Owl and the Pussycat." 224pp. 5⅜ x 8½. 27165-X Pa. $5.95

COMPLETE SONNETS, William Shakespeare. Over 150 exquisite poems deal with love, friendship, the tyranny of time, beauty's evanescence, death and other themes in language of remarkable power, precision and beauty. Glossary of archaic terms. 80pp. 5³⁄₁₆ x 8¼. 26686-9 Pa. $1.00

BODIES IN A BOOKSHOP, R. T. Campbell. Challenging mystery of blackmail and murder with ingenious plot and superbly drawn characters. In the best tradition of British suspense fiction. 192pp. 5⅜ x 8½. 24720-1 Pa. $6.95

THE WIT AND HUMOR OF OSCAR WILDE, Alvin Redman (ed.). More than 1,000 ripostes, paradoxes, wisecracks: Work is the curse of the drinking classes; I can resist everything except temptation; etc. 258pp. 5⅜ x 8½. 20602-5 Pa. $6.95

SHAKESPEARE LEXICON AND QUOTATION DICTIONARY, Alexander Schmidt. Full definitions, locations, shades of meaning in every word in plays and poems. More than 50,000 exact quotations. 1,485pp. 6½ x 9¼. 2-vol. set.
Vol. 1: 22726-X Pa. $17.95
Vol. 2: 22727-8 Pa. $17.95

SELECTED POEMS, Emily Dickinson. Over 100 best-known, best-loved poems by one of America's foremost poets, reprinted from authoritative early editions. No comparable edition at this price. Index of first lines. 64pp. 5³⁄₁₆ x 8¼.
26466-1 Pa. $1.00

THE INSIDIOUS DR. FU-MANCHU, Sax Rohmer. The first of the popular mystery series introduces a pair of English detectives to their archnemesis, the diabolical Dr. Fu-Manchu. Flavorful atmosphere, fast-paced action, and colorful characters enliven this classic of the genre. 208pp. 5³⁄₁₆ x 8¼. 29898-1 Pa. $2.00

THE MALLEUS MALEFICARUM OF KRAMER AND SPRENGER, translated by Montague Summers. Full text of most important witchhunter's "bible," used by both Catholics and Protestants. 278pp. 6⅝ x 10. 22802-9 Pa. $12.95

SPANISH STORIES/CUENTOS ESPAÑOLES: A Dual-Language Book, Angel Flores (ed.). Unique format offers 13 great stories in Spanish by Cervantes, Borges, others. Faithful English translations on facing pages. 352pp. 5⅜ x 8½.
25399-6 Pa. $8.95

GARDEN CITY, LONG ISLAND, IN EARLY PHOTOGRAPHS, 1869–1919, Mildred H. Smith. Handsome treasury of 118 vintage pictures, accompanied by carefully researched captions, document the Garden City Hotel fire (1899), the Vanderbilt Cup Race (1908), the first airmail flight departing from the Nassau Boulevard Aerodrome (1911), and much more. 96pp. 8⅞ x 11¾. 40669-5 Pa. $12.95

OLD QUEENS, N.Y., IN EARLY PHOTOGRAPHS, Vincent F. Seyfried and William Asadorian. Over 160 rare photographs of Maspeth, Jamaica, Jackson Heights, and other areas. Vintage views of DeWitt Clinton mansion, 1939 World's Fair and more. Captions. 192pp. 8⅞ x 11. 26358-4 Pa. $12.95

CAPTURED BY THE INDIANS: 15 Firsthand Accounts, 1750-1870, Frederick Drimmer. Astounding true historical accounts of grisly torture, bloody conflicts, relentless pursuits, miraculous escapes and more, by people who lived to tell the tale. 384pp. 5⅜ x 8½. 24901-8 Pa. $8.95

THE WORLD'S GREAT SPEECHES (Fourth Enlarged Edition), Lewis Copeland, Lawrence W. Lamm, and Stephen J. McKenna. Nearly 300 speeches provide public speakers with a wealth of updated quotes and inspiration–from Pericles' funeral oration and William Jennings Bryan's "Cross of Gold Speech" to Malcolm X's powerful words on the Black Revolution and Earl of Spenser's tribute to his sister, Diana, Princess of Wales. 944pp. 5⅜ x 8⅜. 40903-1 Pa. $15.95

THE BOOK OF THE SWORD, Sir Richard F. Burton. Great Victorian scholar/adventurer's eloquent, erudite history of the "queen of weapons"–from prehistory to early Roman Empire. Evolution and development of early swords, variations (sabre, broadsword, cutlass, scimitar, etc.), much more. 336pp. 6⅛ x 9¼.
25434-8 Pa. $9.95

AUTOBIOGRAPHY: The Story of My Experiments with Truth, Mohandas K. Gandhi. Boyhood, legal studies, purification, the growth of the Satyagraha (nonviolent protest) movement. Critical, inspiring work of the man responsible for the freedom of India. 480pp. 5⅜ x 8½. (USO) 24593-4 Pa. $8.95

CELTIC MYTHS AND LEGENDS, T. W. Rolleston. Masterful retelling of Irish and Welsh stories and tales. Cuchulain, King Arthur, Deirdre, the Grail, many more. First paperback edition. 58 full-page illustrations. 512pp. 5⅜ x 8½. 26507-2 Pa. $9.95

THE PRINCIPLES OF PSYCHOLOGY, William James. Famous long course complete, unabridged. Stream of thought, time perception, memory, experimental methods; great work decades ahead of its time. 94 figures. 1,391pp. 5⅜ x 8½. 2-vol. set.
Vol. I: 20381-6 Pa. $13.95
Vol. II: 20382-4 Pa. $14.95

THE WORLD AS WILL AND REPRESENTATION, Arthur Schopenhauer. Definitive English translation of Schopenhauer's life work, correcting more than 1,000 errors, omissions in earlier translations. Translated by E. F. J. Payne. Total of 1,269pp. 5⅜ x 8½. 2-vol. set. Vol. 1: 21761-2 Pa. $12.95
Vol. 2: 21762-0 Pa. $12.95

MAGIC AND MYSTERY IN TIBET, Madame Alexandra David-Neel. Experiences among lamas, magicians, sages, sorcerers, Bonpa wizards. A true psychic discovery. 32 illustrations. 321pp. 5⅜ x 8½. (USO) 22682-4 Pa. $9.95

THE EGYPTIAN BOOK OF THE DEAD, E. A. Wallis Budge. Complete reproduction of Ani's papyrus, finest ever found. Full hieroglyphic text, interlinear transliteration, word-for-word translation, smooth translation. 533pp. 6½ x 9¼.
21866-X Pa. $11.95

MATHEMATICS FOR THE NONMATHEMATICIAN, Morris Kline. Detailed, college-level treatment of mathematics in cultural and historical context, with numerous exercises. Recommended Reading Lists. Tables. Numerous figures. 641pp. 5⅜ x 8½.
24823-2 Pa. $11.95

PROBABILISTIC METHODS IN THE THEORY OF STRUCTURES, Isaac Elishakoff. Well-written introduction covers the elements of the theory of probability from two or more random variables, the reliability of such multivariable structures, the theory of random function, Monte Carlo methods of treating problems incapable of exact solution, and more. Examples. 502pp. 5³/₈ x 8¹/₂. 40691-1 Pa. $16.95

THE RIME OF THE ANCIENT MARINER, Gustave Doré, S. T. Coleridge. Doré's finest work; 34 plates capture moods, subtleties of poem. Flawless full-size reproductions printed on facing pages with authoritative text of poem. "Beautiful. Simply beautiful."–*Publisher's Weekly.* 77pp. 9¼ x 12. 22305-1 Pa. $7.95

NORTH AMERICAN INDIAN DESIGNS FOR ARTISTS AND CRAFTSPEOPLE, Eva Wilson. Over 360 authentic copyright-free designs adapted from Navajo blankets, Hopi pottery, Sioux buffalo hides, more. Geometrics, symbolic figures, plant and animal motifs, etc. 128pp. 8⅜ x 11. (EUK) 25341-4 Pa. $8.95

SCULPTURE: Principles and Practice, Louis Slobodkin. Step-by-step approach to clay, plaster, metals, stone; classical and modern. 253 drawings, photos. 255pp. 8⅛ x 11.
22960-2 Pa. $11.95

THE INFLUENCE OF SEA POWER UPON HISTORY, 1660–1783, A. T. Mahan. Influential classic of naval history and tactics still used as text in war colleges. First paperback edition. 4 maps. 24 battle plans. 640pp. 5⅜ x 8½. 25509-3 Pa. $14.95

THE STORY OF THE TITANIC AS TOLD BY ITS SURVIVORS, Jack Winocour (ed.). What it was really like. Panic, despair, shocking inefficiency, and a little heroism. More thrilling than any fictional account. 26 illustrations. 320pp. 5⅜ x 8½. 20610-6 Pa. $8.95

FAIRY AND FOLK TALES OF THE IRISH PEASANTRY, William Butler Yeats (ed.). Treasury of 64 tales from the twilight world of Celtic myth and legend: "The Soul Cages," "The Kildare Pooka," "King O'Toole and his Goose," many more. Introduction and Notes by W. B. Yeats. 352pp. 5⅜ x 8½. 26941-8 Pa. $8.95

BUDDHIST MAHAYANA TEXTS, E. B. Cowell and Others (eds.). Superb, accurate translations of basic documents in Mahayana Buddhism, highly important in history of religions. The Buddha-karita of Asvaghosha, Larger Sukhavativyuha, more. 448pp. 5⅜ x 8½. 25552-2 Pa. $12.95

ONE TWO THREE . . . INFINITY: Facts and Speculations of Science, George Gamow. Great physicist's fascinating, readable overview of contemporary science: number theory, relativity, fourth dimension, entropy, genes, atomic structure, much more. 128 illustrations. Index. 352pp. 5⅜ x 8½. 25664-2 Pa. $8.95

EXPERIMENTATION AND MEASUREMENT, W. J. Youden. Introductory manual explains laws of measurement in simple terms and offers tips for achieving accuracy and minimizing errors. Mathematics of measurement, use of instruments, experimenting with machines. 1994 edition. Foreword. Preface. Introduction. Epilogue. Selected Readings. Glossary. Index. Tables and figures. 128pp. 5³/₈ x 8¹/₂. 40451-X Pa. $6.95

DALÍ ON MODERN ART: The Cuckolds of Antiquated Modern Art, Salvador Dalí. Influential painter skewers modern art and its practitioners. Outrageous evaluations of Picasso, Cézanne, Turner, more. 15 renderings of paintings discussed. 44 calligraphic decorations by Dalí. 96pp. 5⅜ x 8½. (USO) 29220-7 Pa. $5.95

ANTIQUE PLAYING CARDS: A Pictorial History, Henry René D'Allemagne. Over 900 elaborate, decorative images from rare playing cards (14th–20th centuries): Bacchus, death, dancing dogs, hunting scenes, royal coats of arms, players cheating, much more. 96pp. 9¼ x 12¼. 29265-7 Pa. $12.95

MAKING FURNITURE MASTERPIECES: 30 Projects with Measured Drawings, Franklin H. Gottshall. Step-by-step instructions, illustrations for constructing handsome, useful pieces, among them a Sheraton desk, Chippendale chair, Spanish desk, Queen Anne table and a William and Mary dressing mirror. 224pp. 8⅛ x 11¼. 29338-6 Pa. $13.95

THE FOSSIL BOOK: A Record of Prehistoric Life, Patricia V. Rich et al. Profusely illustrated definitive guide covers everything from single-celled organisms and dinosaurs to birds and mammals and the interplay between climate and man. Over 1,500 illustrations. 760pp. 7½ x 10⅛. 29371-8 Pa. $29.95

Prices subject to change without notice.

Available at your book dealer or write for free catalog to Dept. GI, Dover Publications, Inc., 31 East 2nd St., Mineola, N.Y. 11501. Dover publishes more than 500 books each year on science, elementary and advanced mathematics, biology, music, art, literary history, social sciences and other areas.